Unarmed Stage Combat

Unarmed Stage Combat

Philip d'Orléans

THE CROWOOD PRESS

First published in 2020 by
The Crowood Press Ltd
Ramsbury, Marlborough
Wiltshire SN8 2HR

enquiries@crowood.com

www.crowood.com

British Library Cataloguing-in-Publication Data
A catalogue record for this book is available from the British Library.

ISBN 978 1 78500 785 9

Disclaimer
This book is intended to be used as a reference or an aide memoire during or after a stage combat course. It is not intended to replace the instruction of a good teacher. No book can entirely replicate the benefits of having an instructor in the room with you, guiding your learning and guarding your safety.

Neither should this be used as a teaching manual by untrained combat teachers. There are far too many risks associated with creating the illusion of violence. Do not be tempted to add your lack of experience to them. If you wish to become a stage combat teacher, there are organizations available to provide the necessary training in the many other aspects required to be a good teacher, beyond a simple knowledge of technique.

The author and the publisher cannot be held responsible for any injuries resulting from use of the information in this book.

Full-page picture captions

Page 2: Jab punch. TOM ZIEBELL
Page 8: Costume pull. TOM ZIEBELL
Page 11: *The Beggars' Opera*, courtesy of The Storyhouse Chester. MARK CARLINE
Page 12: Shakespeare's Rose Theatre 2019, Blenheim Palace.
Page 20: *Treasure Island*, courtesy of The New Vic Theatre, Stoke-on-Trent. ANDREW BILLINGTON
Page 26: *The LadyKillers*, courtesy of The New Vic Theatre, Stoke-on-Trent. ANDREW BILLINGTON
Page 36: *Henry V*, courtesy of the Guildford Shakespeare Company. MARK DEAN
Page 42: *Stig Of The Dump*, courtesy of The Storyhouse Chester. MARK CARLINE
Page 56: *Robin Hood*, courtesy of The New Vic Theatre, Stoke-on-Trent/ ANDREW BILLINGTON
Page 67: *Robin Hood*, courtesy of The New Vic Theatre, Stoke-on-Trent. ANDREW BILLINGTON
Page 68: *Taming of ohe Shrew*, courtesy of the Guildford Shakespeare Company. MIKE EDDOWES
Page 76: *Shakespeare In Love*, courtesy of National Theatret Norway. ØYVIND EIDE
Page 86: *Treasure Island*, courtesy of The New Vic Theatre, Stoke-on-Trent. ANDREW BILLINGTON
Page 95: *The Lady Killers*, courtesy of The New Vic Theatre, Stoke-on-Trent. ANDREW BILLINGTON
Page 104: Non-contact kick to the head. ROB DAVIDSON
Page 112: *As You Like It*, courtesy of the Guildford Shakespeare Company. STEVE PORTER
Page 119: *Gabriel*, courtesy of Theatre 6. ROBIN SAVAGE
Page 120: Wide-angle slap. TOM ZIEBELL
Page 137: Cross punch. TOM ZIEBELL
Page 158: Crescent kick. TOM ZIEBELL
Page 176: Sleeper hold. TOM ZIEBELL
Page 193: Brush and replace block. TOM ZIEBELL
Page 228: Side descent. TOM ZIEBELL
Page 240: Robin Hood, courtesy of The New Vic Theatre, Stoke-on-Trent. ANDREW BILLINGTON

Typeset and designed by D & N Publishing, Baydon, Wiltshire

Printed and bound in India by Parksons Graphics

CONTENTS

	Dedication and Acknowledgements	6
	Foreword	7
	Introduction	9
Part I: Fundamental Principles		
1	A Brief Theatrical Context	13
2	Do These Techniques Actually Work?	21
3	Act While You Fight	27
4	The Actor's Two Heads	37
5	Safety	43
6	Who Sees What and What Works Where	57
Part II: Performance Specifics		
7	Music of The Fight	69
8	Pain	77
9	Picturization	87
10	The Cueing System and Other Support Structures	95
11	Knapping	105
12	Warming Up and Stretching	113
Part III: The Essential Techniques		
13	Slaps	121
14	Punches (Non-Contact)	137
15	Kicks (Non-Contact)	159
16	Chokes and Releases	177
17	Contact	193
18	The Illusion of Falling	229
19	Stage vs. Camera	241
	Conclusion	245
	Glossary	246
	Bibliography	250
	Index	254

DEDICATION

This book is dedicated to my wife Fredi, without whose support it would never have been completed, and to my parents, who instilled in me a lifelong love of books.

ACKNOWLEDGEMENTS

It's impossible to embark on a project of this size without an enormous amount of support. These are the people and institutions without whom this book would not have been possible: Aaron Anderson, Mark Bentley, Georgie Britton, Sheila Burnett, Wolf Christian, Alex Clifton, Charlotte Conquest, Giles Croft, Martin Dodd, Andrew Dornan, Jane Elliot-Webb, Sarah Gobran, Martin Hayward, Theresa Heskins, Sam Hodges, Harris Cain, Gordon Kemp, Jonathan Kiley, Janet Lawson, Kit Lawson, Jinny Lofthouse, Dr Chris Main, John McFarland, Kate McGregor, Cecilie Mosli, Nathaniel Marten, David Parrish, Matt Pinches, Eunice Roberts, Richard Ryan, Julia Schafranek, Helene Scharka, Kit Thacker, Fliss Walton, Joe Windley, Bret Yount, Carole Vincer; all of my many friends in the BASSC; and the fight team of the ROH 2018 production of *Simon Boccanegra*.

Special thanks to Drama Studio London for providing space for the photo shoot.

Thanks and gratitude are also due to the photographers: Andrew Billington, Sheila Burnett, Mark Carline, Rob Davidson, Mark Dean, Mike Eddowes, Øyvind Eide, Luke MacGregor, Keith Pattison, Matt Pereira, Reinhard Reidinger, Robin Savage, Craig Sugden, Betty Zapata and Tom Ziebell.

Thanks and more gratitude are due to the theatres who have provided photographs: The National Theatre of Norway, The Storyhouse Chester, The New Vic Theatre Stoke-on-Trent, Nottingham Playhouse, Creation Oslo, Theatre 6, Guildford Shakespeare Company, Nuffield Theatres Southampton, Qdos Entertainment, Vienna's English Theatre, UK Productions/Flying Entertainment, and Novel Theatre.

Thanks, too, to all of my friends and colleagues in the industry, all of the students I've taught who have driven me to be better at my craft, and all of the wonderfully creative performers I've collaborated with in my career, many of whom are represented in the images presented herein.

Finally, none of this could have happened without the unwavering support of my wife Fredi.

FOREWORD

When I offered to write this foreword, I must admit my first question was, Why do we need another book on stage combat? There are many already in print, so what does this one add to the accumulated knowledge? Taking a closer look made it obvious that there is a clear difference between this offering and the others available. And that difference is down to the author's combined skillsets.

Philip d'Orléans stepped into my role at The Royal Academy of Dramatic Art when I left to work on the Warner Brothers' film *Troy*. This was at a point when he had been a member of Equity's register of fight directors for a couple of years and his fight-directing career was beginning to take off. Since then he has worked constantly at theatres all over the UK and internationally, as far afield as South Korea. Crucially, in all that time he has never stopped teaching and learning.

This is where the vital difference lies between this book and others in this field: it brings together more than twenty years' experience of teaching stage combat at many British drama schools, including seventeen years at RADA, combined with a successful fight-directing career. There is a symbiotic link between the two professions, where the fight director is constantly being presented with challenges and then brings that hard-earned knowledge back to the classroom, providing students with the most up-to-date feedback of what the industry currently demands. From the opposite perspective, years of teaching not only allow the refinement of the raw material used by the fight director, but also engender an ability to explain complex techniques with clarity.

It is more unusual than you might think to find someone who is not only good at what they do, but can also teach their subject to an equally high standard. Philip is one of those rare professionals who is able to take his deep theoretical and practical knowledge and present it to students in an accessible and effective format.

Not only is this book extremely practical, it also presents elements of the performance of violence that have never been discussed in print before. It digs deep into every process that an actor must consider to create a strong fight performance and it explains in great detail how to do that well, and safely. Safety is overwhelmingly important and has to be the shared responsibility of everyone involved in the training and performing of violence. Above all, this book describes how student, actor, instructor and fight director can best fulfil that mission. It is clear on when and how each role has to focus on safety and breaks the information down into easily remembered principles.

As a stunt coordinator I benefit from working with well-trained actors. They make my work process simpler and the result more effective, and they increase production value. The more skills an actor brings to the set, the easier they are to integrate with the stunt team. I have no doubt that the information presented in this book will not only enhance the training of a new generation of actors, but will also become a useful tool for the working actor.

Richard Ryan
Stunt Coordinator, Vikings

INTRODUCTION

This book is part of a long tradition: ever since people have been fighting and writing, fight masters have recorded their personal theories and approaches to self-defence. Stage combat manuals are the latest variation of those records. What all have in common is that they are written primarily as a reminder of knowledge already acquired through long practice. They are used mainly for reference, or in support of learning in a classroom, rather than solo learning. If this text is used without an instructor present, great care must be taken to **establish all the safety protocols** before committing to any action.

With that in mind, what is the best way to use this book? It contains a series of information chapters looking at the broader aspects of stage combat as a performance discipline, alongside a series of chapters focused on unarmed combat techniques. Read it cover to cover or dip into it, as required. Both are appropriate. If you do choose to dip, I strongly recommend that you read the whole of Chapter 5 on safety before proceeding to the technical explanations. At the very least they may clarify terminology and principles that might be unfamiliar to you; or they may lead you to information that you might not have considered before.

Each technique chapter in Part Three looks briefly at the reality of a kick, a punch, and so on, then generally at the safety elements specific to these techniques and what works where in terms of staging, before moving onto the techniques themselves. Each technique is accompanied by four images: a simple graphic illustrating the staging; a body outline showing the technical sequence; a photo-strip showing four stages of the technique; and a composite photograph demonstrating the technique.

To provide as useful an experience as possible to the reader, video footage has been created and placed online at www.philipdorleans.com. Enter the password **STARTSLOW** for access to the videos. If access to the recordings is limited, all the information the reader needs is in the written description.

The book also discusses how to create a character-based fight and is illustrated with pictures of fights I've choreographed as a professional fight director. I must register a debt of gratitude to all of the theatres, photographers and individuals who have willingly provided photos; this book is far richer for their contributions. Many pictures show weapons, but nevertheless support the various themes under discussion.

I've used the terms 'Attacker' and 'Victim' as they clearly delineate who is the aggressor at each particular moment. Many of the other terms that are specific to the craft will be found either in the safety-specific glossary at the end of Chapter 5 or the full glossary at the end of the book.

This book encompasses a broad range of basic unarmed stage combat techniques, but not every technique or variation devised. It comprises core techniques used to prepare a performer-in-training for their fight performance exam and a solid foundation of knowledge in preparation for the profession.

Stage combat is a constantly evolving craft, responsive to the growing demands of an ever-changing industry and an increasingly perceptive audience. This means that practitioners are often creating variations on a theme, innovative ways to make a technique work for alternative staging, or creating something completely original. It would be impossible for a book to capture them all. I've constrained myself to the basic versions of techniques.

In Parts I and II you will find the role of the fight director mentioned many times. This might seem strange in a book on technique aimed at the student and the teacher. Although unarmed combat can be a standalone subject of study, it exists in the industry only as one of many tools in the performer's integrated toolkit. So the end point of all of the enclosed information and discussion, inevitably, has to be its application by a fight director and a performer in the professional environment. Therefore, many of the points made will be drawn through to those conclusions. However, this is not a how-to manual for fight directing. The techniques described here are part of the craft of a working fight director, but only a small part. A good fight director's knowledge base is considerably broader and deeper. Fight directing is a career that should never be entered into lightly. It demands a great deal of training, as the performers' safety very much depends on the expertise of the fight director in a number of different areas.

This work is the accumulation of knowledge filtered through generations of performers and fight directors. Modern stage combat practitioners are as good as they are because they stand on the shoulders of giants, and much credit must go to our predecessors. A small number of the terms and principles in this book I have formulated myself, but others were codified by friends in the BASSC, and still others by our antecedents in the stage combat industry.

PLEASE REMEMBER!

Read Chapter 5 on safety before you try out any of the techniques.

PART I

FUNDAMENTAL PRINCIPLES

1
A BRIEF THEATRICAL CONTEXT

Arguably, drama is conflict. At its heart there is no drama without confrontation, whether of ideologies, philosophies, countries, characters, or needs and desires. Inevitably, some of that discord will manifest itself physically. The need to perform these moments of violence safely and repeatedly must have led, very early on, to the development of some form of staged violence.

ANCIENT EGYPT

The earliest form of ritualized performance seems to be that of the ancient Egyptian priests. Tales of the gods, with their battles and murders, particularly the killing of Osiris by Seth, almost certainly entailed some representation of actual fights. With the priesthood being at the centre of Egyptian culture, science and medicine (Lorenzi, 2003), attracting the brightest, most enquiring minds, it seems inconceivable that somebody did not turn their intelligence towards working out how to create a performed fight, although there are no records proving this.

EUROPE TO THE RENAISSANCE

The first flourishing of theatre in Europe, as we would recognize it, occurred amongst the civilizations around the Mediterranean. In the theatre of Ancient Greece, it seems that acts of physical brutality usually occurred off-stage. Most historians

The Odeon of Herodes Atticus, Athens.

The Colosseum, Rome.

believe that this was done for reasons of religion and tradition, although the reality may have had more to do with practical considerations (Sommerstein, 2010).

There is little information on the traditions of early Roman theatre, but later popular taste was for broad spectacle, as evidenced by the prevalence of arena games and executions. There seems to be proof that some executions were staged as dramas within which the lead characters were brutally murdered (Bellinger, 1927). Given the propensity of Roman culture towards physical cruelty, it seems unlikely they would have followed the Greek fashion, but there is no clear information regarding their approach towards staged violence (Bradford, 2019).

Staged performances of written texts then disappear from the historical record in Europe for a millennium, until the passion and mystery plays of the Middle Ages. The next evolution of performed aggression probably occurred at this time, in scenes representing religious violence (Groves, 2007). It is not until the late Tudor age that the depiction of violence begins to bear some relation to current perceptions of aggressive reality, notably in the plays of Shakespeare. From this point until the current day, the number of fights written into plays would seem to indicate that they were, and continue to be, popular with audiences.

ACTORS AND THE SWORD

Although it is incomplete, there is documentary proof from the late Tudor era that shows that performers studied swordplay at the time, presumably partly with the intention of adapting its usage for the stage (Berry, 1991). At a time when the playing for prizes by fight masters and their acolytes was considered prime entertainment, and most members of the public would have intimate, visual knowledge of sword fighting, it seems unlikely that acting companies would have retained their audiences if their fights failed to replicate the real thing accurately. Today, the pressure of audience expectation can drive producers to ever greater heights, and there is no reason to believe that this was not the case in earlier times.

Well-known performer and clown Richard Tarlton was not only a member of the Queen's Men, but also a fight master by accolade with the London Masters of Defence – a considerable achievement (Martinez, 1996). During this period, theatre began to adopt a form that would be more familiar to modern sensibilities, and began to flourish. One element of this success was certainly down to the spectacle achieved through a focus on violence and fights. In much the same way as an action movie excites with car chases and explosions, Elizabethan and Jacobean theatre achieved similar results with blood and blades.

The trend of performers training in swordsmanship continued through the 18th and 19th centuries. Domenico Angelo, who, infatuated with the actress Peg Woffington, accompanied her to London from Paris, established himself first as a master of equitation, then opened a school of arms in the city's Soho area in 1763 (Aylward, 1953). While his *salle d'armes* was popular with the upper classes (he was fencing tutor to the Prince of Wales), it also drew actors, and continued to do so under the tenure of his son Harry. Controversially for the time, the school also accepted female students, many of whom were actresses (Aylward, 1953).

Angelo and his wife were close friends of the legendary actor David Garrick and, following the death of her husband, Garrick's widow stayed with

Shakespeare's Rose Theatre, Blenheim Palace. A temporary recreation of a sixteenth-century Bankside theatre.

Shakespeare's Globe - **Macbeth** - © Philip d'Orléans, Fight Director 2010

Angus Removes Cawdor's Tongue

28/5/10

Mr. Ken Shorter, Mr. Nick Court, Mr. Julius D'Silva & Mr. Ian Pirie

Please note that once set this choreography must not be altered without the prior consent of the fight director, as this may compromise the safety of the cast

Phrase 1	**Cawdor**		**Lennox, Ross & Angus**
1	They drag you to the pillar and chain you to it *(eye contact then as they take a gentle grip on your arms you stand and create the illusion that they're dragging you roughly along - as you get to the pillar turn and carefully lean back as though shoved hard against it - lean your upper body forward to avoid the ledge - keep your arms clear of the chain as they carefully wrap it around you - support your own weight, be balanced throughout)*	<——	Drag him and chain him to the pillar *(eye contact as you walk towards him, two of you take a gentle grip on his upper arms creating the illusion of roughly dragging him up and to the pillar - let Ken do most of the work himself - help keep him balanced - let him turn at the pillar and two keep a gentle hold as if restraining him, the other feed the chain around his upper torso under his arms and onto the hook - only tight enough for the illusion of restraint)*
2	They hold you in place, force your mouth open and cut your tongue out *(as they place gentle hands on you, you struggle a little but ensure you're completely still before Ian lifts the knife - he'll place it just in front of your mouth being careful of your eyes and nose - as he cuts he'll pull across your face taking care not to flick the point into your face or mouth - his grip on you and on the knife will be soft - only react once the knife is gone)*	<——	Lennox and Ross hold him still and Angus cuts out his tongue *(Julius take a soft grip on K's torso, Nick have a soft R hand on his forehead, and the palmed blood bag in your L hand under his chin - Ian places his L hand with a palmed tongue in it on K's chin - as K drops his jaw carefully place your blade flat in front of his lips and cut down and back to you - place no pressure on the knife, do not cut him - all keep their grips very soft)*
3	They leave you slumped in the chains, bleeding from the mouth *(as they release you, you slump a little - ensure you find a balanced position, as comfortable as possible for the ten minute stand)*	<——	Throw his tongue away and leave him *(Ian throws the palmed tongue carefully into a space in the audience being aware of not hitting anyone with it - Nick has burst his blood bag splashing up over K's face, take the blood bag off with you)*

Fight notes from a production of *Macbeth* at Shakespeare's Globe. Prior to the advent of smartphones, this was one method for ensuring all safety notes were recorded.

The auditorium of the Royal Opera House from the stage; note the height and width.

the Angelos for a while (Oman, 1958). Apparently, Angelo also designed sets for some of Garrick's productions (Oman, 1958). Clearly, there were strong ties between the premiere fencing *salle* in the country and the London theatrical establishment. There is no record that Angelo ever took the role of fight arranger, but it is surely reasonable to suppose that, with those strong ties, he may have been actively involved in creating fights.

In the early 19th century, the diaries of actor-manager William Macready mention the lessons he undertook as a young performer at Angelo's *salle d'armes*, studying with Henry Angelo, the second generation of the dynasty (Aylward, 1953). In the late 19th century Felix Bertrand, son of Baptiste Bertrand, founder of Salle Bertrand (and his own fencing dynasty), was another instructor who was actively involved arranging fights for London theatres (Cohen, 2002).

THE DEVELOPMENT OF THE ROLE OF FIGHT DIRECTOR

Fights continued to be an integral part of live entertainment through the 20th century. The development of the film industry saw their expansion into a different medium, one with greater reach and public impact. Filmmakers followed theatrical tradition, using fencing masters to train performers and choreograph fights (Thomas, 1973). The exposure movies brought led to an increased awareness of the role of the fight choreographer (Richards, 1977) and by incremental stages that role moved away from fencing coaches towards the development of professional fight directors. The wave of new writing in the mid-20th century, with its emphasis on domestic situations, helped create the need to combine in one role someone who was expert in unarmed, as well as sword, fights.

This impetus coalesced into the formation of the Society of British Fight Directors (SBFD) in 1968 and the development of the Equity Register of Fight Directors. The SBFD led directly to an American counterpart, the Society of American Fight Directors (SAFD) in 1977. Their work has led to a point in theatrical history at which it is almost universally accepted that fights should be choreographed by trained professionals, who can advocate for the performer's safety, and who understand the complexities involved in telling violent stories.

THE TRAINING ARC

So how does a performer train to fight on stage? In the UK most train at drama school before entering the profession, with most schools recognizing the benefits of developing a fighting skillset during their training. Before graduating, almost every trained performer in the UK will have taken the Fight Performance Test, covering, at a minimum, unarmed combat and one sword style.

There are currently three primary organizations in Britain that train performers and certify combat teachers. Each organization's examination procedures differ in detail, but are broadly the same in execution. Students perform one or more scenes, containing a fight, for an external examiner. The examiner observes their practical understanding of safety, their mastery of the weapon style, and their integration of character, text and fight into a seamless, fully motivated whole.

The exam is the endpoint of the training process. Performers acquire a skillset, gaining an understanding of fundamental concepts and experience in their practical application. They then learn choreography, utilizing many of the techniques learned. Part of the focus is on understanding how they personally best learn choreography. This then shifts to the integration of choreography and scene and exploration of the rehearsal process. The final stage is managing the transition from rehearsal room to performance space, where learning to trust the solid foundation of technique, training and rehearsal will support their performance when they commit to the character's experience.

Contrary to the process performers undergo in the rehearsal room, as described throughout this book, in any given fight exam, the students all use the same choreography and fit it to their chosen scene rather than the other way around. This gives students the opportunity to demonstrate to an examiner the breadth and depth of their knowledge and ability. Unlike the work of a fight director on a specific show, the training choreography is not completely rooted in the individual character impulse, but is more generalized. This is understood by all involved to be a compromise born out of the exam situation compounded with the inevitable time pressures inherent in any training programme. It is made clear to the students that, once the skillset has been gained, the process shifts to a much more character-specific method.

BASSC teacher Andrei Zayats: fight rehearsals are continually adjusted by the instructor, working towards the clearest story-telling.
ROB DAVIDSON

Records show that group drills have been a staple tool of the fight instructor since the very early times of the formal training of fighters.
ROB DAVIDSON

Moshinsky's 2018 ROH production of *Simon Boccanegra*: a rare opportunity to bring very experienced performers together in a fight team that was capable of fighting aggressively, but safely, surrounded by an eighty-strong opera chorus.

2

DO THESE TECHNIQUES ACTUALLY WORK?

How many times have you seen a theatrical unarmed fight and thought that it did not really work? But through politeness, or a belief that it is not actually possible to make a fight look real on stage, you say nothing. You praise your friend in the company, or the person who directed the production, but you do not mention the shortcomings of the representation of the violence. By saying nothing, you have become complicit in the pretence that a bad fight is acceptable, and not an embarrassment.

The reality is that theatrical fights are unsuccessful far more often than should be the case. There are many reasons for this: maybe the performers were less than physically able; or the director did not care how real the fight looked; or nobody bothered to check the sightlines; or the fight has migrated over a long run; or perhaps they are not running fight calls; or the production could not afford a fight director; or they chose a bad fight director. Or it might be that nobody believes it is possible to portray a realistic fight on stage, so they simply gloss over those moments in their list of expectations.

Well, they are wrong, but they are also right. Wrong, in that it is perfectly possible to create exciting, realistic, dynamic fights, which have an audience on the edge of their seats, tell a great story in synch with the rest of the show, and allow performers to remain safe whilst freeing them to apply their acting skills to the violence. They are right in that many of the techniques taught to performers, and presented in this book, do not work in certain performance venues.

A fight crafted for an end-on stage, allowing a clear view of both faces at a climactic moment. *Dial M for Murder*, courtesy of Vienna's English Theatre.
REINHARD REIDINGER

THE IMPORTANCE OF CONTEXT

Of course, the question then has to be, why teach these techniques? Why do fight directors use them? Why do we subject our performers and audiences to them if they don't work? Why are they

This victim had to look defeated, with a dominant attacker swinging them into position by their neck. *The Kite Runner*, West End and National Tour, courtesy of UK Productions/ Flying Entertainment.
BETTY ZAPATA

in this book? The answer, simply put, is that not all techniques are created equal. Not every technique works in every venue and there is no 'one move fits all' solution when it comes to choreographing a fight. The techniques all have their place, and will all work beautifully in the correct context, whether that is for a single point of view such as a camera, or in a studio theatre, in-the-round staging, or perhaps in a high house.

The problem comes when a fight director, or the director, makes choices that are inappropriate to the venue. Unfortunately, there are fight directors who will put a small theatre jab punch on to a large West End stage without thought to the sightlines for most of the audience. There are also directors who consistently allow such choices without questioning the reason why the moves literally do not work, and without insisting that the fight director find a better solution to the story-telling challenge. They may assume that the audience will not notice, or that, if they do, they will not care.

CAN IT BE DONE?

Creating a fight that works on every level of safety, physical logic, character logic and story-telling, which is also consistently replicable by the performer, and works for every sightline in the venue is not easy. This is a difficult job by any definition. The performance of a fight is also extremely complex. Being safe, accurate, fast, aggressive, and engaged in the character's internal life, all whilst replicating choreography, is challenging for anyone. If a performer struggles physically, the fight will need to be tailored very much to their abilities.

Despite all this, it is absolutely achievable. All the techniques in this book hold great validity as long as their limitations are acknowledged, and they are applied in a context working to their strengths. In Part III, each technique chapter begins with an examination of which staging format works best. It is important for a performer to learn not just how to do a technique, but also how the illusion works, when it does not work, and how to stretch it if

Careful repetition of the choreography in rehearsal enables the development of flow and clarity of character choice. *Dedication*, courtesy of The Nuffield Theatres, Southampton. LUKE MACGREGOR

possible. Performers are not simply puppets to be moved around by fight directors: they will produce better work if they understand the mechanism making a technique work and when best to apply that version, rather than simply just how to do a move. They must understand on a technical level what they are trying to hide from the audience, and what they are trying to reveal.

CONSTRAINTS AND CREATIVITY

I once worked with an award-winning designer, who reflected on an Italian production of *Aida* with which he had been involved. His budget had been effectively unlimited. He had been denied nothing. Every demand he made had been met, no matter how outrageous. Looking back, he was aware that it had been the worst design he had ever created, overshadowing the entire performance. He felt that his most successful work had been created on a limited budget, where the financial constraints required him to be far more creative.

Stage combat is not a dead art. It is not fixed in amber without any hope of change. It is a vivid, lively craft, ever responsive to the demands that a changing theatrical environment makes upon it. Often, it is the constraints placed on it by difficult staging, awkward costumes and sets, or less physically able performers, which encourage it to flourish. When a fight director cannot make the established techniques work, he or she may be pushed to conceive a new way forward. When a teacher has an injured student, a new variation may be created. Restrictions and boundaries fuel creativity.

IMPACTS AND INFLUENCES

The Changing Audience

One force driving the development of the craft is related to the demands of an increasingly sophisticated audience. There was a time when the only performed violence available was on stage, and audiences' expectations were in line with their experience of other shows and the current norm for their cultural paradigm. Therefore, a sword fight in the 1930s would have been little different from a sword fight in the 1850s, particularly if

A restraint hold has to look as though it would work and fit the professionalism, or not, of the attackers. *Gaslight*, courtesy of The New Vic Theatre, Stoke-on-Trent. ANDREW BILLINGTON

the 'Standard Combats' were used. These were a pre-learned series of choreographed phrases, commonly in use throughout the Victorian and Edwardian eras, which could be strung together in any order to create a fight. They were familiar to most performers and it was not unknown, if the audience were enjoying the fight, for the star to extend it by the simple expedient of calling out phrase names to his partner (Wolf, 2009).

Henry Marshall, Master at Arms at RADA from the early 1970s until 1993, left a series of writings to the Theatre Museum in London (now fully subsumed into the Theatre and Performance Department in the V&A museum). He describes visiting, in the 1970s, an elderly performer near the end of his life, who, in the prime of his career, had actively fought the Standard Combats. They were so well known to him that he was still able to recall some of their names, if not the actual moves.

The Film Industry

With the evolution of the film industry, followed by television, the palate of the theatre audience began to change. Outside the constraints of a stage, and with the ability to break fights into easily rehearsed sections that could then be filmed repeatedly until the appropriate effect was created, fights became more spectacular. And as tastes in screen work began to be refined, they also became more realistic and more vicious. Coupled with the camera's ability to support astonishing illusions for woundings and deaths, this led to a sea change in violence on stage. Simply put, the audience began to expect more. Combined with a growing trend for realism in theatre, stage combat had to move forward, and new versions of old techniques were created, crafted to be better suited to the new realism.

This is an ongoing process. As tastes change and films become ever more technically sophisticated, audiences expect still more from their live performance experience. Younger directors with tastes directly influenced by growing up in a technological world have different expectations from the older generations, and therefore different demands. Fight directors work to incorporate these influences into their work, inspired to stretch the craft ever further.

Whilst designed for comedic effect, the characters must still be fully invested in their desperate reality. *Shakespeare in Love*, courtesy of National Theatret Norway.
ØYVIND EIDE

A safe illusion of a leg sweep into a controlled descent whilst managing a large prop. *Robin Hood*, courtesy of the Guildford Shakespeare Company.
STEVE PORTER

Alternative Staging

The 20th century saw a shift from traditional proscenium arch staging to a wider range of staging choices, including traverse, thrust, in-the-round, site-specific and, more recently, immersive theatre. While these all create difficulties for a fight director, they also present opportunities. As soon as the audience's physical relationship to the action alters, many of the illusions that have been relied on in the past to tell the story without hurting a performer are no longer effective. These alternative stagings have really pushed practitioners to expand techniques to accommodate the altered sightlines, and no doubt will continue to do so.

Every technique in this book works – if it is performed in the correct staging context. The relevant information is listed at the beginning of each technique and is fundamental to understanding how to apply the related technical information effectively. If every member of the artistic team involved in the development of a fight moment understands the constraints involved, and how to maximize the effectiveness of each technique, no audience will ever have to sit through another embarrassing failure of a fight, pretending it was worth the price of the ticket.

3
ACT WHILE YOU FIGHT

THE CHALLENGES OF STAGE COMBAT

Is it easy to perform a fight on stage for a live audience? If you have ever had the experience, you will know that it is actually very difficult to do, both well and consistently. The performer is being asked to achieve a number of complex and demanding tasks, all while staying in character:

- They have to remember the choreography in its entirety, with very little room for error.
- They have to remember any text that may be interleaved into the fight.
- They have to remember and apply every relevant safety principle.
- They have to ensure they hide everything that needs to be masked and reveal anything that must be seen to support the story.
- They must stay in synch with their fight partner throughout, giving and receiving precise physical and verbal cues at the right moments.
- They must handle the small errors in distance and placement that inevitably creep into any fight, which could spoil the illusion if unchecked, without allowing the audience to see them fixing those moments.
- They have to remember, and accurately play, their musical score for the fight whilst protecting their vocal instrument.
- They have to stay balanced both physically and emotionally, whilst their character undergoes an exhausting confrontation.

On top of all this, while keeping each of these technical balls effortlessly in the air they must also act. Is it any wonder that it's more common to see a fight performed with a generic wash of emotion than it is to see a fight focused through a clear lens of moment-by-moment character impulse and response? Keeping control of all these elements, and stitching them into a seamless whole to create a really good fight, is hard to do well.

Just like juggling, when the juggler has to shift their attention to one specific ball, they are more likely to lose control of the others. In a stage combat scenario, the first ball to drop is usually the one marked 'Acting'. This is usually because it is the last ball fitted into the sequence, but also because, when the brain makes a choice between focusing on concrete, physical technicalities or the most recently overlaid, nebulous, emotional story-telling, it almost always chooses the former.

As a result, an audience's experience of a fight in a show is often that it feels tacked on to the narrative, rather than being rooted in – and justified by – character and text. It often feels like performers fighting, rather than the characters that the audience have been getting to know. The story-telling beats may feel crude compared to the rest of the performance, or there may be a lack of variety in pace, intention and reaction. This is usually because it is just plain difficult to perform a fight convincingly. Sometimes, due to a lack of rehearsal, inexperience, a poor fight director, or even fear, performers fall back to a slower, apparently safer, less engaged version of the fight, rather than stretching themselves to achieve the best they can.

STARTING WITH CHARACTER

How can a performer avoid this situation? They have little control over rehearsal time, or the

The anticipation of pain can be a terrible fear for some characters if they have never been hit before. *Wait Until Dark*, courtesy of Vienna's English Theatre. REINHARD REIDINGER

partner they end up with, but they do control when and how they introduce the character beats into their fight. It is tempting to think of 'acting' as the last element to be added – something that is laid on top of all the other technical work. I used to work with the analogy that the technical skillset is the skeleton, the choreography is the flesh, and the character choices made are the costume that clothes the technical body. However, I have recently come to the conclusion that this was back to front. In fact, the skeleton must be the character work, the flesh the technical skillset – as acquired by the character – and the choreography the clothing, as chosen by the character. Acting, or the character, must infuse and be at the very heart of the fight, for, without that, the fight is simply a demonstration of technique.

THE FIGHT DIRECTOR'S INPUT

A good fight director develops a fight impulse by impulse with the input of the performers and the director. If all involved are strongly focused on the character intentions and objectives, the fight will be created with a strong internal structure of actable beats, already informed by character. This means that, as the performer's motor learning absorbs the technical moves in rehearsal, their performer memory takes in and fleshes out the character's moment-by-moment story, linking meaning and choice to each move as they work.

What should the performer do if their fight director does not choose to work in this way, using their input, and the fight becomes a generic 'plug-and-play'? At this point the performer should remember exactly what they know and can still bring to the fight – how to act and tell a story – and then apply everything they know of their craft to the choreography, exactly as they would if they were given a less than inspiring text.

This is the real secret: a fight is simply a dialogue. It is an argument between two or more people, enacted physically rather than verbally. A fight happens when words are no longer enough to express how the people feel, but it is not the end of the conversation. It is a continuation. A performer should treat the choreography in exactly the same manner in which they treated the text leading up to the fight.

Not every character is emotionally prepared for violence and the shock continues to reverberate through them. *Gabriel*, courtesy of Theatre 6.
ROBIN SAVAGE

CHOREOGRAPHIC ANALYSIS

The performer needs to sit down and do the same homework for a fight as they do for their lines, in exactly the same way. They might choose to use the following specific processes for analysing text:

- Work out the units.
- Clarify the beats in each unit.
- Action each line, perhaps even each word in certain lines.
- Define the super-objective and map out the linked objectives.
- Understand the through-line; how does each moment link to the next?
- Seek the variety, colour, light and shade, the subtlety and nuance within the text.
- Pull into focus the relationship between the characters.
- Analyse the obstacles and the tactics used to avoid them.
- Calculate the stakes for the character.
- Specify the given circumstances.

How does this type of analysis apply to a physical fight performance?

Units

In the phrasing of the choreography, each discrete phrase of the fight is seen as a unit. Rather than burning through from beginning to end, most performed fights break down into separate sections, with pauses for text, or non-fight action between them. Each section is a phrase of choreography. 'Phrase' is a fight director's term, while a performer might use the term 'unit' for the same concept.

Beats

Each beat sustains for as long as one character drives the fight, which may be for just one move,

FIGHTS Tuesday 29th Jan

3 1	p.55	Tom JO Ed Billy Gerrard	Dermot Skelton Farrell O'Connor Browne	Dermot drinks piss · Tom on stool, struggles with piglet · Gerrard takes piglet from Tom · Ed holds Tom's nose closed, puts cup on Tom's chin · JD holds Tom's right arm, lifts cup with Ed · Billy sits on table, holds Tom's left arm · Tom falls on floor, Ed tucks stool under table
3 2	p.56	Tom Gerrard	Dermot Browne	· Tom lunges at Gerrard · Gerrard deflects Tom with one arm out to chest, one to shoulder
3 3	p.56	Tom Gerrard	Dermot Browne	· Tom runs at Gerrard · Gerrard checks him, grabs his neck, spins Tom 90°, keeps hold of Tom's throat, later turns him 180° (upstage)
3 4	p56	Tom Gerrard	Dermot Browne	· Gerrard takes Tom's shoulder then grabs back of his hair, other hand on Tom's shoulder · Tom grabs Gerrard's hand on back of Tom's head
3 5	p57	Tom Gerrard (Ed-nap?)	Dermot Browne	Dermot's Head Slam · Gerrard slowly lowers Tom's head onto table · Gerrard raises Tom's head a little (Tom left leg back) · Tom slaps table as his head passes down near it · Tom staggers to the floor
3 6	p60	Tom Billy Colm	Dermot O'Connor Finnigan	Lazarus Arose · Billy on Tom's right, Colm on his left, lift him up under his arms · Billy puts Tom's right hand behind back, holds neck

Fight story notes broken down beat by beat, written up for the performers and artistic team. *I'll Be the Devil*, Royal Shakespeare Company.

or for as many as six moves. The next beat begins as soon as another character takes control and fights back. So a phrase, or unit, will be comprised of at least one beat, but will usually contain more.

Action

In using action verbs to define what the character is trying to achieve in each moment of the interaction, the more specific the choice of verb, the more defined the playable intention will be and the more depth there will be to the performance. Each move in a fight must be played with a precise, rather than generic, intention. For example, not 'I'm going to punch you in the face', but rather 'I'm going to shatter your jaw'.

Super-Objective

The performer will have worked out the character's super-objective in relation to the engine driving them through the play. The fight must logically feed into, and support, that super-objective, not play against it. The fight will have its own super-objective; entering the fight, the performers need to know exactly what the character hopes to achieve.

Objectives

These usually change with each new phrase of fight, as a result of the pauses between phrases enabling assessment and renewal, or adjustment, of the character's immediate need. That is not to

It is not uncommon in a fight for a character to pause and reassess the situation. *Merry Wives of Windsor,* courtesy of The Storyhouse, Chester.
MARK CARLINE

say that objectives cannot alter mid-phrase. A character might, for example, decide to abandon attempting to scalp the enemy, shifting focus to just escaping with a whole skin.

Through-Line

Each moment of the fight must be linked to the one before and the one after. What has just happened to them in the previous moment must shape and inform the character's immediate next choice. The logic of that choice applies on different levels and in different ways, and depends, to some extent, on how good the fight director is:

- Physical logic: what position is the body in and what is the next, logical choice of move? What position is the partner's body in and how does that affect the logic of that choice?
- Energy logic: has energy just been expended and needs to be renewed, or has energy just been chambered by the latest shift in position, ready for release?
- Emotional logic: where is the character emotionally? Does it make more sense for the next move to be offensive or defensive?
- Character logic: What is the character's backstory? Is it logical for them to throw a spinning back kick, or are they more likely to flail a foot and fall over?

If the performer gets this right, the linked character impulses generate physical and emotional energy that fuels and drives the fight, without the performer needing to artificially generate that energy.

Variety

A real fight is filled with infinite variety. Even if a move is immediately repeated, the intention and energy behind it will be different. Every single move is delivered with varying levels of energy and intent. Each moment feeds off, but is different from, the one that precedes it. Different choices lead to differing levels of energy, to differing rhythms and pace, to shaded nuances of intent. A fight should be an ever-changing, richly textured tapestry of violence.

Relationship

The relationship between the fighters must be very clear as it will have an impact on the style of the fight and the choices that the characters make. Siblings will fight in a different way from a child and parent. A fight between two work colleagues will be different from one between two friends. The nature of the relationship colours and informs all the choices and responses that fighters make to the moments, and to each other.

Obstacles/Tactics

A fight is the physical expression of the adoption and alteration of tactics to get around an obstacle. The enemy is in the character's way and trying to stop them: they attempt something that works, partially works, or does not work. The next choice is an adaptation of their tactics, depending on which outcome it was.

Stakes

Why is the character fighting? What do they stand to lose? What could they gain? The higher the stakes, the more compelling the fight is for the

Each character fights as their body allows. *Carrie's War*, Apollo Theatre, courtesy of Novel Theatre and Mark Bentley.
KEITH PATTISON

audience, and the broader and deeper the range of choices open to the performer. The stakes should always be pushed as far as possible.

Given Circumstances

The who, why, what, where, when, and how, of the fight.

- Who are they? Who are they fighting?
- Why are they fighting?
- What are they fighting with? What are they fighting for? What is their fighting style?
- Where are they fighting?
- When are they fighting – time, day, month, season, year? When does the fight happen in the arc of the story?
- How did they come to this point? How do they fight? How well trained are they?

Audience Perspective

What makes a good fight from the perspective of the audience? When asked, most people answer with a range of the following points:

- The characters look as if they are vulnerable and in danger.
- The fight is explosive and surprising, for characters and audience.
- The fight is aggressive.
- The attacks are fast and believable, and the reactions match.
- The pain seems real, is sustained, and continues to affect the characters.
- The stakes are high.
- The fight rhythms change throughout, avoiding repetition.
- The choices fit what is known of the characters and their circumstances.
- Each moment seems to be an organic, logical development from the previous moment.
- The characters are seen making choices affected by what has just happened to them.
- The characters are seen to be affected by the violence, assessing what is happening and trying different tactics based on that judgment.

If these elements are considered, there is a good chance that the audience will be invited into the character's reality.

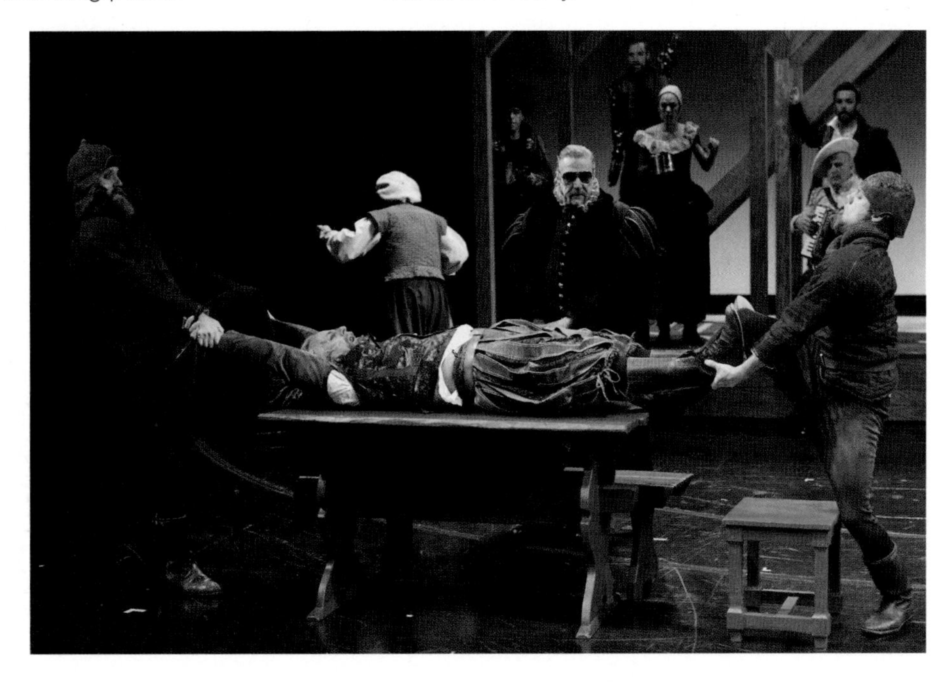

The witty tone of this production dictated this comedic version of stretching on the rack. *Shakespeare in Love*, courtesy of National Theatret Norway.
ØYVIND EIDE

Fights rarely go the way the character hopes they will. *Treasure Island*, courtesy of The New Vic Theatre, Stoke-on-Trent.
ANDREW BILLINGTON

Stanislavski's 'Circles of Attention'

Of course, the application of any of the points described here is in itself a technical process requiring a sequential series of steps, from first rehearsal to performance. Slightly torturing Stanislavski's 'Circles of Attention' gives us an easy analogy to work with. The first circle is the performer's work with their partner, clarifying the various elements of the fight story as a collaborative process: vocal, physical and emotional. The second circle is an expansion outwards, including the physical environment of the stage and set, with the consequent requisite adjustments. The third circle is the final expansion outwards including the audience, ensuring all components of the violence are designed to create the best possible fight story for them. This team work is predicated on the solo work each performer undertakes as homework, in preparation for the shared effort.

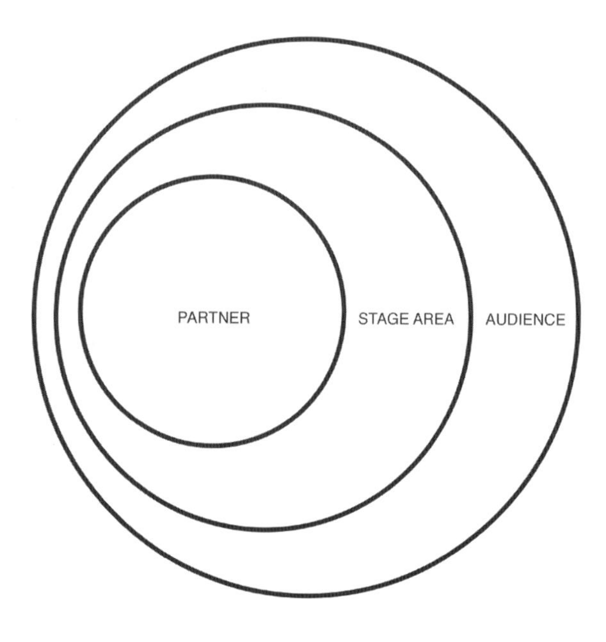

Figure 1: The performer's three circles of focus.

PRODUCTION STYLE

Of course, every choice the performer makes is filtered through the style of the production. Playing a fight as a vicious domestic beating would be anomalous in a Restoration Comedy, as much as a slapstick fight would be in a kitchen-sink drama of the 1950s. Not only must the performer's choices fit the appropriate style, they must also be strongly rooted in what is already known of the character, going on to reveal more than has been seen to this point. They must actively move the story forward, allowing the audience to take a journey with the character to the new, post-fight destination.

CONCLUSION

When an activity is complicated or difficult, the instinct is often to simplify it, making the task easier. This often happens in performed fights. On the surface, a real fight may look like a series of simple choices, but it is far from it. The reality of violence is complex and layered, and over-simplifying the process and the end product would be doing a disservice to the performers and the audience. From an acting perspective, a performer's responsibility is to make clear the fractured chaos, the intricate tangle that is, beat by beat, a fight, and not to allow the audience an easily viewed simplistic representation. Violence should not be a comfortable thing to watch. The risk is that it will become a voyeuristic experience that the audience can view from the outside, without actually having to engage with the reality of, and the consequences for, the characters.

Acting is at the very core when performing a fight. The technical skillset serves the performative skillset, not vice versa, and fight skills and choreography must be integrated into the character's world and physicality. Weaving a great fight from the many different threads discussed above requires continual hard work, as well as a willingness constantly to revisit the detail of the pattern and unpick one colour in favour of another, or to incorporate more subtle layers until each element of the story is clear.

Not every character is trained to fight, and success and failure can create strong reactions. *Twelfth Night*, courtesy of the Guildford Shakespeare Company.
STEVE PORTER

4

THE ACTOR'S TWO HEADS

It can be a schizophrenic experience being a performer. They have to sustain two completely different foci when they are performing, without allowing one to adversely affect the other. A performer in full flow has two heads in operation at the same time: a technical head and a character head. They are able to stay open to the impulses of both, reacting to one and not disrupting the output of the second.

The first head is a technical focus, which means that the performer does not fall off the stage or over the set; it ensures they find their light, or their marks if filming; it enables them to assess their vocal production, so that it reaches where it needs to; it lets them judge whether they are have the impact on the audience that they wish to have. The technical head keeps the performer safe and able to deal with the logistics of performance, whilst still paying attention to the act of acting.

The second head is a character focus, which allows the performer to experience the character's world; it allows them to be responsive moment by moment to the situations in which the character finds themselves; it ensures they are receptive and open to other characters, and that they are listening and hearing for the first time, feeling, reacting and discovering afresh. Through their character head, the performer is fully immersed in the character and their journey, whilst still listening to the promptings of the technical head.

Tybalt carefully releases the dagger while making it seem a natural part of the reaction. *Romeo and Juliet*, courtesy of the Guildford Shakespeare Company.
MATT PEREIRA

INTEGRATION

Together, the two heads complement each other's work, creating a fully embodied performance. It may seem self-evident that a performance cannot be complete without enabling both elements, but when it comes to the illusion of violence it can be harder for performers to find the appropriate balance between technique and acting. For the long-term safety of the performers, the fight needs to be carefully choreographed, with each moment technically crafted, rehearsed and clearly set, with very little room for variance. Yet, for the purposes of the story, the characters need to be able to release the full range of aggressive impulses with appropriate ferocity.

If the balance falls too much on the side of technique, the fight seems too safe and too choreographed, lacking in impulse and connection to the character's instinctive response to violence. If it falls

This set forces the performers to fight right on the inner edge of safe distance. *Corpse!*, courtesy of Vienna's English Theatre.
REINHARD REIDINGER

more to the side of character, there is a risk that the performers may succumb to 'red light fever'. This is a term from the world of filming, which describes the moment the camera's red light goes on and the performer's eyes glaze over, as all memory of choreography flees, to be replaced by instinct and impulse alone. It is a terrifying experience for their partner. Too strong a focus on the acting impulse runs the risk of detaching the fight from the solid foundation of the formalized choreography and of the performer's acquired skillset.

The ideal situation is where a performer is able to combine both skillsets. They are able to fully realize the character's moment-to-moment responses through the arc of the fight, whilst remaining technically aware of their situation as a performer, and making their own, in the moment, adjustments in the performance environment. In a sense, the technical head side-coaches the character head, as an acting tutor might side-coach performers in a scene, without disrupting their character engagement or awareness. This comes only through practice and experience. It is one strong rationale for the fight performance exam that most performers go through during their training. In pursuing their studies for the exam, they will experience the warp and weft of the integrated skillsets during a short performance, and gain an understanding of what is required in the professional environment, and of their own personal rehearsal arc, achieving this to the best of their current ability. The smartest performers also continue their fight training as their career progresses.

INSTINCT vs. CRAFT

There is a perennial discussion about the balance between instinct and craft. When does a performer rely on instinct and when on craft, or does a good performer rely completely on one or the other? The clearest answer is that it surely needs to be a balance of both aspects, with the performer developing an ability to employ both choices simultaneously. The discussion then revolves around the location on the scale of the fulcrum point that tips the performance in one direction or the other.

Why is this a discussion point in a volume on stage combat? Two reasons: the first lies in the risk of using badly trained performers who believe instinct is truth and can therefore only strengthen their performance, usually at the expense of craft, and feeling this justifies altering choreography on the fly without warning their partner. It might seem

Both performers must demonstrate technical precision to avoid injury whilst investing character into the action. *Wind in The Willows*, courtesy of The New Vic Theatre, Stoke-on-Trent. ANDREW BILLINGTON

incomprehensible that someone would make a choice that will place a colleague in a situation in which they could be hurt, particularly if they have had formal fight training. During that training, it will have been drummed into them that, once it has been set, choreography is not changed, except by the fight director or instructor, for all obvious health and safety reasons. However, irresponsible performers do exist and they are a very real danger to themselves and others.

Addressing this issue with clarity, it must be made clear to all performers that the only acceptable instinctual responses allowed in a choreographed fight are in the acting choices made in the moments between the physical violence; or in the vocal work. However, any element of adjusted response in those elements must never alter or affect the position or timing of the choreography. Once it has been rehearsed and signed off by director, fight director and stage management, the fight does not change without the specific input of the fight director.

Only a short-sighted producer allows alterations to a fight by performers or stage management. If there is an accident, the production company might be deemed to have failed in their duty of care to their employees, opening themselves up not only to litigation, but also to the possibility that their insurance policy might be declared void.

The second reason to examine instinct vs. craft is that a performer's body tends to fall into instinctive patterns when creating the elements of a fight. These patterns may exist because of prior training in other martial systems or sports, or may be the product of the performer's life experiences, or the physical development of their body. Asked to enact a particular movement, each person unconsciously follows a specific path determined by the shape and health of their body; or by strongly embedded physical responses; or by their

The alignment of this collision was carefully choreographed, as were the angles of the bodies and swords, avoiding injury on the contacts and the controlled descents. *Robin Hood*, courtesy of The New Vic Theatre, Stoke-on-Trent. ANDREW BILLINGTON

observation skills and proprioceptive accuracy. It is rare for a person to replicate a move perfectly the first time: there is almost always a process of adjustment and refinement towards the template ideal. The time this takes relates to the person's experience and the strength of their brain's connection to the three-dimensional spatial mapping of their body. Movement training should produce a performer who is the master of their body. When asked, they should be able to replicate a physical move with precision, or take a physical note and apply it, without needing to hear the note more than once.

Regarding this second issue, wise performers take responsibility for strengthening their sense of proprioception. This is the ability to sense stimuli from the various receptors within the body, sending the brain information regarding balance, movement and the placement of different elements of the body in relation to each other (Johnson et al., 2008). Effectively, it allows a performer to be physically accurate, precise and balanced whilst moving at speed. Accuracy defines the difference between the desired position for a movement and where it actually ends up. Precision combines accuracy and repeatability. There are many exercises specifically targeting proprioceptive inaccuracies, which are also often helped by engagement with sports or martial arts systems. The study of Laban is also an excellent tool for sharpening proprioception and its ability to sense heaviness, force and effort. The end result of stronger proprioceptive ability is a performer who is better able to replicate combat techniques safely at speed, and to troubleshoot the distance issues that inevitably arise in every performance of a fight.

REALITY vs. TECHNIQUE

It is not only the conflict between the performer's instinct and craft that can destabilize the safety and effectiveness of a fight, but also their innate sense of what a move should really look and feel like. There can be resistance to the structure of a technique, whether it is from an instinctive feeling that a move should be done in a particular manner, or from a trained response interfering with acceptance of information. Further complicating the matter, until the physical information is rehearsed and fully integrated into brain and body, the instinctive shape held in the brain can resurface as soon as the performer removes conscious attention from the technique. Why is this an issue? Well, a technique is structured with two specifics in mind: how to make the moment safe for performers, and how to tell the story most effectively to the audience. The position of the preparation and the action will have been very carefully considered, in such a fashion as to achieve both aims, but they will almost certainly not reflect the reality of the technique, as if it were used on the street. This becomes a stumbling block for some performers. Either they will say 'it's not real', or their body will revert to what it considers to be real when accessing the character's impulse and intention.

One example is the roundhouse punch. In reality, most people prepare this near their hip, then swing it up with the arm fully extended, making contact with the opponent's face then dropping down in an arc to the opposite side. The fist essentially describes an arch, with impact achieved at its apogee. In the stage version, the fist prepares at the height of the target, wide to the side of, but not behind, the performer, whilst leaning in that direction. For the action, the body weight shifts to the opposite side as the arm is swung in an almost fully extended semi-circle crossing the target, remaining at that height all the way through. It is an entirely unnatural physical action that bears very little resemblance to the real version of the punch. However, if the real version is done on stage, it just will not work. If there is supposed to be an illusion of contact, it will be convincing for only a small section of the audience. If there is an avoidance, it will make the punch look fake, as if the performer is deliberately aiming to miss. If the stage version is done slowly, then it too will seem fake, but if it is done at speed it will be entirely

Strong technical focus is required to avoid character energy creating real pressure across the victim's throat. *Romeo and Juliet*, courtesy of The Storyhouse, Chester.
MARK CARLINE

convincing, whether performed with the illusion of contact or of avoidance.

There are many instances where reality does not work as well as craft on stage. Reality is not designed to tell a story to multiple points of view. Reality is not designed to allow safe repetition of an action eight times a week. Reality is reality: a one-off moment, an attempt to achieve something that either succeeds or fails, but only by the standards inherent in the inception of its action, not in relation to the perception of a multitude of observers. Craft, on the other hand, allows the story to be told so that it works for every viewpoint in the auditorium. Craft allows the action to be safely repeated at speed with full aggressive intent for the length of the production run. Craft creates the successful illusion of reality. To shift performance paradigms, it is an aphorism in filming that what a performer does feels fake in real life, but looks real in fake life.

CONCLUSION

Just because a move feels right, or feels good from the character's or the performer's point of view, does not always mean it works. It does not mean that it is good, that it tells a clear story, or even that it is safe. Conversely, just because a move does not feel natural in the performer's body, or to the character, does not mean that it is not safe and is not good storytelling. Trust the techniques and work with them until they do feel natural. Make them the character's reality and train with them until this way of moving or attacking is the way the character would choose to do it. At that stage, you will have created a stage reality that works and is safe. Resolve this balance between craft and instinct, and you will facilitate an easier working relationship between your character head and your technical head.

The lifters support the victim, holding their hand, while the victim tightens their core, making themselves easily liftable. *Treasure Island*, courtesy of The New Vic Theatre, Stoke-on-Trent.
ANDREW BILLINGTON

PATRICIA
LANES
500

5
SAFETY

PERFORMANCE

It is axiomatic that stage combat has to be safe, surely? This is the very foundation of the extended philosophies of most stage combat organizations worldwide. It was certainly one of the reasons for the foundation of the Society of British Fight Directors (arguably the progenitor of all those groups) and, at base, the rationale for establishing Equity's Register of Fight Directors. It must seem obvious to all involved in the creation of illusory violence on stage that it is desirable for everybody to survive the experience, and to be able to replicate it consistently for every performance.

However, there are a few practitioners who believe that stage combat cannot be made entirely safe and, indeed, that if it is safe, it loses its effectiveness as a performance skill. The idea is that the audience will see performers being safe and will be unable, or unwilling, to suspend their disbelief: performers who are focused on keeping each other safe will be unable to play the aggression and danger inherent in a real violent confrontation at a level that convinces an audience.

There is a kernel of truth here. It is undoubtedly valid to say that there is an increased risk in creating a violent performance on stage. It is also undeniably true there is a fine line between the reality and the illusion of violence, and it is easy for performers to slip over that line in the heat of performance, with unpleasant consequences. Performers are hurt every year creating fights on stage. Indeed, although it is a very rare occurrence, performers have been killed on stage (Wolf, 2009) or died later as a result of injuries sustained in the course of a fight performance (Topham, 2018). This is why the role of fight director exists – to minimize the risks to performers, while at the same time creating a physical story that serves the production.

The term 'minimize' is used advisedly. It is impossible to remove all risk from a performance, although the focus of all the professionals involved is to reduce those risks to an acceptable level. To that extent, the idea that stage combat cannot be made entirely safe does have some validity, just as no physical endeavour in everyday life (for example, crossing the road) can be made entirely safe. It can be made mostly safe, but it only takes one performer to misstep or suffer a memory lapse of what is coming next for an accident to occur. This explains why a good teacher will clarify safety concepts for their students throughout their class-time, rather than simply focusing on technique, as will good fight directors when they choreograph.

However, that does not address the main thrust of the argument: the belief that a performer focused on safety is unable to look dangerous, or, perhaps, that playing dangerous leads to playing dangerously. Of course, this is a fallacy. Any performer worthy of the title should be able to divorce the character's violent impulses from the actual flow of physical energy through the fight, and should be able to completely hide safety principles and rehearsed choreography from the audience whilst investing in the character's aggression. With enough rehearsal time and sufficient professional support from a good fight director, it has been proved many times that a company of performers can sustain strong, exciting fight performances that convince audiences, whilst remaining safe and injury-free. A good performer can act aggressively without being aggressive. Whilst it is not possible to make every moment of a performer's time

The lighting state is assessed for safety, ensuring performers can see the swords at all times. *Dedication*, courtesy of The Nuffield Theatres, Southampton. LUKE MACGREGOR

on stage completely safe, it is possible to create a mindset that focuses on safety before all other considerations and ensures that the safety of all involved takes precedence.

THE CASCADE

The study of accident theory in various industries suggests that many major accidents occur from a cascade of seemingly trivial errors, rather than from a single catastrophic incident (Roberto, 2013). Most stage combat techniques are designed to incorporate a 'belt and braces' approach to safety, so, if one principle fails, a built-in safety redundancy catches the error before it can begin the cascade. For example, in the case of a parrot punch, if red light/green light (do not punch until the victim has begun to avoid) fails, and the performer punches without waiting for their cue, displacement of target (punching to a safe space) should still prevent an accident. In other words, the performers usually have to make more than one mistake to trigger an accident. When an accident happens in a fight, it is most often the result of multiple errors.

WHO WATCHES OUT FOR WHO?

Performance safety works on differing levels in the theatre. At its most basic, the individual performer is focusing on the safety principles for each technique and is responsible for themselves and for their partners' safety. Subsequently, there is the company of performers actively looking out for each other's safety. Above them is the stage management team taking overall responsibility for the safety of the company and the audience. The ultimate responsibility for everyone's safety lies with the producers, who will have had every element of the process risk-assessed, and will have ensured that they have hired qualified professionals to fill each role.

What working practices should producers put in place to support performers if a fight is involved? Ideally, if there is a fight, a push, a fall or a lift, a good fight director will be contracted to work with the company. Enough time must be allocated within the rehearsal period to create and rehearse fights that serve the production. The fights must be within the performers' ability to perform, and easily and consistently replicable eight times a week for the length of the run. If there are understudies, they must be rehearsed in, and procedures must be established to keep them regularly rehearsed and to manage the process if there is a sudden need for them to step into a role. The structure and length of fight calls must be established, to be held by stage management before any run and, once the show is open, before the first performance of the day. If it is a matinee day and there is enough time, fight call is also to be held before the second performance. Clear paths of communication must

Anything around a performer's neck is designed to make it impossible to cause injury in any circumstances. *The Beggars' Opera*, courtesy of The Storyhouse, Chester. MARK CARLINE

be maintained between stage management and the company, ensuring any safety issues are addressed immediately. A risk assessment of every area of the production must be completed and made readily available to the company.

MENTAL HEALTH

It is obvious, given a moment of consideration, that the illusion of violence is extremely close to the reality of violence. However, what may not occur to some is that each performer, member of the crew or of the stage management and artistic/concept teams will have an individual history of, and relationship to, violence. It is possible that for some that history is traumatic, and being exposed to work on violence in the rehearsal room may adversely affect their mental health. All steps should be taken to ensure that everyone is aware of the range of material that might be covered, before the session begins. They should also be given the opportunity to raise any issues they might have, in a safe and non-judgemental atmosphere.

Staging violence can be a trigger for those with certain life experiences in their past, and it is not uncommon for students' engagement in the learning environment to be affected by this. Every effort should be made to develop protocols to ensure clear communication of all relevant information in a timely manner, and to support those in need of assistance when exposed to material that could be damaging to their health.

Performers and all others involved in the process should also be honest, with themselves and with colleagues, about what they feel they can manage, and when they might need additional help. All those involved in the teaching or creation of performed violence have a responsibility to work towards creating a safe, supportive space, in which everybody can participate fully in the creative process without fear of being harmed in any way. The BASSC now includes Mental Health First Aid as a requirement for its teaching staff, and this will probably become more common throughout the industry as there is better recognition of the importance of supporting the mental well-being of colleagues and students.

CONSENT

No matter how many structures are put in place for everyone's safety, there can be no work at all unless all involved give their consent in the first place. Consent is very much at the heart of the creation of the illusion of violence. Nothing can be done except with the agreement of everybody involved in the process and that agreement must never be assumed, but always explicitly sought. Whatever response is received should be heard with respect and given clear consideration (Turner, 2019).

No participant should ever be placed in a situation where they feel explicit or implicit pressure to do something they are uncomfortable with, whatever the root of that discomfort. There must always be procedures in place to ensure that everybody involved in the process feels they can clearly say no to a suggestion, without fear of being pressured into it, or of losing their job, or placing future work in jeopardy.

Consent should be renewed on an agreed regular basis, and can either be refused or withdrawn at any point. If it is withdrawn, there should be no demands to explain why; the fact should simply be accepted and alternative approaches discussed. Hopefully, those involved will be able to make counter-offers to move things forward. It is also important to note that, as the various intimacy direction organizations make clear, permission does not mean consent. Those in authority can give permission for things to happen, but that does not mean that those involved have given consent.

Each establishment will have its own working procedures dealing with this issue, and should inform all employees about them. However, as freelancers, performers, fight directors and teachers are advised to make themselves aware of good practice (Chicago Theatre Standards, 2017).

Unarmed combat on stage includes a lot of physical contact, which must always be negotiated and then further curated regularly to ensure that everyone is still content with the boundaries established. The physicality of violence must never become an excuse for inappropriate or unwanted physical contact. If the violence is sexualized, best practice is to collaborate with an intimacy director (theatre) or coordinator (camera).

The scope of this book does not allow for a detailed exploration of all aspects of consent in the working or teaching environments. Intimacy direction is a growing field, which will undoubtedly develop further very quickly, and it is worth investigating the different organizations involved for more up-to-date information.

Consent builds trust and, with trust, the work will be freer. It will be all the better for it, which must surely be a positive outcome for everyone.

CLASS

This book is primarily directed at students and teachers, so it is worth examining the safety processes for the classroom. Obviously, the teacher will have assessed the safety issues for the space. Is the room well-lit, of a comfortable temperature, and is there adequate ventilation? Is there sufficient space for the size of the class to learn and carry out the techniques safely? Is the flooring safe and are there issues with furniture or set crowding the space? Have the students been instructed in correct footwear and clothing for the session, and have they followed those instructions? Is anyone chewing gum, eating or drinking anything but bottled water? Have all hazardous jewellery and watches been removed? Are bags and personal items stored out of the way? Have students been warmed up preparatory to the work beginning? Have all instructions been communicated clearly and students' comprehension checked?

Safety in stage combat is not confined to the techniques themselves. If this book is used for personal study and the techniques practised without the presence of an instructor, great care must be taken that all of the above elements have been thought through prior to beginning work. Accidents in stage combat can happen because of many different causes, not just the obvious ones.

When working with a partner, two common reasons for accidents are starting without ensuring the partner is ready, and going too fast to begin with. A fight must always begin with eye contact between partners; this is safety in its most basic form. Look and see if your partner is ready for you. If they are not making eye contact, do not start. Get their attention first before you begin. Both partners must be clear about what is about to happen, what specific safety principles are in play, and how the technique is structured. It may seem

BASSC teacher Rosa Nicolas demonstrates how choreography is customizable to the performer.
ROB DAVIDSON

All performers need to be able to free themselves immediately in case of real emergency, as these restraints allow. *Wind in The Willows*, courtesy of The New Vic Theatre, Stoke-on-Trent.
ANDREW BILLINGTON

obvious, but it must also be explicitly stated who is the attacker and who is the victim. It is not unusual for teachers to see two students both punch at the same time.

Once everything has been established, start SLOWLY. Going slow gives the brain and body time to process information, establish priorities and get the technique right. When learning a new physical pattern, the brain begins the process of physically altering its own structure, increasing the connections and pathways between the different areas of the brain required to lock in the new information (Johnstone, 2017). Starting slowly gives this muscle memory, the motor learning, time to absorb the correct forms and information rather than the mistakes you will undoubtedly make if you go too fast, too soon. Aiming for product over process, going fast from the very beginning, not only inevitably leads to errors, but greatly increases the risk of an accident. Students should not pick up speed until both partners have explicitly agreed that they are comfortable with safety principles and technique, and are willing to go faster. Speed is picked up in incremental steps rather than simply blasting from slow-flow to full speed in one go, which is a recipe for disaster.

STRUCTURE

Each technique in this volume has been taken apart to examine the stress points – those moments that are most likely to facilitate or cause an accident. Safety principles have been applied to reinforce those areas, in order to reduce the possibility of injury whilst maintaining the performer's ability to act the fight. Over the years, many practitioners from many organizations have played with these ideas and principles in an effort to make them as safe and robust as possible. Part of that process has resulted in the codification and simplification of the safety principles into efficiently stated and easily remembered concepts. This also encourages the formation of a standardized approach to the body of techniques itself in both presentation and application.

The techniques themselves are however simply the building blocks with which the story of violence is constructed. They need to be cemented

order. There are variations on the cueing system depending on its application to weapons work or unarmed combat, but the basic version is as follows:

1. Eye contact.
2. Look at the target.
3. Preparation.
4. Action.
5. Reaction.

No matter how fast a fight flows, this system is the invisible underpinning that dictates where each performer is at each moment, and that maximizes their chances of staying safe. In exactly the same way as performers learn the cues for their next line, and expect their colleagues to give them the same cues in the same order in each performance, performers in a fight need to give and receive the right cues at the right time. In a scene of verbal confrontation, paraphrasing the cues, whilst probably leading to some confusion, can be worked around, perhaps with a little ad-libbing to get back on track; but giving the wrong cues in a physical

together and held firmly within a matrix that keeps them in a consistent shape, despite the stress of character choice and performance energy. That matrix is the cueing system. This is the standardized sequential flow of information that dictates which element of the technique happens in which

ABOVE LEFT: A rehearsal shot of one of the riskier fight illusions, made safe by the use of extremely stretchy material, cut and marked to exactly the right length. *Dial M for Murder*, courtesy of The New Vic Theatre, Stoke-on-Trent.
ANDREW BILLINGTON

Performers have to carefully rehearse the traffic of bodies and weapons in crowded scenes. *Robin Hood*, courtesy of The New Vic Theatre, Stoke-on-Trent.
ANDREW BILLINGTON

confrontation can lead to disaster. A mistake in fight cueing can place two performers on a deadly collision course.

RESPONSIBILITY

It is worth stating here that a performer should *never* improvise any moment of a fight on stage. Ever. An improvised moment in a stage fight means that it has become a real fight and people get hurt in real fights. The choreography is the formalized physical story, signed off by fight director, stage management and director. It is rehearsed until it is firmly in the muscle memory of the performers, and has been textured and enriched with the creation of acting beats that reveal the characters' story. It is then played consistently, without variation, night by night. Of course, performers may find variations in their vocal scoring of the fight, or in their character's emotional response to the moments, but those variations are never allowed to affect the core stability of who does what move, at which moment, to whom. Making an unauthorized change to that structure invites disaster.

It is also fair to say that a performer should take responsibility for their own safety. This can take a number of forms. Learn as much as possible: increasing your skillset can only make you safer, more employable, and a better performer. Increased knowledge gives you the ability to assess the performance environments you find yourself in and effectively judge whether the production company is looking out for your safety. Consider your health; a fit healthy body is a responsive tool, while a performer with an unfit body will find it hard to adequately support the character's physical demands. Keep yourself hydrated: a fully hydrated brain retains information more efficiently and has better reaction times (Popkin et al., 2010). Come to a stage combat class or rehearsal relaxed and fully fuelled: leave the tensions of the day at the door of the space.

This close-distance fight was carefully rehearsed before being taken to performance speed. *Treasure Island*, courtesy of The New Vic Theatre, Stoke-on-Trent.
ANDREW BILLINGTON

Possibly one of the most useful skills a performer can develop is the ability to isolate various parts of their body. It can be difficult to perform an enraged character without letting that over-riding emotion infuse every part of the body. A safety issue may arise when the hands are as filled with rage as the face, affecting the performer's fine motor control. Tension in the arms and hands adversely affects accuracy. The performer needs to find a way to play and fully embody the strongest emotions without allowing them to infect their hands or their weapons; they have to be able to separate emotional intensity from physical intensity. This is not natural; it is a learned and consciously applied skill, which must be worked on and rehearsed into the performance. Indicators that this is not being achieved might be loss of balance, punches and strikes not fully extending to the target zone, or contact strikes landing too hard. The performer needs to work on bleeding off that tension, allowing it to release into and support the character's story, but freeing up their arms and shoulders. Essentially, the storm must be able to rage in full fury on the performer's face, whilst their hands and feet must be working precisely at the calm, relaxed centre of the violence.

The character's rage can sometimes affect a performer so deeply that they experience 'red light fever'. This term from the world of filming describes the moment the red light on the camera indicates that filming has started, and the character rises to the surface and fully subsumes the performer. It can happen to the extent that the performer completely forgets the choreography and just follows the character's impulses into an improvised fight. This is extremely dangerous; if one performer observes it in their partner, they should immediately step back out of the fight and refuse to engage, if possible. It is unacceptable to place a partner in harm's way simply because it feels 'right' to allow the character full rein, without utilizing the strong foundation of safety principle and formal technique.

CONCLUSION

In conclusion, the primary focus for student, teacher, performer and fight director must always be the safety of themselves and of others. This must take precedence over story-telling, acting, and indeed all other production considerations. All activities linked to stage combat must be risk-assessed, and those assessments revisited on a regular basis. A conscious focus on all aspects and levels of safety must underpin all work in stage combat, as the slightest negligence or loss of focus can lead to life-changing injuries.

Stated in its most fundamental form, the responsibility of the individual involved in any form of staged violence is to keep themselves and all around them as safe as possible.

In this book the techniques themselves are structured into groups by type, but they can also be broken into groups by safety principle. The following glossary of safety principles discusses each element in detail and describes the 'family' of techniques that it works with. When you study a technique, ensure you always read the section on safety at the beginning of that particular chapter, as it will undoubtedly contain more information than the individual technique header will.

In a production performed in the round, these pistols were pointed at different entrances into the space to avoid them being directed at the audience. *Treasure Island*, courtesy of The New Vic Theatre, Stoke-on-Trent.
ANDREW BILLINGTON

GLOSSARY OF SAFETY PRINCIPLES

This section of the chapter contains an alphabetical list of all of the safety principles referenced in this book. Each principle is explained in full and the techniques that utilize it are also recorded.

CONTROLLED DESCENTS: CLOSE TO THE GROUND

This principle describes the first stage of all controlled descents, which is to get as close to the ground as possible before actually releasing the body and committing it to the ground. It is psychologically scary to create the illusion of falling from the full height of the body. It is also easier to control balance and the soft on soft principle when the distance to the ground is short. So each descent has its own structured moment to safely get lower whilst sustaining the illusion of a fall.

Risk: the performer shortcuts this element of the descent and ends up with a section of real fall, with all of the potential consequences.
Applies to: controlled descents.

CONTROLLED DESCENTS: FALL TO SAFETY

This controlled descent safety describes the victim's responsibility to ensure they are descending into a safe space. If they cannot create a moment to look back in character to be certain there is no hazard, they must work out a conscious moment of eye contact with their attacker, who can see the space and will agree to stop them if there is danger.

Risk: the performer takes their safety for granted, and forgets to check, greatly increasing their risk of injury.
Applies to: controlled descents.

DISPLACEMENT OF TARGET

Used when the performers have to be in distance to create the illusion of contact. The target zone is moved to a space near the partner and allows the target to be covered by the strike. The principle requires a clear shift of the attacker's eyes, from eye contact to looking at the target. Partly, this helps cue the partner and telegraph the move to the audience, but mostly it ensures that the attacker's strike goes to the safe place. If the performers maintain eye contact, there is a greater chance of the strike going towards the victim's face. Depending on the target, the distance from target zone to the victim's body will be between 6 and 12 inches (15–30 centimetres).

Risk: the attacker misjudges the placement of the attack.
Applies to: forehand and backhand profile slaps; forehand and backhand profile sweep slaps; roundhouse punch; parrot punches; straight punch; stomach punch; profile kicks to face and stomach; stomp kick to face; elbow strikes to stomach or latissimus dorsi.

DOVE OF PEACE

This is used specifically for the strangle. In a real strangle, the attacker's thumbs cross the victim's trachea to crush it closed. This technique overlaps the webbing of the two hands: the thumb and forefinger of the dominant hand drop on top of the forefinger and thumb of the other hand, removing the dangerous thumbs from the equation. The fingers and thumbs hug the sides of the victim's neck in a horizontal collar, as the webbing between thumb and forefinger makes light contact with the top front of the throat and the natural concavity of the palms protects the vocal instrument. The hands use just enough energy to remain in contact with the neck. The fingertips curl around and lightly dimple the muscles of the side or back of the neck (usually the sternocleidomastoid muscles, or the upper trapezius muscles running up beside the neck vertebrae, depending on the relative sizes of neck and hands). Avoid the tip of a thumb sticking up against the victim's jawbone, as pressure against the bone of the mandible is uncomfortable. Also avoid pointing the fingers up behind the victim's ears, for similar reasons.

Risk: the hands slide too far around and behind, placing the thumbs across the victim's vocal instrument.
Applies to: the strangle.

ENERGY ALONG THE GROUND, NOT INTO THE GROUND

This controlled descent principle describes the angle of descent of the performer's body. The steeper the angle of descent, the harder the impact; the shallower the angle, the easier it is to control that potential bump at the moment of contact. The most useful supporting image is that of the shallow descent of a plane landing at the airport. Each controlled descent contains a structured element to keep the energy moving along the floor. The performer has to avoid meeting the floor and stopping dead, because the energy their body imparts to the hard floor shocks back into them, potentially causing damage.

Risk: misjudging the angle of descent and impacting too hard, with consequent risk of harm.
Applies to: controlled descents.

EXHALE

This controlled descent safety describes how to keep the body relaxed whilst flowing down to the ground. Holding the breath locks the body into a state of tension, making it much more likely to be damaged upon contact with the ground. Actively breathing out when descending releases tension from the body, greatly reducing the chance of injury.

Risk: the performer allows fear or apprehension to cause them to hold their breath, increasing the hazard.
Applies to: controlled descents.

EYE CONTACT

This is baseline safety. The performer makes eye contact with their partner at the beginning of each phrase and ideally between each technique. This eye contact allows performers to check that their partner is focused and prepared. It creates the last opportunity to stop the fight if something is wrong. There are differing schools of thought regarding eye contact in a fight (*see* Chapter 10 for a more detailed discussion). For techniques where eye contact is not possible, it is usually replaced with physical contact or a vocal cue.

Risk: performers pay lip service to the moment of eye contact, but do not actually make a conscious confirmation of what they see.
Applies to: almost every partnered technique in the book, except for chokes from behind.

NEGOTIATION

This contact safety is the formalization of consent, and is specifically used any time one performer has to touch another. It comprises three elements. First, the negotiation of the contact itself, requiring one performer to actively seek the permission of their partner before they touch them. They must never assume that it is okay to make physical contact without first specifically asking their partner. Once that permission has been given, the assumption is that it holds good for the rest of the rehearsal, unless the partner chooses to clearly withdraw it. However, that permission must be sought again at the next rehearsal: it should not be assumed to be a blanket dispensation. Once the production is on its feet, these issues are dealt with at the fight call prior to each performance.

Second is the negotiation relating to how much energy is involved in the contact. For example, if it is a push, how hard will that push be. This will never be a constant; it is a variable that may change day by day, or even within the span of a rehearsal.

Third is the agreement that the victim will have final say on both issues. If the victim says no, there is no arguing or attempt to persuade them; there is merely an acceptance of their right to say no. The victim also has the right to change their mind, or even to rescind their permission or agreement. There should be no egos involved, no judgement of the partner's decision, simply agreement. Performers must bear in mind that for some people these can be very complex issues relying on a number of variables affected by that person's history, physical and mental health, and the current state of their relationship with others in the company.

Risk: in the heat of performance the attacker ignores the negotiated elements in favour of an instinctive response.
Applies to: zero energy and shared energy pushes; hair, ear and costume pulls; contact kicks; contact punches; knee to the stomach; strangle; choke from behind; contact elbow strikes.

OUT OF DISTANCE

This describes any position where there is enough distance between the two performers that they cannot hit each other without actually moving forward. That distance depends on the performance venue, the skill of the performers and their level of trust. The closer the hand (or foot or knee, and so on) is to the target, the more convincing it is for a larger section of the audience, but the higher the risk, and vice versa. The average distance is somewhere between 8 and 12 inches (20–30 centimetres). This principle relies on tricking the relatively poor depth perception of the human eye and is used for upstage/downstage techniques.

Risk: the attacker or victim leans or steps in, thus negating the safety distance.
Applies to: forehand, backhand and wide-angle upstage/downstage slap; jab punch; hook punch; backfist punch; uppercut punch; upstage/downstage kicks to face and stomach; upstage/downstage crescent kick.
In specific circumstances it can also work with: roundhouse punch, cross punch.

PROTECT THE FRAGILE AREAS OF THE BODY

This controlled descent principle focuses on the areas of the human body that can be easily damaged when they make contact with the ground, leading to potentially career-altering injuries. These are the face, the back of the head, the spine, the coccyx, the wrists, the elbows and the knees. Each descent is designed to either avoid, actively remove, or minimize the impact on these areas.

Risk: a moment of inattention leaves one of these areas of the body at risk of damage.
Applies to: controlled descents.

PULL TO SAFETY

Used specifically with the various versions of the pull, this principle focuses on the attacker's responsibility to ensure the victim's landing area is safe for them, as they may not be able to see it easily for themselves. The look into the space is the beginning of the pull and is also the attacker's last opportunity to cancel the technique before the victim is committed to it. This process not only encompasses an assessment of the physical hazards currently in the space, including the victim's proximity to the stage edge, but also scans for dangers about to enter the space. It is a proactive, predictive assessment of potential danger, rather than a passive one.

Risk: the attacker looks but does not consciously see, or looks but fails to predict other movement into the space, therefore pulling their partner into danger.
Applies to: hair, ear and costume pulls.

PUSH TO SAFETY

Used specifically with pushes, this principle focuses on the attacker's responsibility to ensure the space behind the victim is safe for them, as they cannot easily see it for themselves. This process not only encompasses an assessment of the physical hazards currently in the space, including the victim's proximity to the stage edge, but it also scans for dangers about to enter the space. It is a proactive, predictive assessment of potential danger, rather than a passive one.

Risk: the attacker looks but does not consciously see, or looks but fails to predict other movement into the space, therefore pushing their partner into danger.
Applies to: zero energy and shared energy pushes.

RED LIGHT/GREEN LIGHT

This permission safety is used specifically for avoidances. It clarifies the moment when the attacker looks to see if the victim has given permission for the attack by beginning their avoidance: this is the green light. If they have not begun to avoid, the attacker must pause or abort the attack; this is the red light. At speed in a performed fight, the cue to release the avoided attack is the very beginning of the avoidance. If the target is the face, the cue is the victim starting to move the head away from the strike, signalling permission to attack. The attacker must deliberately look for the cue, not look and assume they will see the cue. The attack must be a conscious choice based solely on whether the avoidance has begun.

Risk: the attacker looks and assumes the avoidance has begun without really checking, and attacks through a red light.
Applies to: parrot punches; roundhouse punch; any other non-contact strike that can also be avoided.

REVERSAL OF ENERGY

This describes a redirected flow of energy through the attacker's body, which deceives the audience as to its direction and intention. In reality, the energy of an attack drives into the victim's body. Depending on the technique, the attacker alone, or in combination with the victim, refocuses the flow of energy, either away from or around the victim's body, whilst maintaining the illusion that it moves into that body. If used for the strangle, this shared energy technique requires both partners to 'listen' closely to each other's physical energy, through the physical contact of the victim's grip on the attacker's arms, so that they can balance it, as one pulls in one direction and the other in the opposite. For the choke from behind, the attacker places one arm in opposition to the other – one pulling outwards, the other pulling inwards, in energized resistance to each other. The energy used is apparent to the audience in the dynamic tension of the attacker's arms, but, if it is executed effectively, it is impossible to see in which direction it moves.

Risks: either the partnered energy is mismatched and the strangling hands start to bounce on the victim's throat, or a gap appears between hands and neck, destroying the illusion, or the attacker misapplies the energy in the wrong direction.
Applies to: the strangle; the choke from behind and the sleeper hold.

SOFT ON SOFT

A contact safety specifically designed to minimize the hardness of a moment of contact and the potential for damage. Performers always make a negotiated contact on large areas of muscle, such as the abdominals, the hamstrings, the latissimus dorsi, the deltoids and, possibly, the calf muscles. These muscles vary greatly – in size and thickness and from performer to performer – as does the individual's perception of the strength of a contact. The abdominals will always be tightened to provide maximum shock protection for the internal organs. The other useable muscle groups are usually left relaxed, although some performers like to tighten the deltoids and latissimus dorsi. When used for a controlled descent, it describes making contact with the ground on areas of muscle, avoiding less well-protected areas of the body. The point of the principle generally is to avoid striking areas of bone, or areas lightly covered with a thin layer of muscle.

Risk: the attacker mis-targets and strikes an area that will hurt either themselves or the victim.
Applies to: contact punches; contact kicks; knee to the stomach; parrot punches; blocks; elbow strike to the latissimus dorsi; controlled descents.

SOFT STRIKING IMPLEMENT

This contact safety is an extension of the soft on soft principle, ensuring that whatever makes contact with a performer is as yielding as it can be. If the attack is a kick, the softest part of the footwear or foot is chosen – usually the shoelaces area. The knee to the stomach always uses the thigh muscle, and a contact punch the hollow fist. This relaxed version of a fist relies on relaxation to achieve soft contact, rather than an inherent softness provided by muscle, or breadth of contact area.

Risk: different for each application of the principle. For a kick, the attacker may flex their foot, making contact with the toes. With a stamp, they might lead with the heel rather than the flat of the foot. For the stomach attack, the risk is leading with the knee rather than the thigh; for contact punches, it is punching with a tight fist.
Applies to: contact punches; contact kicks; knee to the stomach; elbow strike to the latissimus dorsi.

VICTIM CONTROL

This principle is often used as a counterbalancing element within a technique, to provide the victim with the opportunity to stop the moment if they feel they are in danger. It cannot be applied to every technique, only those with an element of contact. In the strangle or the versions of the pull, it is used to lock the attacker's hands into position. Simply by letting go, the victim can terminate the moment, as the direction of the attacker's energy and their relaxed grip cause them to immediately release the victim.

Risk: limited, beyond the attacker either reversing the direction of their energy, or gripping too tightly.
Applies to: the strangle; hair, ear and costume pulls.

WITHDRAW THE ENERGY

This contact safety describes the moment the strike reaches the surface of the partner's body. At that precise moment of touch, the attacker reverses the direction of the strike, pulling the energy of the attack back from the target. In a real fight, the aggressor visualizes their attack pushing through the victim's body. With such a strike, even when the body stops the fist or foot from travelling any further, the energy shockwave imparted continues to move through the victim's body, creating damage. This safety principle is designed to specifically avoid that risk. It is sometimes described as 'pulling the blow', although this term should be used with care, as it often leads to an action that slows down at the last moment, or an attack that bounces out faster than its approach. Neither of these tells the correct visual story to the audience. To work well, this needs practice, which should always start slowly. The withdrawal itself must happen immediately: if there is the slightest delay between the moment of contact and that of withdrawal, the energy enters the body and is felt as a heavier strike than it is meant to be. To frame this concept in simple terms, every time somebody applauds, they withdraw the energy from their own hands at the moment of contact. Nobody claps by beating through their own hands.

Risk: the attacker fails to be precise in judging the surface of the target and strikes into it, effectively making a real strike.
Applies to: contact punches; contact kicks; knee to the stomach; elbow strike to the latissimus dorsi.

6
WHO SEES WHAT AND WHAT WORKS WHERE

This may seem an obvious statement, but not every member of the audience in a theatre sees exactly the same thing. The location of their seat affects how much or how little they see. An audience member on the extreme right of the auditorium will have a very different view from that of someone sitting on the extreme left; they will have different sightlines.

Sightline literally means 'line of sight' – the direct line from the eyes to the object being viewed. Understanding exactly what the sightlines are in any particular performance space is integral to making every one of the non-contact techniques in this book actually work. Without that basic knowledge it is impossible to successfully create the illusion of contact. The observer believes that contact has been made when the striking implement (fist, foot, weapon) gets between their eyes and the target. If that obscuring of the target, however brief, is linked with an appropriate physical and vocal reaction, you create belief in the reality of the attack. If any of the sightlines are ignored, those moments of violence will not work for audience members sitting in those positions.

Non-contact unarmed combat techniques only exist in relation to an audience, and specifically to the position of the audience in relation to the fight. Without knowing roughly what that is, it is impossible to choreograph an effective fight. Indeed, part of a fight director's work in the technical rehearsal will inevitably involve checking various elements of the fight work for all of the extreme sightlines in the theatre, side to side, and high to low. It is important to understand that not all techniques work in all

A fight created specifically for thrust staging with audience on three sides. *The Beggars' Opera*, courtesy of The Storyhouse, Chester.
MARK CARLINE

venues, because the sightlines can be too extreme for some actions to cover them all.

THE IMPACT OF SIGHTLINES

Taking the upstage/downstage slap as an example, Figure 2 shows that, although the illusion of contact is successful for most of the audience, those sitting on either end of the front row can look directly through the safety gap between the attacker's hand and the victim's face. Consequently, it looks to them as if the attacker has missed the victim. If the

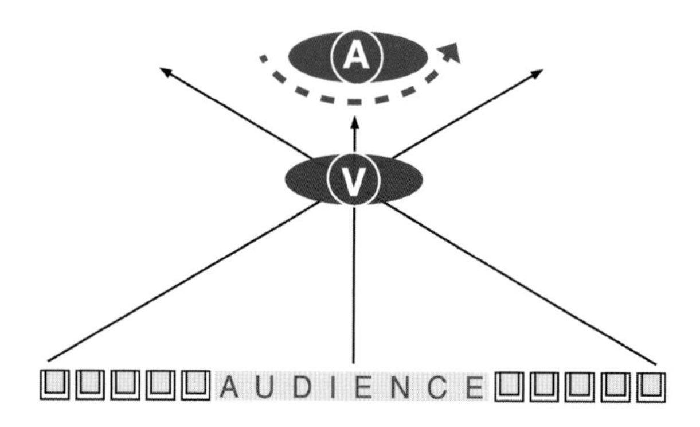

Figure 2: The path of the upstage/downstage slap does not cross the sightlines from the ends of the audience, looking as if it misses.

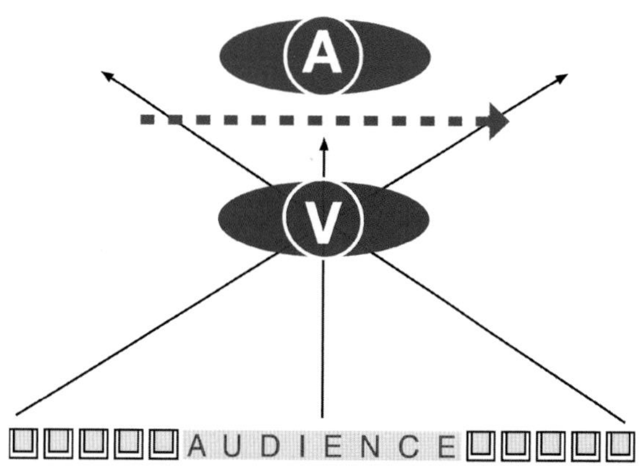

Figure 3: This wide-angle slap does cross the sightlines from the extreme ends of the audience, looking as if it hits.

wide-angle slap is substituted, as in Figure 3, the action now works for every position on the front row.

Alternatively, pulling the original fight moment further back upstage, as in Figure 4, would result in the narrowing of the cone of sightlines, making it possible for the upstage/downstage slap to work for all points of view. It is a simple solution, if it is compatible with other variables in the choreographic equation, such as set, lighting or depth of stage.

A high house poses a number of challenges. To some extent, all auditoriums have height to them, even if they are a single raked bank of seating. However, as architects and managers attempt to squeeze as many paying audience members as possible into a finite space, most theatres have at least one circle, if not two or three. The highest of these naturally create a different bank of sightlines, with audience members looking down towards the action. As a result, where a technique might easily work for seating in the stalls, or even the Royal Circle, it often fails to convince anyone seated higher in the house.

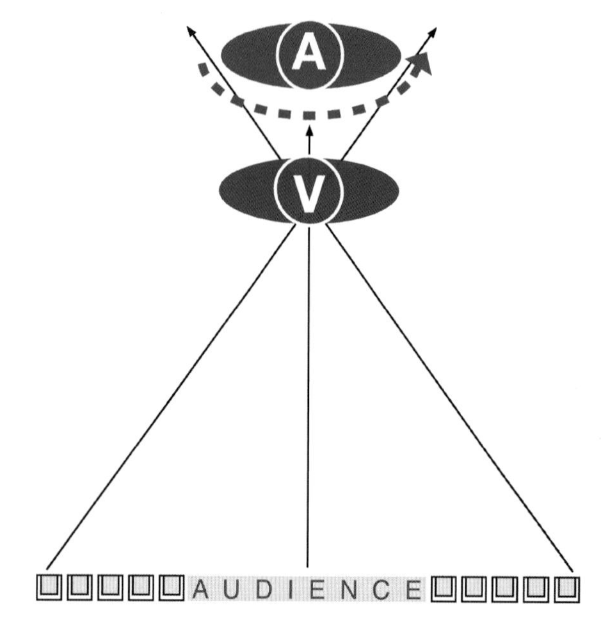

Figure 4: Moving the fight upstage narrows the sightlines, allowing an upstage/downstage slap to be effective.

For example, the profile slap (Figure 5) may work for the lower levels of the auditorium, but not for anyone seated above them. In this case, the profile sweep slap (Figure 6) might be a better option, as the path of the attacker's hand closes off all of the sightlines.

Again, it is also entirely possible to make the original choice work simply by pulling it further upstage to alter the sightlines, as seen in Figure 7.

VARIATIONS IN STAGING FORMATIONS

The sightlines for the more traditional end-on or proscenium arch staging configurations are relatively easily understood, but there are more extreme staging formations, such as traverse, thrust or in-the-round, which all increase the complexity

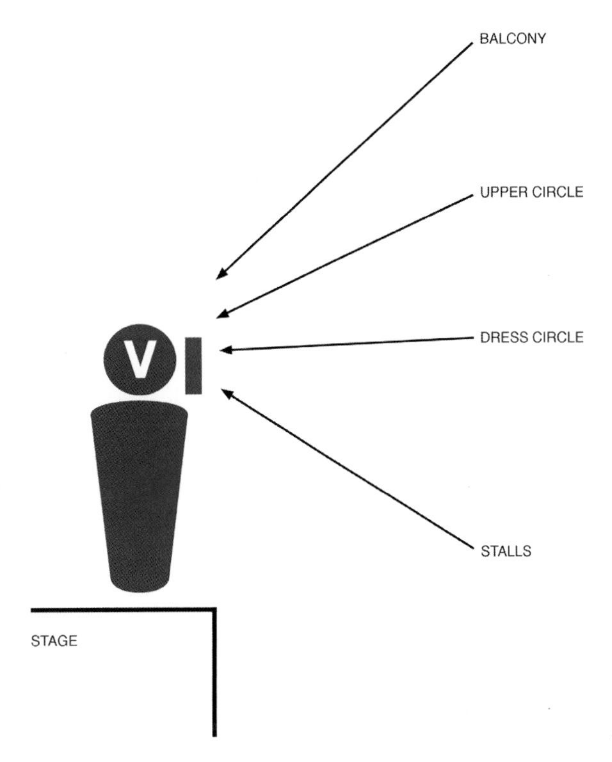

Figure 5: The two top tiers of the audience can see between the hand and the face, destroying the illusion.

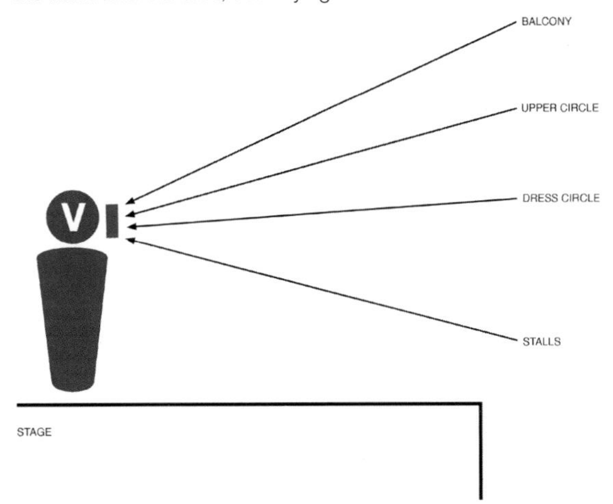

Figure 7: The profile slap works in a high auditorium if pulled upstage, narrowing the vertical sightlines.

of the challenge for fight directors and performers. The demands of these non-traditional formations (Figures 8, 9 and 10) will limit the number of effective non-contact techniques. This is why contact techniques are so important – often the

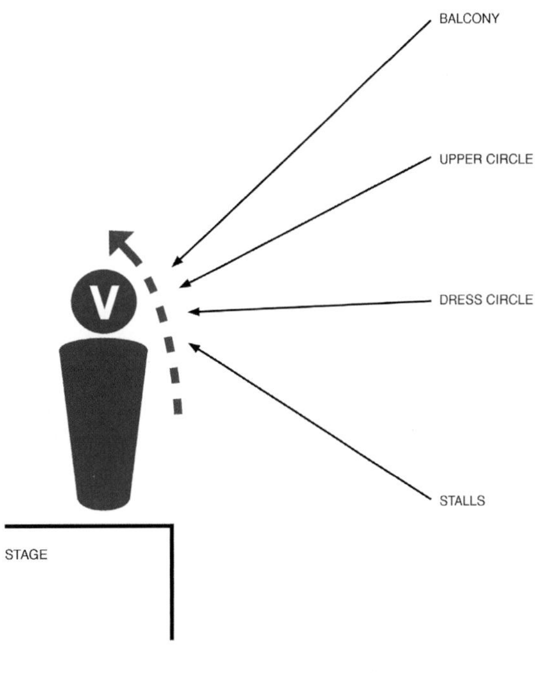

Figure 6: The profile sweep slap covers all sightlines in a high auditorium, creating the illusion of contact.

fight director will have little choice but to explore those options, if they wish to craft a competent story.

With each staging configuration, there are a few simple considerations to take into account:

- **Proscenium arch/end-on**: how wide is the audience? How far upstage is the action?

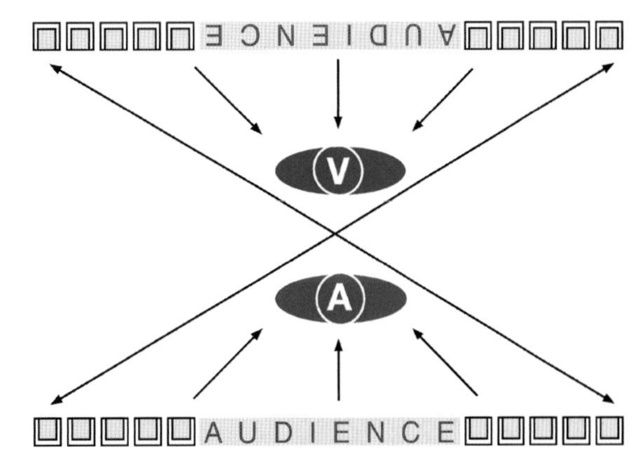

Figure 8: Long traverses make it harder to cover extreme sightlines.

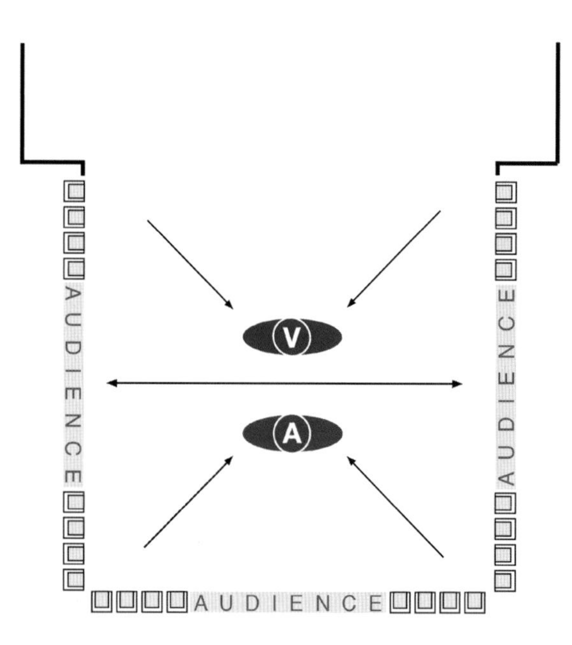

Figure 9: Difficult sightlines for a thrust.

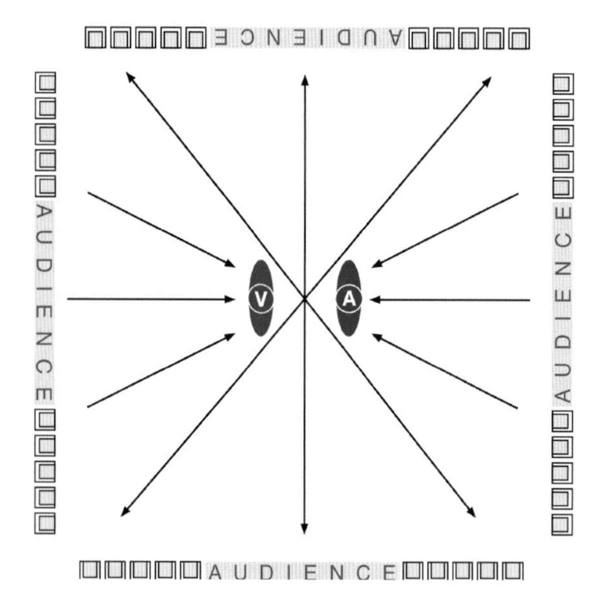

Figure 10: Awkward sightlines for in-the-round staging.

- **Traverse**: how close is the audience? How long is the traverse?
- **Thrust**: how wide and deep is the thrust? How far upstage is the action?
- **In-the-round**: how close is the audience? Where are the voms?

With all of the formations, the fight director also needs to take into account the height of the audience?

WHEN TO REACT

Where the staging is of the more common end-on type, it is clear that, for an attack travelling across the stage, each member of the audience will perceive the moment of illusory contact as happening at slightly different times, depending on the angle of their sightline (*see* the example of the cross punch, Figure 11). This raises the question of when should the victim react. At the first moment of potential contact? At the last moment of potential contact? At some point in between?

The answer lies in an understanding of how the brain works. It is known that the brain does not consciously process all of the information it receives second by second; instead, it filters and prioritizes some input (Markowsky, 2017), often drawing upon previous experience, memory and its predictive structures to link different elements of information to create a logical, seamless story

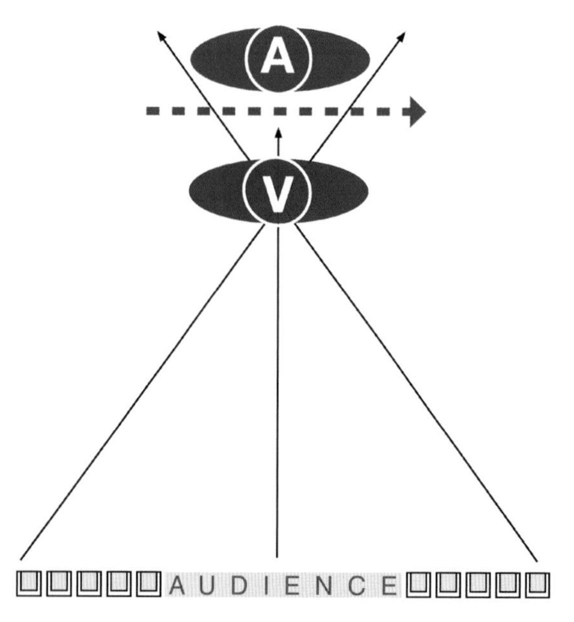

Figure 11: It is clear that each audience position sees the moment of illusory contact at different times.

of the body's moment by moment experience (Shimojo, 2014). This postdictive process happens at a level below conscious awareness.

What bearing does this have on the manipulation of sightlines? Well, it is actually a positive, as it builds some leeway into the techniques. If the attack, reaction and knap are executed as fast as possible, the brain puts together the technical elements of the movement, the aggressive speed and the percussive sound effect, and retroactively creates a logical narrative to support the information, persuading the observer that somebody just got hit hard. This happens even if, for that sightline, the reaction was slightly early or late. Surprise, speed and aggression can completely mask the fact that the moment did not technically work, convincing the observer that they have seen something that they did not actually see.

This comforting fact suggests that the reaction should be played directly for the centre of the audience, with the reaction timed to occur as the attack crosses the line passing from the centre of the audience, through the victim and on upstage. (This is known as the target line.) This centralized position acts as a median, meaning that for equal numbers of the audience the reaction will be slightly early or slightly late, but not egregiously so for any single member. If the reaction is executed well, the disparity will not be noticed by the audience as it will fall comfortably within the range of variance that the brain will, albeit unknowingly, forgive.

TARGET LINE

An accurate calculation of the optimum target line – the crossing of which will convince the audience that contact was made – relies on an awareness of all of the sightlines in play. However, therein lies a hidden pitfall for both attacker and victim. They must consciously work out where the target line lies, because if they leave it as an unconscious calculation, their brains will trick them.

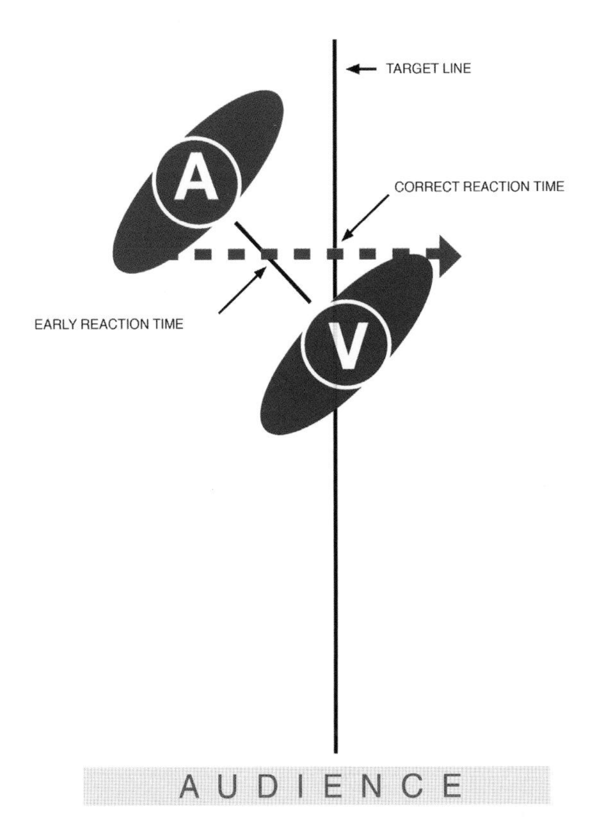

Figure 12: Performers must know the position of the target line to the centre of the audience when timing their reactions.

Left to its own devices, the brain of both performers will decide that the moment of illusory contact occurs when the attack crosses the line between their bodies. However, this is not always the case (*see* Figure 12), particularly if the two performers are on a diagonal, rather than directly upstage/downstage of each other. Two possible errors can result: either the attack will be misplaced, looking good from the attacker's perspective, but not working for the audience; or the reaction will be mistimed, looking far too early or late from the position of the audience.

As with so much in the performance of staged violence, instinct must bow to the conscious use of craft to ensure that each moment works as well as possible, for as much of the audience as possible. Because there are so many fixed points of view within the auditorium, the technical choices the fight director and performers make can only ever be a best compromise, in order to achieve a structured approximation of reality. However, as long as precision is combined with speed, the audience will never realize, because their brains will do half the work for the performers.

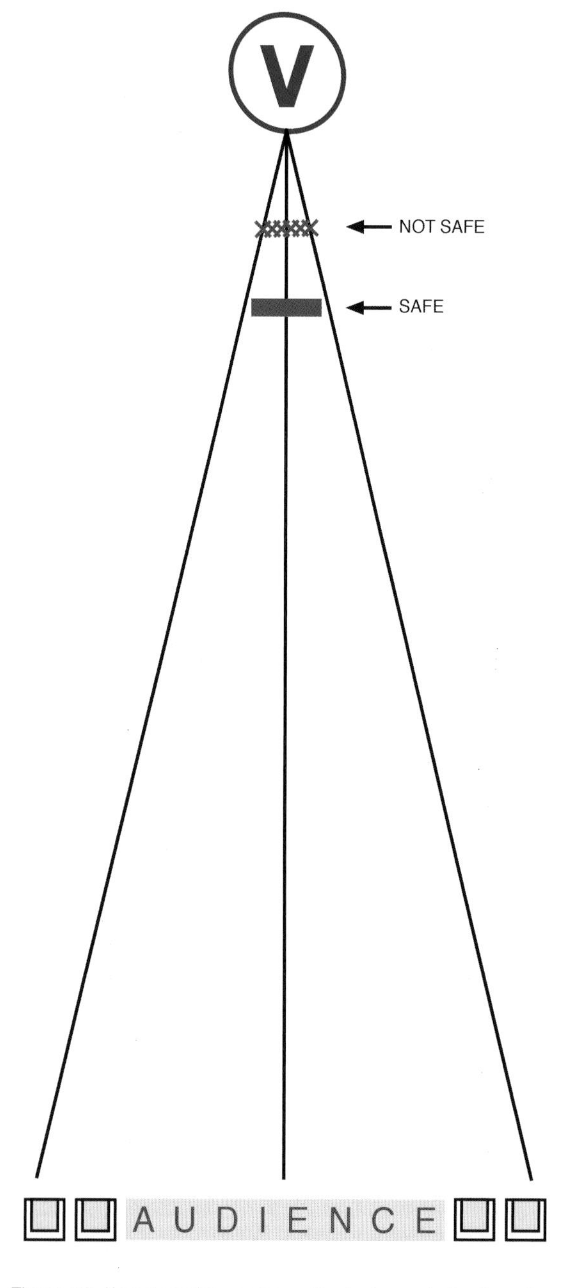

Figure 13: If upstage/downstage attacks towards the target are to cover all sightlines, they will be too close for safety; at a safe distance, they do not cover all sightlines.

ORIENTATION TO THE SIGHTLINES

While many of the techniques rely on crossing the target line to create an illusion of contact, there are many other attacks, the majority of them oriented upstage/downstage, that rely on spiking, or obscuring the target line. Instead of travelling laterally across the stage, intersecting multiple sightlines before they reach the target, these techniques, because they move in towards the target, have to rely on the width of the fist or foot to close off those lines. The only way to achieve this with a narrow object is to get extremely close to the target (*see* Figure 13), which is of course more dangerous. For safety reasons, the fist has to be pulled back, greatly reducing its

The Greek National Opera auditorium demonstrates how high the audience can be in relation to the stage.

efficacy, which is why most upstage/downstage techniques are reserved for small to mid-size theatres.

Sightlines are the hidden secret of unarmed stage combat, and the single most important variable in determining the physical structure of a staged fight. Without an understanding of how they work, a performer will be unable to utilize the techniques in this book effectively, and a fight director will be unable to make any choreography work in anything but the smallest of venues. They simply cannot be ignored if you wish to convince your audience that there is any reality to your violent conflict.

WHAT WORKS WHERE

Clearly, not every technique works in every performance space. The sightlines unique to each venue will have an impact on the design of choreography

TABLE 1 TECHNIQUES FOR A PROSCENIUM ARCH/END-ON STAGE

Slaps
Upstage/downstage slap
Backhand upstage/downstage slap
Wide-angle upstage/downstage slap
Profile slap
Backhand profile slap
Profile sweep slap
Backhand profile sweep slap

Punches
Jab punch
Hook punch
Upstage/downstage backfist
Roundhouse punch + with avoidance
Parrot punch
Straight punch in profile
Cross punch
Uppercut punch
Stomach punch

Figure 14: Proscenium arch staging.

Kicks
Upstage/downstage kick (head)
Upstage/downstage kick (stomach)
Upstage/downstage crescent kick
Profile kick (head)
Profile kick (head – kneeling)
Roundhouse kick (stomach)

Chokes
Strangle
Sweep break
Choke
Elbow strike to the stomach
Sleeper hold
Horizontal elbow strike to the lats

Contact
Zero energy push
Shared energy push
Costume pull
Hair pull
Ear pull
Kick to the thigh (standing)
Kick to the thigh (lying down)
Knee to the stomach
Hollow-fist stomach punch
Flick-hand stomach punch
Open-palm strike to the stomach
Blocks
Kick to the groin

Controlled descents
Big step descent
Front descent
Side descent (curtsy)
Side descent (parachute style)

and therefore on the detailed acting choices made by the cast. In Part III, each technique chapter lists the style of venue best suited to the individual technique.

This section gathers that information together in one place to allow the reader to search for viable techniques by venue, prior to reading up on their specific details, but it does not sift these techniques out according to those that work well in high auditoriums. The reality is that, beyond the contact and descent techniques, only a few of these methods are particularly effective in such venues. The situation is usually handled by cheating the position of the performers on the stage, and adjusting the expectations of all involved in the creation of the story.

Sometimes, pragmatism requires fight directors to make choices of techniques that are not optimal for a particular staging configuration. The result is that the illusion of contact is sacrificed for a small fraction of the audience. Obviously, this is not ideal, but if it is handled skilfully, using the tools of speed, aggression and misdirection, the negative impact on the story-telling for that part of the audience can be minimized.

Something that must be made clear is that the skill of unarmed stage combat does not (indeed cannot) exist without an explicit understanding of

TABLE 2 TECHNIQUES FOR A THRUST STAGE

Slaps
Profile slap – variation
Backhand profile slap – variation
Profile sweep slap – variation
Backhand profile sweep slap – variation

Punches
Roundhouse punch with avoidance
Parrot punch
Stomach punch
Hollow-fist stomach punch
Blocks
Kick to the groin

Kicks
Roundhouse kick (stomach) – variation

Chokes
Strangle
Sweep break
Choke
Elbow strike to the stomach
Sleeper hold
Horizontal elbow strike to the lats

Contact
Zero energy push
Shared energy push
Costume pull
Hair pull
Ear pull
Kick to the thigh (standing)
Kick to the thigh (lying down)
Knee to the stomach

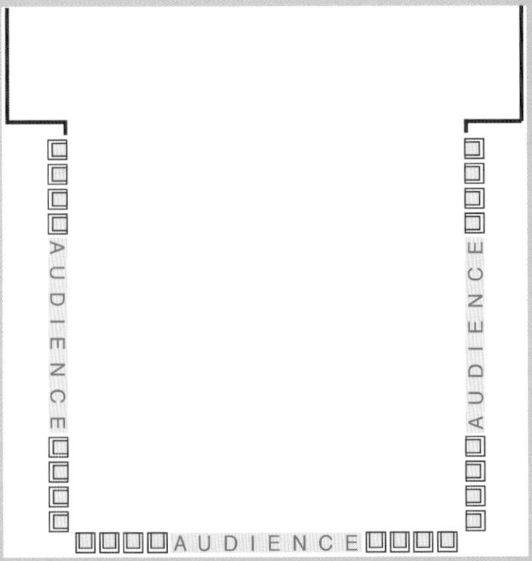

Controlled descents
Big step descent
Front descent
Side descent (curtsy)
Side descent (parachute style)

Figure 15: Thrust staging.

where the audience is at every point in relation to the performers. Apart from some of the contact methods, the core of the techniques under discussion rely on knowing the sightlines from the extremities of the audience seating. Not every move is going to work for every type of staging. In fact, the position of the performers on the stage itself – whether they are further up or downstage, opening or closing sightlines – can influence the choice of attack. Only a bad fight director is going to choose a move that does not work for a large proportion of the audience, and only an inattentive director is going to allow them to do so.

The array of techniques available has been developed in response to the constraints that various auditoriums have placed on fight directors. It is their creative responses to those restrictions that have led to the variety of choices available when it comes to attacking a character.

Each of the four staging configurations below is clarified using a simple illustration. Bear in mind these are generic and that each particular venue is a variation on the theme, with its own specific challenges.

TABLE 3 TECHNIQUES FOR A TRAVERSE STAGE

Slaps
Profile slap – variation
Backhand profile slap – variation
Profile sweep slap
Backhand profile sweep slap

Punches
Roundhouse punch with avoidance
Parrot punch
Straight punch in profile
Cross punch
Stomach punch

Kicks
Profile kick (head)
Profile kick (head – kneeling)
Roundhouse kick (stomach)

Chokes
Strangle
Sweep break
Choke
Elbow strike to the stomach
Sleeper hold
Horizontal elbow strike to the lats

Contact
Zero energy push
Shared energy push
Costume pull
Hair pull
Ear pull

Figure 16: Traverse staging.

Kick to the thigh (standing)
Kick to the thigh (lying down)
Knee to the stomach
Hollow-fist stomach punch
Blocks
Kick to the groin

Controlled descents
Big step descent
Front descent
Side descent (curtsy)
Side descent (parachute style)

TABLE 4 TECHNIQUES FOR AN IN-THE-ROUND STAGE

Slaps
Profile slap – variation
Backhand profile slap – variation
Profile sweep slap – variation
Backhand profile sweep slap – variation

Punches
Roundhouse punch with avoidance
Parrot punch

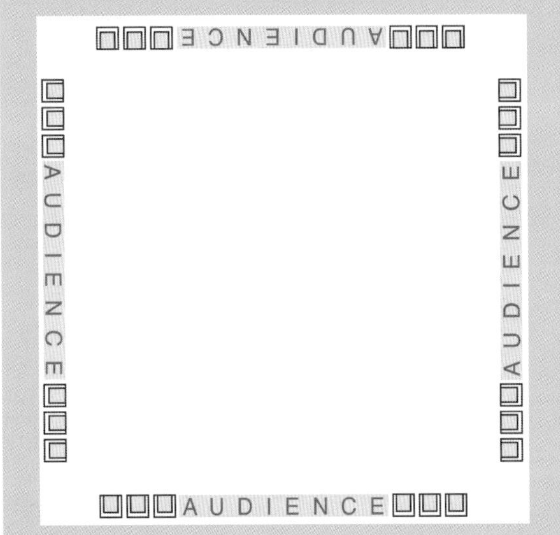

Figure 17: In-the-round staging.

Kicks
Roundhouse kick (stomach) – variation

Chokes
Strangle
Sweep break
Choke
Elbow strike to the stomach
Sleeper hold
Horizontal elbow strike to the lats

Contact
Zero energy push
Shared energy push
Costume pull
Hair pull
Ear pull
Kick to the thigh (standing)
Kick to the thigh (lying down)
Knee to the stomach
Hollow-fist stomach punch
Blocks
Kick to the groin

Controlled descents
Big step descent
Front descent
Side descent (curtsy)
Side descent (parachute style)

An example of open-air in-the-round staging. *Two Gentlemen of Verona*, courtesy of The Storyhouse, Chester.
MARK CARLINE

PART II

PERFORMANCE SPECIFICS

7
MUSIC OF THE FIGHT

SOUNDSCAPE

When the human animal engages in physical violence it does not do so quietly. Noise is created in every real fight, both deliberately and inadvertently, whether it be war cries, kiai, curses and insults, or the sounds of pain, effort and impact. When creating a staged fight, these noises will also inevitably be present, because it is almost impossible to engage in physical action without sound leaking from the body. The error that is often made by performers is to accept the sounds that they instinctively make as the totality of their performance. Instead, the moment may be seized as an opportunity to consciously craft a musical score designed to achieve specific aims.

This is an idea that was fully embraced in its early years by the movie industry, and has been fully mastered in its many forms. An audience can be inspired to have a particular emotional response to a certain character at a specific moment, and those emotional responses can be shifted at the director's whim. It is a skilled, nuanced art form, utilizing music and sound to bypass the logical areas of the brain and to directly stimulate the emotionally responsive areas, creating the exact response desired. The sophisticated twenty-first century movie audience may be well aware that it is being manipulated, yet, despite that knowledge, it is mostly unable to prevent itself responding to those aural stimuli, to at least some degree (Lipscomb, 2019).

Most people would agree that a soundtrack can alter the emotional response to the character situations portrayed, but how important is that background noise to an audience's experience of action and tension? To give an indication, try experimenting with your favourite action or horror movie: choose a sequence you find particularly exciting and watch it with the sound on mute. Watch it again with the sound engaged, and reflect on the difference in your response, emotional and physical. Which version created clearer emotional reactions? Did you note a difference in physical effect, such as altered breathing patterns, a shift in heart rate, adjusted posture, or muscular tension? How much more physically invigorating is the action sequence when taking advantage of every Hollywood sound effects trick (Zarrelli, 2016)? How much better could a fight be if a similar approach was followed in live performance work?

STRUCTURE

It may seem obvious that, in the creation of a fight, there will also be an accompanying vocal soundtrack supporting the story of the action. But the most common response performers have to this situation is to allow instinct to shape their soundscape moment by moment as they perform the fight. The problem with simply allowing the body to make noise when and how it wishes is that it will tend to the generic rather than the specific, and that it will be responsive only to what is actually happening to itself. In other words, whilst the character is experiencing pain, the performer is only experiencing effort. At worst, the sounds made will reflect exertion, not pain; at best, they will be a generalized attempt at pain. To achieve maximum effect and to make their fight as individual and realistic as possible, the performer needs to work out exactly how they want the audience to respond to each moment. This will then give

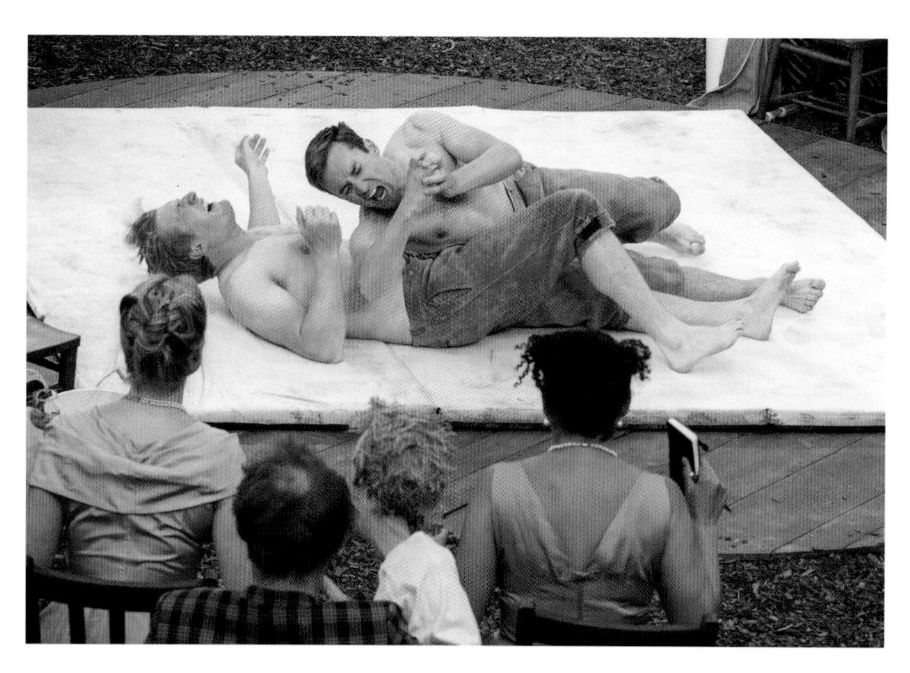

A moment woven from three carefully timed vocal stories: the attacker's effort vocals, the victim's pain vocals and the shock vocals of the onlookers, all in a clear sequence. *As You Like It*, courtesy of The Storyhouse, Chester.
MARK CARLINE

them the framework upon which to hang specific choices for each element of the fight.

Consider how a stand-up comedian constructs and refines their routine. They create their gags and place them into a particular order, in an attempt to get laughs, and building the ability to gather later laughs with shorthand triggers. They will then try out the routines and see what works and what needs adjustment. They may shift gags within the sequence, to see whether different timing or placement makes them more effective; if not, they may dump the gag completely and plug in an alternative (Small, 2019). A performer creating a fight sequence needs to be just as proactive and conscious in their manipulation of sound to achieve the greatest impact on their audience. If a particular sound is not working, it should be replaced with a different choice with an alternative payoff.

THE IMPACT OF STORY

The creation of a musical score for a fight must take account of a number of variables (Raphael, 2001). What is physically happening to the character? If it is simply effort, then how much? What is their physical condition? Their age? How tired are they at this point in the fight? If there is pain, then what type? What area of the body? Is that area already injured? Is the pain expected or unexpected? How does the pain affect the body in the longer term? What experience does the character have with violence? What is the character's emotional response to both violence and pain? What is their relationship with the attacker?

In exactly the same way as they would analyse text line by line and word by word, the performer must do the same with their fight, teasing it apart move by move and scoring each moment exactly as if they were writing music. A page of an orchestral score has multiple staves for different sections of the orchestra: woodwind, brass, percussion, and so on. The fight performer's score should be constructed in a similar fashion, with staves for exertion, pain, emotional response and text, all interweaving to create a personal symphony of agonized aggression.

Audiences are trained by a lifetime of experience to draw complex information from the subtlest of sounds. For example, most parents can instinctively tell by the quality of the sound of a crying child whether that child is in severe distress or is only seeking attention. That ability for an audience to discern detailed information from simple sound means that performers must make a conscious effort to create precise, well thought-through vocal choices, which reflect and clarify unique story-telling beats. Anything less is simply bad acting or professional laziness.

THE PRODUCTION OF SOUND

At any single moment in a fight, a specific sound may need to convey not only information relating to the physical condition of the body, but also to its emotional state and response, and to the level and quality of pain it is experiencing. To do justice to this level of complexity, the performer needs access to their full, responsive vocal range, tone and pitch. However, if the performer continues to make instinctive choices in the fight, they generally only utilize the comfortable middle zone of their vocal range, and often simply make generic grunts of exertion. In stage combat circles this is often referred to as 'grunts-per-minute' or GPM. These choices are, at root, poor story-telling. On the other hand, they may find themselves losing control and committing their voice completely to the reality of the violence, consequently damaging it (Ryker, 2001).

The production of a chosen sound must be approached at a technical level, taking into account not only the various story-telling components but also the constraints of the performance space. Will a sound that might, under normal violent circumstances, be unstructured, need to be consciously structured, to ensure it reaches the entire audience? For example, an exhalation after a real strike to the stomach might only be a release of air from the lungs, a sound that may only, in the theatre, reach partway into the stalls. To craft a sound that reveals the correct story elements, and reaches to the back of the highest area of the auditorium,

This performer will have carefully rehearsed safely producing sound in this position. *King Lear*, courtesy of the Guildford Shakespeare Company.
STEVE PORTER

the performer will have to work with structured sound designed to interact with the acoustics of the space, and created with a clear awareness of what they are trying to achieve (Brereton, 2014).

Under the stress of conflict humans often make very strange noises and certainly utilize the full gamut of expressive sound. Everyone is aware of this, which is why any sound created must mirror and reflect the audience's experience of the reality of pain, heightened emotion or effort under emotional strain (Munro, 2001). If it fails to do so, there is a risk of building a barrier between them and the character, which will be difficult to surmount. How can they engage with the character if they cannot unconsciously believe what they are hearing?

TWO INSTRUMENTS

Performers often forget that they have two instruments at their command. Not only can they make vocalized sound to convey information to the audience, they can also use their breathing. Sound and breath can be used together or separately to cue the audience as to the character's state. The first tool the performer instinctively reaches for is vocalized sound, but to ignore breath is to ignore a subtle and muscular form of communication (Coetzee, 2001). Every member of the audience has spent their life unconsciously studying the non-verbal cues produced by the human body (Puce, 2013), as a means of ascertaining the levels of risk around them. The sound of breathing is one of these.

Everyone in the audience will be aware of how the breathing changes when a person is nervous, or out of breath, or fearful (Ricard, 2014). Everyone knows that stertorous breathing can be a sign of illness, or that a sudden sharp nasal inhalation can be a prelude to an immediate physical attack. They may not, however, be aware of the fact that the body responds to the visual cues of the rise and fall of the chest or the flaring of the nostrils (Olsen, 2013). All these elements combined create a means for passing information to the audience that is received subliminally, yet can be completely under the conscious control of the performer. It is entirely possible to reach inside the audience's collective head and adjust how they feel about a character with a simple shift of breath.

VOCAL SAFETY

An additional benefit to placing strong focus on communication through altering the pattern, rhythm and audibility of the breath is that it reduces the risk of damage to the vocal instrument. An actual violent confrontation can leave the fighters struggling vocally in its aftermath. Hoarse, croaking, sore in the throat, their voices are temporarily damaged by the unsupported screaming and shouting usually involved in a real fight (Voice Foundation, 2006). Sadly, performers are also sometimes left in a similar condition after performing a staged fight (Munro, 2001). This happens for a number of reasons, but the most common is that they have simply forgotten to apply everything they know about how to support, protect and use their vocal instrument in such a way that it remains healthy, no matter what physical demands are placed on it. In the heat of performance, instinct can override technique, putting the performer's voice at risk of damage.

When it comes to the safety of the performer's voice, and therefore their career, it is necessary to go further and consider it as vocal choreography, to be afforded the same importance as the physical moves (Olson, 2001). The sounds the performer makes must be considered in terms of their physical position. Is the body aligned to allow physical and breath support for the sound they need to make at that point? Does the position of the head and neck allow them to release the sound rather than constraining it? Has physical tension been introduced momentarily in a manner that will cause poor vocal production (Olson, 2001)? The performer must be able to survive the performance, and scale the same mountain again the following day. Survival must refer to vocal safety and health as much as physical safety and health.

Vocal work for this technique is crafted to avoid stressing the vocal instrument by shifting focus on to the articulators in the mouth. *Henry V*, courtesy of the Guildford Shakespeare Company.
MARK DEAN

This focus is particularly relevant for opera singers, who physically cannot produce the sound they need if their body is in the wrong position. Fight directors working with extreme singers very quickly learn what is achievable physically, and what places too much demand on breath production and placement, or which body positions misalign the voice (Newcomb and Meyer, 2001). The singers themselves are very clear about what is possible and what is not, and will always inform the artistic team if they are asking too much.

Clearly, damage can be caused to any vocal instrument that is inadequately prepared for the work or has not been taken into consideration whilst creating the physical choreography and its attendant musical score. Given this risk, it is surely important to think about choreographing body and voice in conjunction with each other. This may not be as radical a demand as it might at first seem: the difference between a supported and an unsupported position can be subtle. Often, it is as much a matter of awareness as anything else.

There is a further complexity to consider. The illusion of vocal violence must be created in exactly the same way as the illusion of physical violence. A completely genuine vocal response will be unsustainable over an extended run of a production (Ryker, 2001). Whatever sounds the performer chooses to create, they must be able to recreate them for the entire run, perhaps as many as eight times a week, without stressing their vocal instrument. They need to look for ways to bypass the throat and, by directing air through the lips or the nasal cavity, find sounds that mimic those created by the vocal folds. The trick is not only to work with placement, but also to adjust the parameters of volume, pitch, rhythm and duration to marry the technical requirements of the sound with the artistic needs of the story beat (Lowry and Walsh, 2001).

There is a full-throated roar as Kate breaks free – the sound chosen reflects and reinforces the inner character. *Taming of the Shrew*, courtesy of Guildford Shakespeare Company. MIKE EDDOWES

RESPONSIBILITY

Who should be responsible for the performer's vocal health? Is it legitimate to expect the stage combat instructor or the fight director to shoulder this obligation? Or is this something that should be left to the voice coach with their many years of specialized training? Or is it the performer who must take responsibility for their own instrument? At its core, the issue here is knowledge and timing. Who has the requisite knowledge and when should it be applied? How much knowledge and experience are required, and by whom, to protect a voice in the extremes of a violent performance?

Certainly, a performer-in-training is unlikely to have enough knowledge or experience to be able to protect themselves during training sessions. At this point it must become the stage combat instructor's responsibility to at least make them aware of the potential risks to their voice, just as they do for their body, and to monitor the vocal production within the session for signs of strain. However, it is not common for a stage combat professional to have gained the same skillset as a fully trained voice coach, and it is unlikely that they will be able to do much beyond increasing the performer's awareness of the issue. What is the voice coach's position in this debate? They may well have the skills to mitigate the risk to the performer's instrument, but how much does the student have to learn before they know enough to be able to even approach the subject of extreme vocal production? Where in the arc of the training can the voice coach profitably approach the material, and will it be early enough to support the stage combat sessions? The reality is that everyone should be consciously aware of the problems and working to protect the performer, because the journey of the performer-in-training rarely allows the full acquisition of the necessary skillset prior to the onset of fight training. The sensible performer will always approach a session of fight skills with an awareness of vocal risk, and an intention to apply whatever vocal training they have received to protect proactively their voice.

It is hoped that a professional performer in the industry will have garnered the skills, and eventually the experience, to understand when their vocal instrument is under strain. They should also know how to manage those moments. However, it is not uncommon even for professionals to suffer, no matter how experienced they are. It is so easy to allow instinct to take control that performers need to be constantly reminded of the issue. The best result for all concerned is a collaboration between performer, voice coach, director and fight director to maximize safety in all aspects, along with a robust story-telling that serves the text (Raphael, 2001). Circumstances, budget and lack of awareness of the issues can,

The vocal expression of sudden physical pain has to be carefully crafted to avoid damaging the vocal instrument. *Robin Hood*, courtesy of The New Vic Theatre, Stoke-on-Trent.
ANDREW BILLINGTON

unfortunately, often work against that outcome, to the detriment of the performer's health.

CONCLUSION

At the end of the day the only person who can really take responsibility for the health of that particular vocal instrument is the performer themselves, with, of course, the support of their professional colleagues on the artistic team (Wiley et al., 2001). They should ensure they get a full vocal warm-up before beginning to work, and should consider the benefits of a brief vocal warm-down at the end of the session, if it has been demanding on their instrument. They should have considered the demands that a particular fight or moment of violence will make, and have flagged up any concerns to those who can best help them. And above all, they should have taken the opportunity to collaborate on a vocal choreography that will create the most compelling and complex storytelling beats possible.

> 'The music of the fight – using breath and/or voice to help the audience understand what your character is feeling physically and/or emotionally, moment by moment.'

8
PAIN

Perhaps luck is with a particular performer and they have been cast in a West End production, in a small but important role. The description is simply 'office worker, mid-40s, lives locally, recently divorced'. The question to ask at this point is 'Is this the sum total of the character and all the performer will use to base their characterization upon?' Or is it simply a starting point, from which they will then mine the text for direct, indirect and inferred information about the character, which they will then use to craft a unique, fully embodied individual to entertain the audience?

If the answer is the former, the audience is likely to see a generic representation of an office worker, painted in broad strokes, ill-defined and weakly rooted in the world of the text. However, the latter choice should present a complex, fully formed character with a clear backstory, strongly defined relationships and traits, capable of interacting with their environment in surprising and truthful ways.

What has this to do with pain? Well, in exactly the same way as a performer looks at character development with its many complexities, they must also look at the story of pain in the fight with the same level of attention. Unfortunately, it is far too common on stage to see a pain story that is simplified and stereotypical, relying on cursory grunts and non-specific physical acknowledgement of damage. Bad acting, essentially.

Too often, a performer is missing an opportunity. An individual's response to pain is unique to them and this is a chance not only to enrich and deepen the general story-telling of the fight, but also to reveal a side of the character that might not be seen otherwise. The performer has to be as specific about – and delve as deeply into – the reality of the pain as with every other aspect of their performance.

The attacker carefully uses enough force to dimple the victim's cheek without actually causing any pain. *Gabriel*, courtesy of Theatre 6.
ROBIN SAVAGE

THE TECHNICALITIES OF PAIN

So what is pain? It could be described as an evolutionary tool that acts as a warning when the body is in danger of damage or destruction; it is a protective mechanism, often working below the level of conscious thought (Yusuf, 2019). It is an unpleasant, distressing sensory and emotional experience, resulting from potential or actual injury or illness. It is multi-layered: there is a physical sensation of the pain, but there is also a perception of it – its type (sharp or dull), how intense it is, and where in the body – as well as a psychological and an emotional response to it (Williams and Craig, 2016). All of these elements combine, as in a triangulation procedure, to give the clearest picture of what is happening to our body.

Briefly, there are a number of different categorizations of pain, but the most useful in terms of performance is almost certainly nociceptive pain (related to damage to the physical tissue of the body). Pain receptors are located throughout the body, externally and internally. When stimulated, these nociceptors send a pain message to the spine and thence to the brain. Nociceptors are either specifically attuned to chemical, mechanical or thermal stimuli, or will be polymodal and receptive to all. The sensation of pain differs according to the nerve fibre type the message utilizes: for example, messages on the A-delta fibres (travelling faster) give the sensation of sharp, sudden pain, while those on the thinner C pain fibres (which travel more slowly) will lead to a feeling of duller, more amorphous pain arriving a fraction later (Dafny, 1997).

Pain is often broadly triaged as chronic or acute. The former is, in essence, pain that is suffered long term, although opinion differs on how to define the time scale. Acute pain is defined as short term – it is far more likely to be an actable element of a fight performance. The word 'short' may be slightly misleading; at the very least it is usually measured in days, if not weeks and months (Sein, 2018).

PAIN THRESHOLD

The arc of the pain story begins with the pain perception threshold, where the character becomes aware of the pain message, and continues on to the pain tolerance threshold, where the character reaches the point at which the sensation is no longer tolerable. It then moves into the intolerable zone, causing the character to become entirely incapacitated, or to begin to make choices they might never otherwise be able to make. These different levels vary from person to person and each stage gives the performer an opportunity to make their characterization unique (Kanner, 2009).

A story beat where the essential nature of the character comes to the fore at the moment of their death. *The LadyKillers*, courtesy of The New Vic Theatre, Stoke-on-Trent. ANDREW BILLINGTON

BE PRECISE

Various elements of pain can be measured: duration, intensity, type, onset and severity. Other elements can be defined by how the pain affects the character: body movement, breath audibility and vocal delivery. This ability to measure on various scales, or to assess the effect on the body, gives the performer a series of playable, quantifiable criteria to use when defining their character's pain. If they break the pain story down far enough, every moment and every component can be described. If it can be described, it can be played.

Pain is of course different depending on the specific area of the body and the type of injury caused – soft tissue, joint or bone damage? If soft tissue, what type and where? A stab to the eye causes a very different type of pain from a cut to the forearm. A broken toe feels different from a broken femur. Type of injury is also important: is the bone fractured? If so, how? Is it non-displaced, displaced or comminuted? Is it open? Is the broken bone protruding from the flesh (Nordqvist, 2017)? The choices available to the performer are broad enough to encourage and support a very wide range of stories.

Exactly what triggers the pain? How does it start? Is it sudden or slow? Hot or cold? Is it a sudden flare of agony that subsides into a dull throb, or a mordant ache that gradually grows into a spike of incapacitating anguish? Pain is never static, so how does it change? Is it simply shifting in severity or does it actually move around the body? Where might it re-present? How might it affect different areas of the body? How can it affect the way the body moves? The way it breathes? What happens to the pain when the character moves? What specific movements affect it and how, and for how long (Cooney, 2017)?

PHYSICAL DEGRADATION

What happens to the rest of the body when one particular area is hurt? Does a character walk normally with a broken foot? Of course not. They almost certainly limp. But what is a limp? It is a gait that is uneven or impeded by injury or some form of limitation. But is it antalgic, ataxic, double-step, drag-to, equine, festinating... or one of fifteen other abnormal gaits? (There is no need to seek definitions of these terms; they serve merely as an example of how detailed a performer's research can be.) Consider how generic most performed versions of a limp can be and reflect on how phenomenally specific it is possible to be when discussing walking difficulties. Recognize that each of these gaits affects how the rest of the body moves and balances, each in different ways from each other. Why would any performer, who understands that great acting is rooted in specificity, choose to be any less detailed than this in every aspect of their fight work?

It is clear that a limp must affect every element of the walking body. The rest of the figure makes adjustments in most of the other muscle groups, attempting to reduce pain in the damaged area by shifting the centre of gravity, continually adjusting balance, and trying to minimize disturbing or impacting the injury. So an observer sees overall movement that is a refraction of the damage throughout the body, but is centred on that locus of the wound. What if the character is carrying more than one injury? How do those competing levels and types of pain interact? How does the complex mechanism of the human body react to multiple stimuli in different areas? Does one outweigh the other? Do they at moments cancel each other out? Does the body, or the character psychology, prioritize one or the other?

Apparently, simply touching an area of pain can reduce the intensity for a brief period of time. In very generalized terms, this happens because the touch sensation travels down larger-diameter nerve fibres than does pain. According to Gate Control Theory (which posits that large-diameter nerve fibres can block signals from smaller-diameter fibres), this inhibits the pain sensation (MyDr, 2012). A suitable analogy might be to consider the pain message as a local train and the touch message as a fast train: the local train pulls into a siding to allow the fast train through, thus allowing the touch message to arrive with priority (Wlassoff, 2014). Consider the accidental hammering of a thumb and how the victim shakes then holds the abused digit, all the while cursing. Indeed, recent studies seem to show that cursing itself actually physically reduces the sensation of pain also (Stephens and Umland, 2011), perhaps keying into the more primitive fight/flight response, with its attendant hormonal release.

Pain in any area of the body affects how that area is carried or moves, and also how adjacent areas adjust to compensate for the abnormal circumstances. Without any other information than what their eyes see, the audience should be able to tell that the character is injured, and even make a fair guess as to where and how badly. The

Pain affects every part of the body, not just the site of impact. *Julius Caesar*, courtesy of the Guildford Shakespeare Company.
STEVE PORTER

performer must be clear on how the damage limits what the character can do physically. It is the physical degradation of the body that is compelling, watching it fall apart as it desperately tries to stay functional.

THE SOUND OF PAIN

Pain also affects the breathing, which will change in terms of its pattern and rate, as well as its audibility. Breaths might become longer or shorter, faster or slower, but they will almost always be easier to hear. The purpose of the breath might also alter from a simple expression of pain. Some people instinctively use breathing to manage pain, perhaps in a similar manner to using touch. The conscious breathing element of the Lamaze birthing procedures is one example of pain management through breath (Lothian, 2011). Effectively, performers can use their breath as a musical instrument to guide the audience through their character's journey of pain.

Changes in breathing are usually coupled with vocalized sound. Under the duress of sudden pain most people make some sort of vocal noise, ranging from the mildest 'Ouch' all the way up to a shriek of excruciating torment. Those sounds will all be moderated not only by the differing sensations experienced in the bones, joints and soft tissue when they are exposed to crushing, tearing, lacerating or piercing wounds, but also by the character's expectations regarding violence. Their anticipation or apprehension of being the victim also comes into play. Within the bounds of protecting their vocal instrument, the performer needs to make specific choices regarding the intensity and type of pain they are experiencing and create sounds that not only support that story choice accurately, but continue to reflect the changing circumstances of the wound, and also of the character.

Pain also affects speech. Nobody speaks normally when they are in pain – the voice reflects the condition of the body. If the body suffers, the vocal delivery comes under stress. The pitch and timbre alter, the colouring of the voice changes, the speed and volume of the delivery shifts, the choice of words will be affected. One character may try to conceal the fact that they are in pain, while others will shout it out to the world. The performer must find a way to create that tension in the vocal delivery without introducing tension into the vocal instrument. This is done by using the muscles and formation of the mouth to shape the sound without stressing the vocal folds. The

No one can anticipate how intense pain will be. *Romeo and Juliet*, courtesy of the Guildford Shakespeare Company.
MATT PEREIRA

character's approach to, and use of, language will be changed when their body is hurt, and this must be reflected in the performer's vocal choices.

PSYCHOLOGY OF PAIN

As well as the physical and vocal manifestations, each specific moment of damage will also have an emotional and psychological impact. The performer's choices can only be focused through a deep knowledge of the character's given circumstances. What is their experience of violence? Is it an everyday occurrence or limited to a playground beating as a child? What is their relationship with the other character, and what do they expect of them? What is their anticipation of how they should be treated: do they have low self-esteem or a strong sense of entitlement? Do they react with fight/flight (high arousal) or freeze/fold (low arousal)? How damaging is the violence to their sense of self? How resilient are they? What is their particular Achilles heel? A pianist will not react in the same way to having their hand crushed as an accountant. How fast can they bounce back, or respond to violent stimuli? What is their immediate response, fear or anger? How does the context affect their choices? A parent with children to protect will make different decisions from a person who only has themselves to defend. The richer and broader the performer's knowledge of their character, the more refined their internal responses will be to the devastating violence engulfing their character.

The character's psychological response can also be thought of as a measure of their level of suffering. But suffering can very much be mediated by cultural expectations and practices (Hansen and Streltzer, 2005). A special forces soldier would probably be able to sustain a greater level of physical or emotional stress before they considered themselves to be suffering than an average office worker. Status is another important element

The victim expresses physical pain interwoven with suffering at the prospect of imminent death. *Sleuth*, courtesy of Vienna's English Theatre.
REINHARD REIDINGER

in determining a person's response to what is happening to them. Both expectation and anticipation will play a role in their mental response. Are they routinely beaten, or is this a world-shattering first? Does the extended anticipation of damage to come give them time to acclimatize or does it make it eventually worse?

SECONDARY SYMPTOMS

Pain brings with it associated symptoms, such as dizziness, nausea, tremors and shock. As the pain itself develops and shifts, the secondary symptoms, both physical and emotional, grow and change. As a realization of what has happened to them sets in, the character's immediate world view and sense of self alter. Their ability to be themselves is no longer guaranteed, and their relationship to themselves and others can be drastically reconfigured. They can suffer a loss of mental acuity and their ability to remain focused on the task at hand can be compromised. The performer must chart and play the continuous physical and mental changes over the course of the scene, or perhaps the entire play. Nothing is static with regards to pain and a human being's response to it.

It might also be worth looking at external factors such as alcohol, medicine or age. They can all have an impact on the apparent perception of pain, as can the hormonal balance of the body chemistry. The flood of adrenalin caused by the fight/flight response can reduce the awareness of pain, as can the rush of endorphins associated with exercise or stress.

DESCRIBING AND DEFINING PAIN

Having considered the multitude of choices open to the performer when examining pain from different angles, there are a number of tools that can be applied to the task of refining those choices. Rather than re-invent the wheel, it makes sense to examine the medical profession's approach to helping patients define their pain accurately, and apply their expert knowledge to performance work.

LOCATES

L: Location – specifically what part of the body is in pain? Does it move to other areas?
O: Other – what other symptoms are there? Shock, loss of fine motor control, difficulty breathing?
C: Character – what type of pain is it? Stinging/aching? Nagging/unbearable? Sharp/dull?
A: Aggravating/alleviating factors – what makes the pain worse/better? Movement, touch, breathing?
T: Timing – is the pain pulsing, continuous, intermittent? What is the duration?
E: Environment – what has caused the pain? Where are you?
S: Severity – on a scale of 0–10 grade the level of pain from none to worst.

(University of Florida, College of Medicine)

COLDER

C: Character – type of pain? Check descriptor list.
O: Onset – acute or gradual? Sudden or slow?
L: Location – where in the body exactly?
D: Duration – how long?
E: Exacerbates – what makes it worse?
R: Relieves – what relieves the pain?

(Zasler et al., 2007)

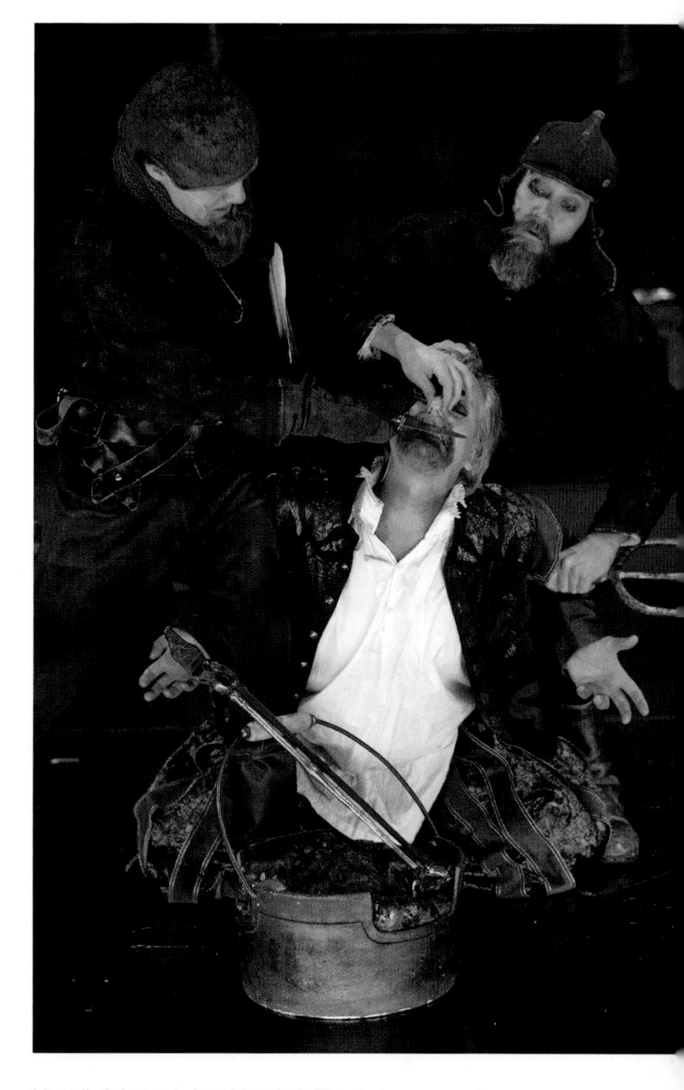

Not all violence is hot-blooded. This torture scene is an example of more considered brutality. *Shakespeare in Love*, courtesy of National Theatret Norway.
ØYVIND EIDE

The acronyms LOCATES and COLDER, created by healthcare professionals, are a good starting point.

It is also worth examining descriptor lists of pain used in the medical environment to draw as clear a picture as possible of the type of pain experienced. The most commonly used is the McGill Pain Questionnaire. The full-length version lists seventy-two words representing pain and is an effective tool for a performer to refine their character's pain experience. There are versions readily available online; with its easily definable approach to describing pain, it should be a part of every performer's toolkit.

The use of similes can be even more effective for a performer as a tool for honing exactly what the character experiences, as these can strongly engage the creative imagination. Examples might include 'It feels like…a rake digging in to my eyes… lightning strike…insects crawling under my skin.' These are images that not only describe the sensation clinically, but also carry a strong emotional response to the experience, which can greatly enrich the portrayal of each moment (Semino, 2010).

RESPONSE TO PAIN

Once the precise image of the pain and its moment-by-moment journey have been created and described, it is time to consider more precisely how different people respond to pain. Do they fear it? Deny it? Laugh through it? Embrace it? Focus it? Do they anticipate its onset like a toddler about to be beaten? Does it cause them to break down, so that they are no longer able to function? Do they catastrophize the experience? Or do they drive through it, using an external task to pull their attention from the pain? How does the character cope with the onslaught of negative

The moment after the first hot flare of pain, when the victim looks inwards and realizes how bad the damage is. *Gabriel*, courtesy of Theatre 6.
ROBIN SAVAGE

physical sensation? What is their personality and how does it respond to being harmed? For example, research seems to show that a more neurotic personality structure is actually more sensitive to pain (Banozic, 2018). How does the context affect their choice to reveal their level of discomfort? Are they trying to not lose face in front of others? Or does it not matter? How do their given circumstances affect their response to pain?

It can be difficult as a performer to remember how pain really feels and how it actually affects the body and the mind, which is why these approaches can be particularly useful. Once the pain has been defined and focused, it then has to be sustained. People do not simply shake off pain; it stays with them for a measurable period. They may be able to continue to function, but everything they do, think and say is filtered through the pain, and that continuing story must be clarified in all its twists and turns.

To this end it may be useful to consider the 'pain train'. Each element of the train delivers a new aspect of the pain experience. The engine is the moment of impact or injury. The first carriage is the initial perception of pain, with appropriate vocal and physical response. The second carriage is how that pain then changes, increasing or decreasing, again with physical and vocal responses. The third carriage might be how the pain then flares up when that body part is moved or struck again. And so on. The train can be as long or as short as required to tell an interesting story.

Of course, the performer cannot become indulgent in their depiction of pain. It must always serve the story. As in reality, the character's need to speak, or to achieve a goal, allows them to work through the pain regardless. They are changed and affected by it, but still focused on their objectives, particularly if the stakes are high.

To summarize, the character's individual story of pain can be incredibly complex, fascinating, and revealing on many levels. It can help make that character unique and compelling to watch, but only if specific choices are made with clarity for every single moment. Those choices must be responsive to the continual changes in the character's circumstances, and precise in every element of the scene and fight. It is important that the performer makes detailed acting choices, because if they action the physical dialogue of the fight in a generic fashion, their pain story will inevitably be just as generic. At that point they will have lost the opportunity to deepen their audience's engagement with their character.

Pain can prevent the body from working normally, often necessitating the help of others. *Romeo and Juliet*, courtesy of Guildford Shakespeare Company.
MATT PEREIRA

9
PICTURIZATION

The term 'picturization' is commonly used to describe the process of visualizing something, from any media, as a picture. It may seem odd to consider this in reference to staged violence, which is already by its very nature a series of connected physical images. However, that can be its downfall. The artist follows a process of purposeful, calculated composition, in which they consider balance, structure and line, as they look for the clearest way to reveal their vision. Choreographing a fight is different, as it involves a set of competing priorities, which can draw the attention away from the pictures that are being created.

Size disparity between the hands and the neck means that the little finger is not able to fit, despite good technique. *The Crucible*, courtesy of The Storyhouse, Chester.
MARK CARLINE

VISUAL STORY-TELLING

Because of the focus on safety, story, character impulse, pain, technique and performance logistics, it sometimes happens that the importance of the pictures is forgotten. Every element of the physical picture must reinforce the story-telling. An artist will often start with broad strokes and general shaping and finish with the fine detail work. In the same way, fight performers need to follow a process on all levels of their fight creation that ends with a strong focus on the tiniest of details. Part of that work involves ensuring that there are no anomalous elements left in the physical representation of the violence – a strangle where the attacker's fingertips are splayed out rigidly from the back of the victim's neck, instead of curling around, pressing into the flesh, or a punch thrown with a hand so loose that it no longer looks like a fist. These are simple physical errors that will completely undercut the performer's attempt at muscular veracity. Put another way, for a sense of authentic violence, each part of the physical picture must look right. The audience may not have experienced a strangle themselves, but they will have an intuitive sense of how it should look.

REPRESENTING REALITY

Achieving an accurate embodiment of violence demands not only an attention to detail, and a basic level of physical clarity and mastery of the body, but also a fundamental understanding of what each technique is attempting to achieve and how it should look, and perhaps feel. The performer must know how an attack or defence works in the real world, so that they have a clear template of what reality they are attempting to convey to the audience. Where does the body weight sit? How does the centre of gravity shift? Are the elbows bent and, if so, is it vertically or horizontally? Is the physical energy sustained, or broken and renewed? How does success or failure, moment by moment, affect the body and its position?

What, for example, is the reality of punching? How a character throws a punch depends on a number of variables. Are they trained or not? If they are, in what style? What is the intent of the punch – minimal or maximal damage? Is it the beginning or end of a combination? Not only does the performer need to get the physicality of the moment correct, they also need to get it correct for this type and style of punch, and this particular character. On a side note, the move must also match what is known of the character and their history: this could perhaps be seen as picturization on a meta level. If a mild-mannered hero suddenly jumps into the air for a back-spinning hook kick, this had better happen because the character has a martial arts backstory, which has now become germane to the plot, not because the fight director discovered the performer was able to create that flashy move.

To continue with the example of punching, many performers have never thrown a punch in anger, or been trained to throw a punch at all, never mind in any one style. Without that experiential learning under their belt it can be hard for some to make their punches look powerful and effective. Some people need to feel the technique from the inside by actually doing it, before they can create the illusion. This is possible with many unarmed techniques and the use of a kick-pad, but not usually possible with weapons skills. This is where the feedback from the instructor is so important, as it can bring the performer more quickly to a greater understanding of the necessary adjustments. If a performer has never actually punched or kicked before, it is certainly worth learning how to do so, to create a foundation of physical experience to build upon.

BASSC teacher Janet Lawson demonstrating an arm lock; the student's smile shows that there is no pressure applied through the arm.
ROB DAVIDSON

Isolation

Ideally, a performer needs to be in control of their body to a level where they can be given a physical note and are able to apply it with the minimum of difficulty. They need to be accurate with their replication of any movement. More importantly, rather like a mime artist, they need to be able to isolate various parts of their body during a movement sequence. The mime's skill in making the observer believe in the existence of the invisible is partly down to their ability to break down the articulation of every physical action into the smallest, clearest sections, to fully maximize their communication with the audience. If a fight performer can achieve this, they stand a much greater chance of successfully selling every single moment of a fight with clarity.

The Knowledge of the Audience

This clarity is important because if there is any generalized quality to the depiction of violence the audience will see it. Every member of the audience has studied how the human body works, from the inside, for their entire lives. They understand the flow of energy in the body, where power comes from, what it feels like to work with inertia and mass. If a mime artist tries to create the illusion of pushing a broken-down car with straight legs, upright body and straight arms, nobody will believe them. If they bend their legs, lean forward with bent arms, the audience immediately understand the story. They may never have pushed a car, but they understand instinctively what it would feel like to do so. It is exactly the same with fights. Any move which is physically generalized and not engaged from the core of the body will not engender in the observers an instinctive belief in the reality of the moment.

Engaging the Core

In the process of the body moving, there will be a triggering event that sparks a thought leading to a decision. Once this is made, air is drawn into the body to fuel the intended action, the muscle structures engage preparatory to movement, particularly the abdominal core, the stance may widen, the legs will probably bend to gather energy from the ground, pushing it up through the core and out to the attacking or defending extremity of the

Not every character with a weapon is trained in its use, influencing the choices of the performer on the right. *Corpse!*, courtesy of Vienna's English Theatre. REINHARD REIDINGER

body. The most important element of this is the idea of energizing the body's core. Every move that is made, even the smallest, is supported through the core muscles. If they are not engaged throughout a fight, the audience will have no belief in the reality of the character.

Once again, punching presents a strong example for this case. It is common to see a performer who is uneducated in the art of punching throwing a fist with straight legs and without bending or turning at the waist. The lack of core engagement makes the punch look entirely fake. As soon as the movement is energized through the centre of the body, it begins to look like a true, aggressive impulse, and a realistic attack.

Angel and Demon

Another important element of physicalized violence is the counterintuitive ability to isolate the character's aggression from the performer's technique. This means keeping absolute control over the precision and placement of attacks and defences, whilst fully embodying the character's overwhelming destructive desires. If the performer allows the raging emotional storm fully into their body, it can introduce tension into the muscles controlling their movement. This can then adversely affect both their balance and accuracy, increasing the level of real danger to all involved. A skilled fight performer will have the face of a demon, but the hands and feet of an angel.

Character Throughout

Of course, the flip side of this is that the fighter can disengage too far from the character's impulses, and then elements of the fight stop looking real. Without the character driving the moment-by-moment choices in the fight, it becomes merely a dance, lacking anything but the broadest emotional strokes underpinning each move. Even to

The hook needs to look threatening without actually being dangerous to the performers, so it has an inward-curving point. *Peter Pan*, Richmond Theatre, courtesy of Qdos Entertainment. CRAIG SUGDEN

the eyes of an untutored audience, this sort of fight will lack an indefinable sense of reality.

BE PRESENT: SURF, DON'T DROWN

There is a variation on this issue, within which only certain elements of the fight continue to lack reality, like small unfinished areas of a painting that is otherwise bursting with colour and detail. In juxtaposition with the more effective elements of the violence, they stand out in stark contrast, shockingly obvious to the audience, completely undermining any belief they may have developed in the fight. This can happen to any technique in a choreography, but is most common when it comes to attacks that are designed to miss or to be avoided.

The brain seems to be designed to look for patterns (Alonso, 2011) and also, once it has found them, to seek ways to reduce the body's energy expenditure through the repetition of the pattern. The aim is to trade minimum energy output for maximum efficiency (Yu and Yu, 2017). What is choreography, rehearsed again and again, but a complex, repeated pattern? Empirical evidence appears to show that the brain decides that, because an attack misses, it needs less energy because there is no illusion of contact and therefore

The anticipation of violence is as much part of the story of the fight as the actual action. *The LadyKillers*, courtesy of The New Vic Theatre, Stoke-on-Trent.
ANDREW BILLINGTON

no requirement to really sell it. The result can be a fight sporting a couple of rehearsal punches limply performed in the middle of a vicious flurry of attacks. Time and again, even with experienced fight performers, in the middle of a violent fight there is suddenly a slow, mono-rhythmic attack delivered with no aggressive intent. It stands out like a black and white sequence in the middle of a technicolour film. It is another example of why it is so important for the performer to be consciously present in every moment of a fight. Not only is it vital in terms of safety, but also to keep each momentary intention focused and played clearly. No element of a fight can be run on auto-pilot without compromising both safety and story.

The skilled fighter achieves a balance between the competing priorities of truthful story-telling and technical safety and clarity. They are able to surf the character energy without drowning in it, using it to infuse and inform the physicality, without being overwhelmed by it.

All experienced performers will be aware that what they feel when performing is not always

Physical performance demands both fitness and flexibility from the prepared performer. *Treasure Island*, courtesy of The New Vic Theatre, Stoke-on-Trent.
ANDREW BILLINGTON

what the audience experiences as they watch the performance (Vasiliades, 2004). Not everything crosses the footlights in a predictable way and it can be hard to determine from onstage what is actually working in the auditorium. Feeling that a moment is engaged and truthful is not a reliable indicator that the audience has received the same perception. This is as true of performed fights as it is of any other element of a performance. Just as a director becomes the eyes of the audience and feeds back to the performer on what is actually working, so the fight director or instructor fulfils the same role for fight moments. Of course, technology can also be used to record fights in the rehearsal room, allowing the performer to view them with a critical eye, ensuring that every physical element of the story rings true.

MARKING THE FIGHT

The first time a fight is run each day it is always walked back in and run slowly, giving the performers time to remember it and to get into synch with their partners. In the business this is often referred to as marking the fight. The common format is the performers sketch in the fight without engaging their cores, without putting any intention into the attacks, without playing the moments. The problem with this is that they are using a section of their rehearsal time undermining all of the work they have achieved up until this point. Under the stress of performance, when they will not have the time to think consciously about each element of the fight, but must rely on everything absorbed in rehearsal, they may fall back on the sketch rather than on the fully realized oil painting.

It is necessary for the first run of the fight to be slow every time, but slow does not mean that all elements bar the sequence of shapes should be forgotten. Once moments are set, they should be played fully, whether fast or slow. Every attack, every defence, every choice is fully energized and realized in the body, emotions and voice, so that every time the fight is run it reinforces all performance elements, consistently building towards a fully embodied performance rather than undercutting the previous work. A marked fight should simply look and sound like a slow-motion run of the final version of the vicious confrontation (Wiley et al., 2001).

Finally, do not be complicit. Do not be part of substandard story-telling. Do not accept fight moments that patently will not convince physically, either because they are under-energized or because the sightlines are wrong for the audience. Do not allow the craft to be undervalued in the eyes of the audience, or other creative colleagues. Fights should not be comfortable to watch. They should be difficult, awful, and above all convincing in every aspect. Get the picture right physically and emotionally.

Each body convincingly supports the audience's understanding of the physical action. *Two Gentlemen of Verona,* courtesy of Guildford Shakespeare Company. STEVE PORTER

10
THE CUEING SYSTEM AND OTHER SUPPORT STRUCTURES

The cueing system is central to a fight performance, along with other supporting elements that will enhance a performer's application of the techniques of stage combat. As with all physical or performative skillsets, looking deeper below the surface of what the audience sees will reveal more about the mechanisms that underpin an effortless performance. Without these components reinforcing it, that performance will be much weaker.

Every stage combat technique is structured and sequential. They have been analysed and stress-tested in performance, to ensure not only that they are safe, but also that they create an effective illusion and tell a character story that works. Not every technique works in every context (*see* Chapter 2), and some are more convincing than others, which is why the performer needs to understand the technical elements, so that they can be as effective in performance as possible. This means all of the elements, not just the obvious ones. If the 'attack' and the 'reaction' are the glamorous onstage component, then the fundamentals – the cueing system and the other support structures – are the hardworking backstage crew that make the performance possible.

THE CUEING SYSTEM

The cueing system is vital from the point of view of safeguarding (*see* Chapter 5). It has a number of

The victim's hands are around the garrotte, cueing the attacker to tighten it to a pre-agreed pressure. *The Beggars' Opera*, courtesy of The Storyhouse, Chester.
MARK CARLINE

constituent parts, which need to be examined in more detail from a practical perspective.

Eye Contact

This is the simplest safety principle – looking to see if your partner is ready before you launch the next attack. Arguably, it is also the most important safety element, as it is the very final check, and opportunity to stop, before committing to the physical moment. The performer must be consciously present in the moment. This should not be a perfunctory glance within which they see what they expect to see, rather than what is actually there. They must actively expect at some point not to achieve eye contact and to have a protocol to deal with that eventuality. If that meeting of the eyes does not occur, the violence must pause until it does. If that happens in rehearsal once or twice, and the performers stop, it will reinforce the need to stick to the convention and, ultimately, strengthen the performance. There is an explicit red light/green light safety principle in play at this stage of every technique.

Ideally, eye contact is made between every move, but in practice, at performance speed, that is not always feasible. Eye contact should be made at the beginning of each new acting beat, which can be defined by a shift of power between the characters. Each time a character takes control of the fight, it marks a new beat and an opportune moment to renew eye contact. If character A has three continuous attacks against character B, that constitutes an acting beat; if B responds with two attacks of their own, that is the next beat, followed by A's response as the third beat, and so on. If it is possible to achieve eye contact between each move, then the performers should absolutely do so.

Within the stage combat community there is an ongoing discussion regarding eye contact. Some practitioners believe that eye contact should be sustained as a continuous, unbroken link between the two performers, to maximize their safety. There are a couple of issues to address on this: first, particularly in a weapon-based fight, it is possible to misjudge the position of the weapons if not actually looking directly at them, leading to both safety and performance consequences. Second, it can make the visual picture a little odd, as it is not natural behaviour for humans to sustain eye contact, particularly in a fight situation. It is important to remember that every member of the audience has studied body language all their lives, making them unconscious experts in it. It is possible to pick up body language cues and interpret them at a surprising distance and, unless the intended story is that the fighters are falling in love with each other, it is unlikely that fixed eye contact will enhance the performance.

Some practitioners make an argument for maintaining eye contact using an interpretation of the traditional Japanese swordsmanship training of seeing all things, near as if they are far, far as if they are near, combined with a form of seeing through the opponent. This is a rather literal-minded take on Musashi's discussion on strategy in his *Go Rin No Sho*, describing a process of unfocused attention, allowing the fighter to see all, to be ready for anything, and to react to everything (Zehr, 2015). The counter-argument must surely be that, while this may be effective in a battle or duel, or as a strategic tool, it takes a certain amount of training before it works at an unconscious level, which is necessary for performance, with all its counter points of focus. In addition, it takes no account of the visual story-telling beats necessary in a staged fight to explicate the drama to the audience. Neither does it include the possibility that different characters are trained, and fight, with different styles and methods, or of the need for the performers to tell different stories.

Look at the Target

If attacking, it surely makes sense to look at the target, to ensure the maximum chance of successfully hitting it. Having failed or succeeded,

The victim focuses on the attacking weapons, as the attacker looks at the target that he is attacking.
ROB DAVIDSON

the attacker then scans the victim for a new target and focuses on that. The victim will almost certainly look at the incoming attack to maximize their chances of avoiding or blocking it, then either look for an opportunistic target to attack themselves, or look at the next incoming attack. Some might argue that an experienced fighter might not choose to look at the target in an attempt to fool their victim: this is possibly true, but it is of little use to performers in live performance. That is far too subtle a nuance for most of the audience to understand and they will almost certainly misread the choice. It also misses the opportunity to build in an intuitive cue to remind the partner what the next move is, and to telegraph to the audience what will happen next, leading them through the fight story with the performers and maximizing their enjoyment.

Preparation

Each move will have a preparation built in to it; it may be small or large, but this does not matter as long as it is present. Would somebody prepare a move by chambering energy for it in a real fight? If they were a trained fighter, they probably would not, or at least they would attempt to minimize it, particularly if they were fighting another experienced combatant. Telegraphing a next move is unlikely to lead to a successful outcome, as the victim will have time to prepare a response, unless it is being deliberately set up as a trap. However, on stage, technique preparations are vital elements that give a cue to the performer's partner as to the timing and content of the next move; they also tell the audience clearly what is about to happen. The latter can be of benefit to the performers because, when they are well trained and fighting at their top speed, it can be very difficult to follow them once they commit to the action. The audience can be reduced to playing catch-up as the fight moments progress. At full speed, to the perception of the audience, a fight can descend into a cartoon-style ball of dust, with fists and feet sticking out at odd moments. Their appreciation of the story of the fight will be intensified and clarified if they are able to follow the moment-by-moment

The attacker's non-weapon hand physically cues Caesar for the timing of the attack across his back. *Julius Caesar*, courtesy of the Guildford Shakespeare Company.
STEVE PORTER

travails of the two characters. Allowing the audience to take the emotional roller-coaster ride of the fight with the characters will enrich their experience, and deepen their understanding of the characters' journey.

Whether small or large, a preparation is necessary for safety and clear story-telling. However, each preparation must contain an unrestrained sense of threat, feeding into the aggressive sense of fight, otherwise it simply becomes a technical element with little meaning.

Action

Most people would probably consider the action to be almost the entirety of the technique – they would not even spot the various other elements listed here – yet, without those other elements, the action would be unsafe and probably meaningless in story terms. The action will be the attack, punch, slap, kick, and so on, but it is only to be released when the preceding steps have been followed. Without these, there is a heightened risk that one of the performers will be out of synch, perhaps in the wrong place, and therefore exposed to danger. The performer can only commit fully to the character's aggressive impulse if they are certain that all safety procedures have been followed, and that their partner will not be in harm's way. Once triggered, the attack must be fuelled by the preparation's menace and threat, which must be developed into an appropriately vicious release.

Reaction

Arguably, the reaction is what pulls everything together and sells the story. In terms of the perception of the audience, a strong reaction can go some way towards rescuing a poorly executed action. However, a poor reaction will kill a good action. The reaction must match the angle, speed

Ensuring all sides of an in-the-round audience can see, the performers are subtly cueing each other's turn with body pressure. *Wind in The Willows*, courtesy of The New Vic Theatre, Stoke-on-Trent.
ANDREW BILLINGTON

and energy of the attack. The timing must be exact – if it comes too soon or too late, the illusion will be destroyed. A clear reaction comprises not only the physical component, which tells the visual story, but also a strong vocal or breath element to clarify the character's response for the ears of the audience. It will also reveal their emotional response to the moment of violence and pain. The performer must make strong, unique choices in all of these areas, in order to avoid becoming generic in their story-telling.

The cueing system provides a road map for the performers to follow at every stage of the fight. It ensures that they know where they and their partner should be at all times, and what should happen when. It will establish and secure their safety. Even at performance speed, when each step occurs so rapidly that it might seem almost impossible to distinguish the order, it is vital that everyone adheres to the cueing system, otherwise the performers may fall out of synch with each other. This will greatly increase their danger and it will almost certainly degrade the illusion they are creating.

It is important to remember, though, that a cue should be perceived as a threat to the victim by the audience, rather than a moment of communication. As complicit performers they may be signalling the sequence moment by moment for each other, but as characters they are creating moments of threat, leading to aggressive moments of attack.

THE SIX ELEMENTS

Part of the technical process of this form of storytelling is knowing exactly what you want to reveal to the audience, and what you want to hide from them, and at what point. You also need to know precisely how you go about hiding something: by masking it, or by redirecting the audience's attention at an opportune moment? The choices

THE SIX ELEMENTS OF THE ILLUSION OF CONTACT

- Action
- Reaction
- Knap
- Illusion of contact
- Timing
- Character impulse

made as to how to reveal or hide will depend on the staging and the auditorium, which, of course, will often dictate the choice of moves in the choreography. The performer needs to understand the logic of how a move works on a technical level within each type of space, or they will not comprehend clearly what needs to be hidden at exactly which moment. Without this level of knowledge, they will struggle to be consistent in their manipulation of the audience's perception of what is happening. Technical knowledge aids understanding and creates a more effective performer.

Each non-contact strike comprises six simple, consistent elements, each of which must be present. The first three must occur in the correct order, if the appropriate illusion is to be successfully created for the audience.

Action

For the performer, this actually comprises, and is shorthand for, most of the elements of the cueing system: eye contact; look at the target; preparation; action. These must be physically accurate and safe.

Reaction

The physical, vocal and emotional reaction to the moment of violence must match the energy and speed of the action accurately. It must also be performed in a way that keeps both performers safe.

Knap

This term is used in the stage combat profession to describe the sound created to help the audience believe that contact was made by the attacker. For a more in-depth discussion, *see* Chapter 11.

Illusion of Contact

In order to create the opportunity for the audience to believe that something has actually hit the victim, the physical picture must be correct and what they hear must reinforce that story. Whatever is hitting the victim has to either cross or obscure the target. The knap must be audible and the physical reaction appropriate to the action.

Timing

If the technique is mistimed, the illusion does not work. If the reaction is too early or too late, the moment is clearly fake and the belief of the audience is broken. However, as the target line is set to the centre of the audience (*see* Chapter 6), the brain's ability to retroactively create a story gives a moment of grace. This allows slightly early or slightly late reactions still to sell, as long as they are fully energized. The knap must happen at exactly the moment when the strike reaches the target line, and the physical reaction must be timed to the delivery of the action. The vocal reaction must be timed so as not to obscure the sound of the knap, yet still support the story of pain.

Character Impulse

Most importantly, each moment of a technique must be driven by an impulse from the character; this must be rooted in both the text and the character's backstory, and justified by their emotional and physical response to what has happened immediately prior to this moment. The attack must

This assisted suicide needs clear cueing and negotiation as to who controls the blade. *Julius Caesar*, courtesy of the Guildford Shakespeare Company.
STEVE PORTER

be triggered by a clear choice and delivered with specific intention. The reaction must reflect the victim's actual experience as something to which the audience can relate, rather than being a formulaic response to the attack. Without this the technique is simply a short piece of choreography rather than a living moment of action.

BREATHING

Many of the techniques described above are predicated on the basic premise that the performer is breathing. Setting aside the obvious jokes, the very foundation of any performance is the performer's choice of when and how to breathe. Not all breathing is the same or serves the same function. Consider how a singer decides how to phrase a song or how a swimmer judges from experience and training how much air they will need and for how long. Anybody who has used weights or resistance machines in a gym will have been instructed on when to inhale and exhale while their body is executing a physical action. They will also have discovered – sometimes through getting it wrong – that it has an impact on how efficiently they are able to do the exercise. Sports practitioners train in the use of effective breathing for their particular needs. In much the same way, performers train to ensure that they have enough breath to support the character's need to speak, and that they will not run out of breath midway through a line or thought.

The performer must also examine how to breathe whilst fighting. When do they need to breathe? When does the character choose to breathe? How much air do they need for a move, and how long does that one breath need to sustain them? Are they speaking as they fight? How desperate is the character's need to breathe? On a technical level, when can the breath be taken and when should it be released? How much oxygen does the body need to fuel the next moment? What other purpose does the breath serve? Is it conveying information to the audience on the character's physical condition, or on their emotional response to the moment?

Should the character's breathing be allowed to be instinctive? Surely, everyone breathes all day every day and the body's autonomic reflexes can be left to get on with this aspect of the performance? As with so many things in the performing crafts, instinct is a two-edged sword. The belief that instinct creates reality, lighting the path

towards truth on stage, ignores the fact that the stage itself is an artificial environment, presenting a simulation of reality. Craft is most often the effective operative word and must, most assuredly, be applied to breathing in a fight. Instinctive choices may not take into account the fact that the auditorium is deep, or wide, or has a poor acoustic. They may ignore the technical demand that the character has to spit out a Homeric curse in the middle of the fight, without time to grab enough air at that point.

Everybody will have experienced that moment when they realize they do not have enough air in their lungs to complete what they were saying, and have to stop for an ungainly gulp of air. It is also common for tension to tighten the breathing apparatus and seemingly reduce the body's ability to take in a full breath. Performers train specifically to avoid this, yet nerves can affect even the most experienced, particularly if they feel they are outside their comfort zone, as many do when confronted with a stage fight. This is why it is important to make specific, conscious decisions regarding the breathing within the technical structure of a fight – do you need to fuel the next physical action, or need breath to vocalize a clear reaction or sustain a continuing soundtrack of pain? The breathing in a fight needs to be scored in the same way as a musical score is marked by a composer for their wind instruments.

To create their own solid foundation of breath from which to fight, the performer needs to

ABOVE LEFT: Fire, combined with an inability to see the attacker, means that precise cueing is vital for the next moment. *The LadyKillers*, courtesy of The New Vic Theatre, Stoke-on-Trent.
ANDREW BILLINGTON

LEFT: The victim has rehearsed their breath control carefully, ensuring they retain sufficient air to speak clearly. *Two Gentlemen of Verona*, courtesy of The Storyhouse, Chester.
MARK CARLINE

discover, primarily through active rehearsal, how much breath they need and when they need it. They will find that the physical shape or position of the body can sometimes restrict the ability to take in a deep breath. Equally, they will learn that holding the breath, inadvertently or not, introduces tension into the body, usually in a way that hinders performance. They will almost certainly realize that breathing in on the character's impulse or decision to act, then releasing the breath on the physical action, allows the body to be most free and responsive in the fight. This will be an ongoing process during rehearsal, but, in order to gain the most benefit, it should be formalized at some point to fix it as conscious choice.

DOMINANCE

This is perhaps a minor point, but the majority of performers are right-dominant and will feel most comfortable using their right hand to hit somebody. However, in a real fight, most people use both hands, either because the need to hit overcomes the lingering difficulty of using their 'stupid' hand or because a momentary physical position forces them to use their non-dominant hand. It is fairly common in a staged fight to choreograph a flurry of blows using both fists, so performers should consider exploring how to become more facile in their use of their non-dominant hand. They might practise daily chores with that side or holding their drink with that hand – anything to begin the process of re-educating the brain and building new neural pathways, to allow the uncommon to become common.

CONCLUSION

To take theatre itself as a paradigm, most people have only the haziest understanding that there is a whole world of support staff behind the glamour of the lit stage and the performance. Without those support structures, the theatre would not exist. It is the same with unarmed stage fighting; it could not function in any meaningful way without the elements described here. The more clearly the performer understands them and is able to apply them, the more effective their illusions of violence will be.

A punch preparation designed to suit the tone of this show as well as to cue the partner. *Robin Hood*, courtesy of the Guildford Shakespeare Company.
STEVE PORTER

11
KNAPPING

In reality, a hand or foot striking a body makes a sound. It may be flesh on flesh or on clothing, or, depending on costume, leather on flesh or clothing. That sound is an integral part of the fight experience and therefore a vital element of a fight performance; without it, the fight illusion is greatly diminished. To create that sound on stage, a performer cannot simply hit their partner, for obvious reasons. Instead, they hit themselves. This is called making a knap, or knapping, and comes in a variety of forms. Knaps are always structured to be hidden within a natural flow of movement, so that they are masked from the audience's perception.

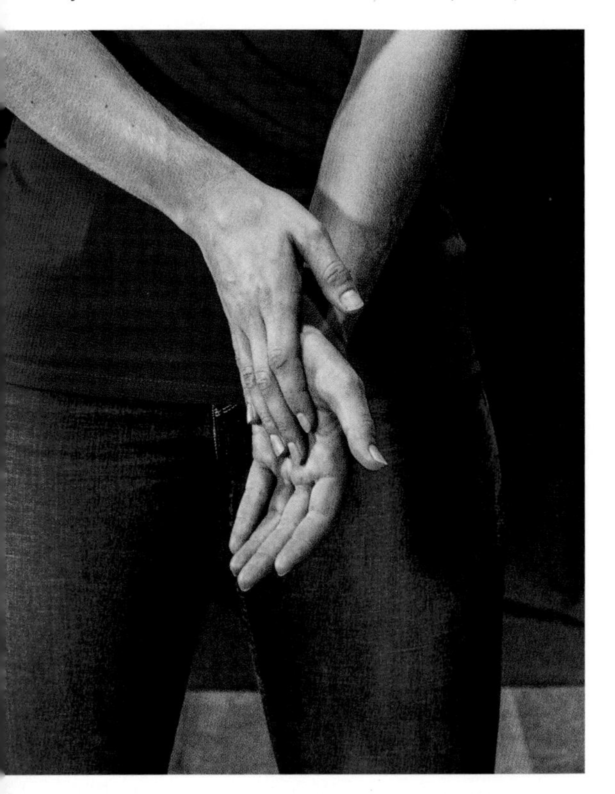

A clap knap with fingers to palm.

Knap

The simulated sound of a violent attack created by striking one body part against another.

The term 'knap' is most commonly used to describe the use of a hard stone or bone to strike percussive blows on a flint core, or the resultant flakes, to create useable shards of flint for weapons or tools. Whoever coined the term for stage combat purposes was probably visualizing that process of hitting one thing against another.

The knap is almost always created with a hand, except for contact kicks, where the actual sound of the foot hitting the target makes the knap. In theory, a knap can be created off almost any body part, except, of course, the head and neck. In practice, the following are the most common types of knap.

TYPES OF KNAP

Clap Knap

As in applauding, the two hands clap together to produce a sharp sound. The quality and loudness of the sound can be altered by the speed and force of the clap, and by the specific area of the hand struck.

Chest Knap

The chest knap is created by striking a flat hand against the upper chest. Each performer will need

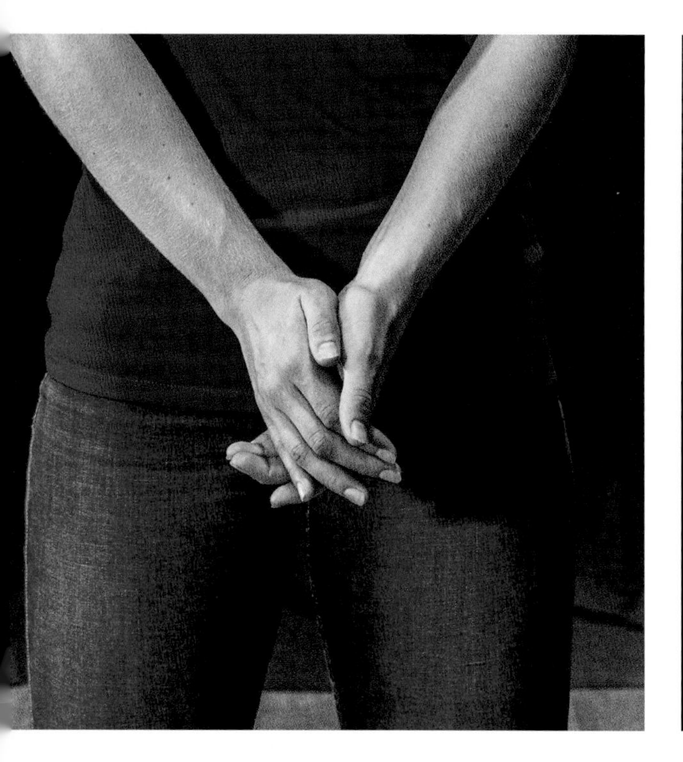

A clap knap with cupped hands.

A chest knap; note the flat hand.

to experiment to find the most comfortable but resonant areas of their chest for knapping. Different areas will produce sounds of differing depth and quality. The uniqueness of the physique of each performer means that this is an area where the technique will always be slightly customized to achieve the best results.

The shape of the knapping hand will also have an impact. A cupped hand tends to create a duller thudding sound. A stiff, flat hand, where the contact is made with fingers only as the hand brushes sharply across the chest, produces a much brighter, crisper knap, which reaches further through space. This is useful, as chest knaps are

A knap brushing the side of the chest.

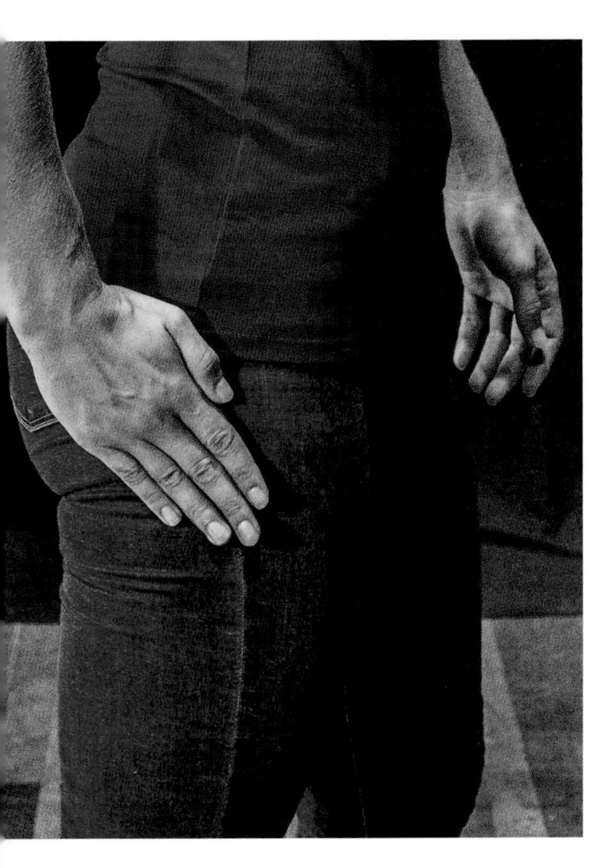

An upstage brushing thigh knap.

primarily made upstage, with sound bouncing off the upstage set to reach the audience. The hand should be lifted off the chest as quickly as possible, or the sound will be muted, making it less effective.

Thigh Knap

A thigh knap is created by brushing stiff fingers across the front or side of the thigh. A relaxed hand with slightly separated fingers creates a less percussive knap, while stiff fingers, tight together, create sharp sounds that carry further. It is usually used for kicks, but can also usefully be used for punches, masked in the natural rotation of the body.

It is possible to create knaps off other areas of the body, such as a forearm, according to need and availability. It is worth each performer exploring what works as each individual's tolerance to the sting of a knap is different.

DEFINING KNAPS

Knaps may also be defined by who creates them.

First Party Knap

Created by the attacker, and usually masked in the natural movement of the attack.

Second Party Knap

Created by the victim, and usually masked in the natural movement of the reaction.

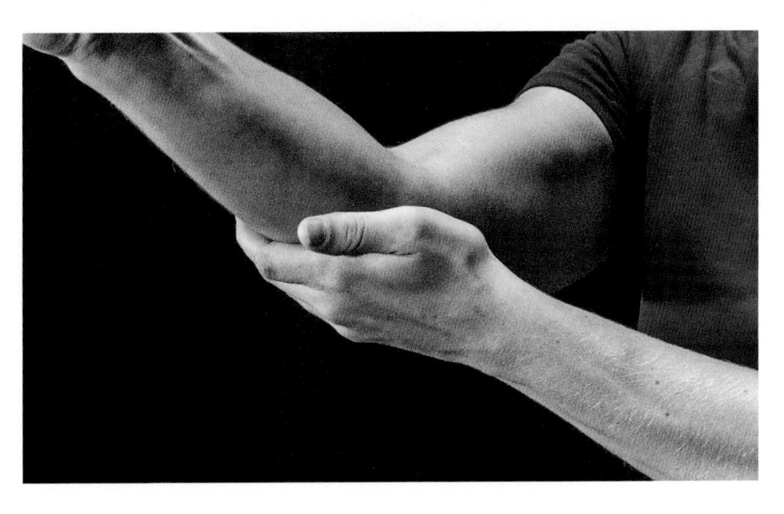

A knap off the forearm.

Third Party Knap

Created by someone else on the stage, and primarily masked by dint of them not being the focus of attention. The third party must be close enough to the action for the sound seeming to be centred there, masking the knap with their body, or that of another performer. The slight increase in difficulty with this knap is the risk of mistiming it.

Shared Knap

This knap is created by one performer on another performer's body. There are a variety of possible shared knaps and the choice to use them is often driven by necessity, when circumstances close off other options. They are more complex, as performers often struggle to create a consistent and satisfyingly loud knap. When knapping off your own body, your brain coordinates both sides of the action, but when knapping off someone else's body, the slightest alteration in angle, distance or pace between the two bodies dramatically affects the quality of the sound created.

THE NEED FOR VARIETY

So many elements of the knap can adversely affect its successful production that it is important that performers understand many variations. Costume has a major impact; anything thick, soft or padded muffles a knap, as do multiple layers of fabric. Conversely, vinyl or leather can actually magnify a knap very effectively.

Staging also influences the choice of knap. Performers try to mask knaps from the audience

ABOVE LEFT: A cross punch chest knap with the attacker downstage.

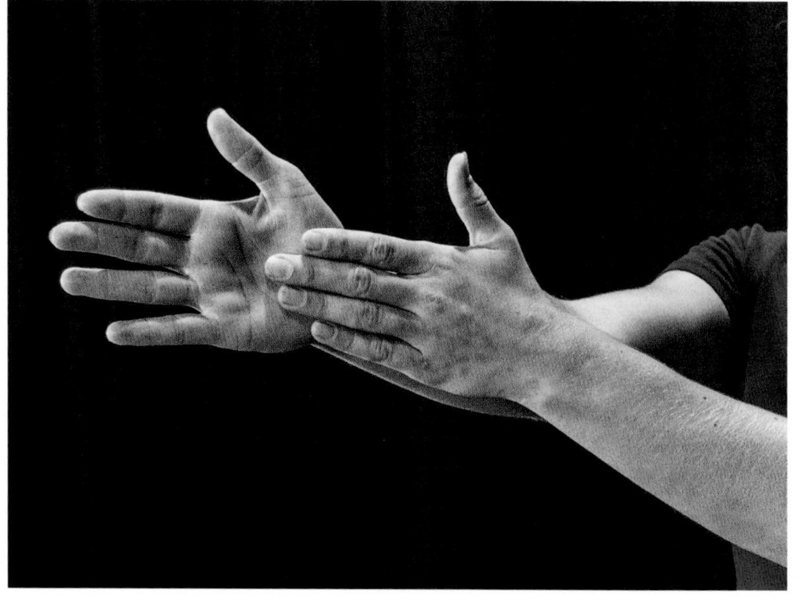

A clap knap formed by shooting the hands past each other.

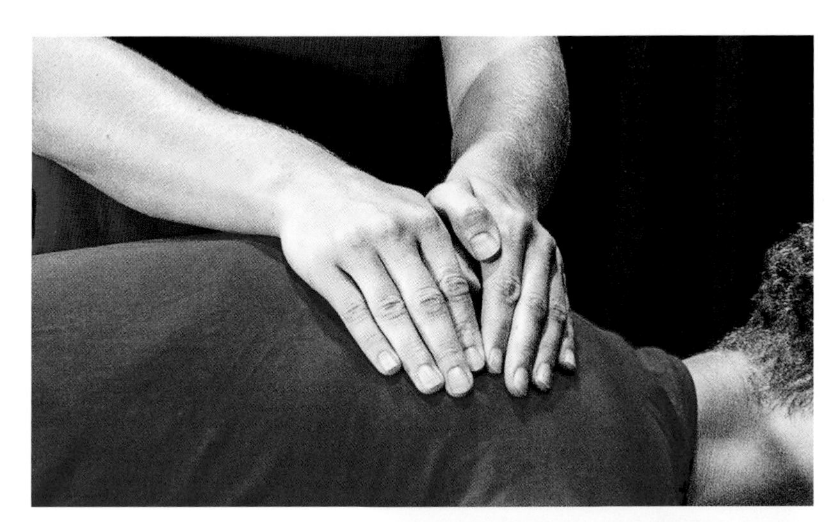

A shared knap created on the partner's back.

A non-contact profile kick to the head, with the victim reacting towards the audience and the upstage hand beginning the thigh knap.
ROB DAVIDSON

to minimize the risk of them seeing how the trick is performed. If the staging is thrust, traverse, or in-the-round, it can be difficult to find a hidden area to knap, unless it is momentarily created by some subtle audience misdirection, or if it can be hidden in the natural movement of the body.

The physique of the performer themselves can also have an impact on the viability of a knap and lead to other choices.

This area of stage combat is very much a moveable feast. In order to achieve the necessary variety, it would greatly benefit performers to practise knapping off various areas of the body, with both dominant and non-dominant hands. An equal facility with either hand is useful.

THE FASTER THE BETTER

A good knap needs to be loud and clear enough to convince the whole audience of the story moment. It also needs to be hidden if the illusion is to be sustained. Ideally, it needs to be executed fast. Whoever performs the knap must find a logical reason for their knapping hand to be close to the area of the knap. If the hand makes too long a journey without good reason, the knap is telegraphed to the audience and the illusion is spoiled. If that hand is in a fist, it will open to knap, but then close again as fast as possible.

The knap must not be prepared, as a preparation cues the audience and reveals what is happening. For example, it is a common error with

Roundhouse kick with a chest knap, with BASSC teacher Jonathan Leverett assessing whether the knap is masked.

a clap knap for the victim to open their hands wide first or lift their elbows in preparation; both actions will give the game away. The faster a knap is executed, the less likelihood there is of it being seen; a performer needs quick hands. The speed of a good knap also feeds energy into the attack or the reaction and enhances the illusion.

Performers need to be aware that knaps often sting. However, after some repetition, knaps that feel quite harsh to begin with may have less impact as the body gets used to them.

CONCLUSION

Of course, a knap can only approximate the sound of a real contact strike. The sound of a fist hitting a bony face is different from that of clapping hands, or a hand thumping a chest. It is a necessary compromise – there are only so many ways to create body contacts safely. The good news is that the brain is designed to retroactively fill in gaps in its information flow, providing as seamless an interface with the world for its body as possible (Mahon, 2018). When it sees a fist fly, observes a victim moving in reaction and hears a sound, no matter how generic, it works to convince itself that it has seen and heard the real thing. This of course is of great benefit to performers in the theatre.

Knapping is a vital aspect of well-performed stage combat. The audience perceive a fight in two different ways. They watch the action movie, but they also listen to the radio play. Without both elements, their appreciation of the story is weakened. Without clear, well-masked and well-executed knaps, an extremely important component is lost, and the performance is the poorer for that loss.

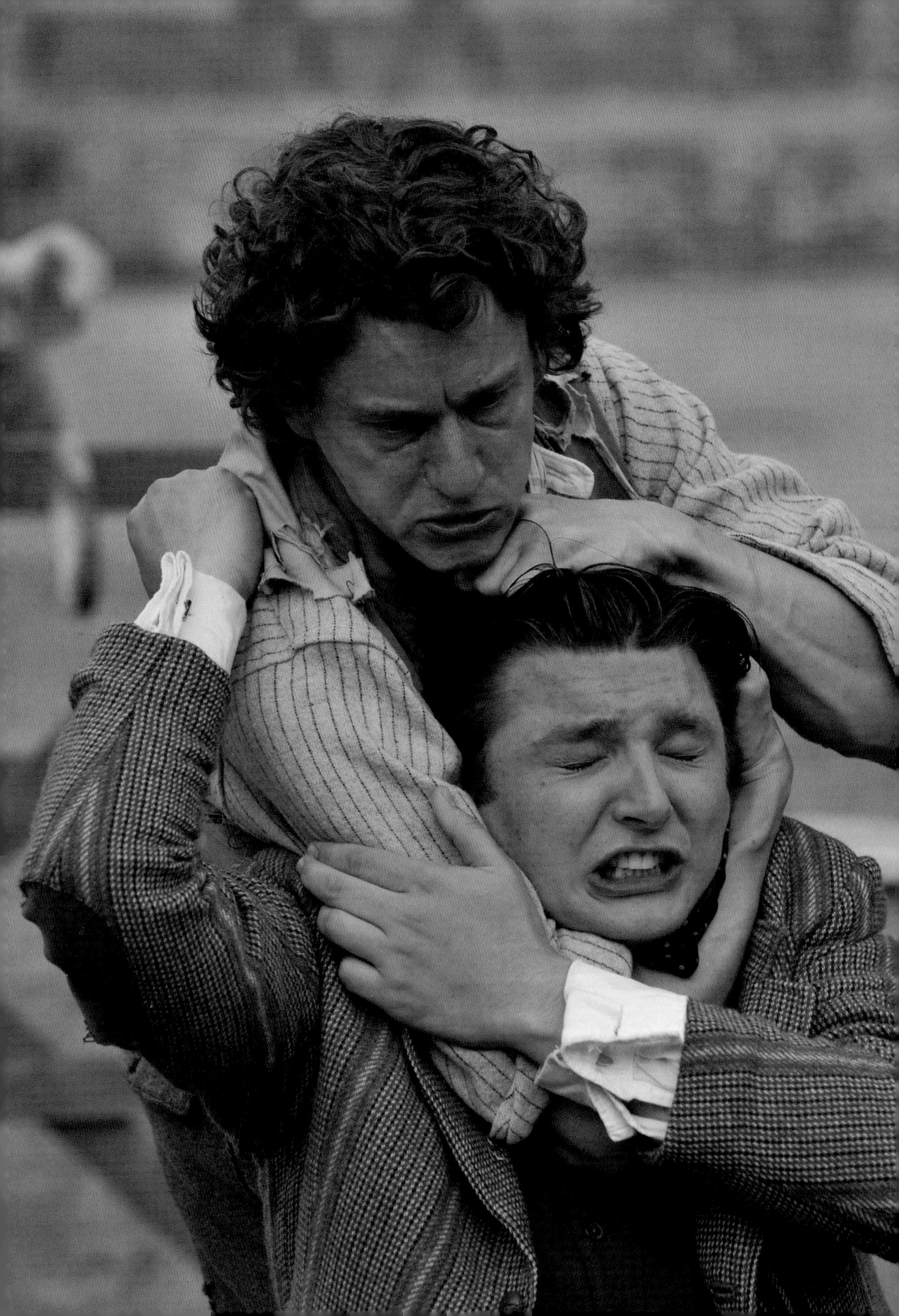

12
WARMING UP AND STRETCHING

The importance of warming up and stretching out has been received wisdom for many years in almost every field of physical exertion. Yet it appears that the matter may not be as clear cut as had previously been assumed. Scientific evidence seems to indicate now that long-held assumptions may no longer be accurate.

What do the terms 'warm-up' and 'stretch' mean in this context? Warming up involves slightly raising the temperature of the muscles through light exercise prior to either stretching, or proceeding to the target exercise for the session. Stretching describes lengthening and loosening various muscle groups to prepare them for the work involved in an upcoming physical session.

Warming up and stretching are not the same thing, or interchangeable, as some believe. They fulfil two different functions. Stretching before a warm-up would entail stretching cold muscles, which is at best ineffective and at worst risks

This illusion is created entirely by the victim; note the attacker carefully supporting them. *Macbeth*, courtesy of the Guildford Shakespeare Company.
CHARLOTTE CONQUEST

damage to those muscles. The body should always be warmed up before attempting moderate to intense exercise (Fisher, 2018). To date, it has been believed by most practitioners that both the warm-up and the stretch are necessary elements of an exercise routine, to prevent potential injury to the unprepared body. It certainly remains true that a warm-up preparatory to exercise is advised by all professional practitioners discussing the issue (Walker, 2016). The jury, however, is out with regard to the most common forms of stretching being used to reduce the risk of injury.

WARM-UP BENEFITS

The primary purpose of a warm-up is literally to make the muscles warmer through light usage. As the muscles warm up, they begin to move and release more easily, which helps reduce the risk of straining or tearing them. Light exercise raises the heart rate, with a beneficial effect on the circulatory system, and increases the breathing rate, bringing more oxygen or fuel into the system. Stress on the heart is reduced as it is slowly eased up to function at a higher capacity capable of supporting the increased need for oxygenated blood to fuel the muscle groups required for the planned exercise. The joints become more lubricated, the muscles more flexible, the body's range of motion increases and it is better prepared for the full exertion to come. The warm-up also acts as a focusing tool, allowing the performer's mind to concentrate on the work ahead (Simon, 2019).

STRETCHING MODALITIES

Putting aside for the moment the question of the efficacy of stretching, or whether it is appropriate, how should it be done? There are a number of different ways to approach this subject, all with differing levels of complexity, ease of use and effectiveness (Knight, 2019).

Static Stretching

This is the form of stretching that most people are familiar with. The body carefully adopts a position placing a group of muscles, or an individual muscle, under tension, holding for 20–30 seconds before release, allowing the muscles to relax and lengthen. It is a relatively easy and safe method of stretching.

Passive Stretching

Also known as partner or assisted stretching, this relies on using a machine or a friend to increase the force applied through the muscle, allowing muscles to stretch further than they do in a static stretch. There is an increased risk attached to partner stretches, so they should be used with care and always closely monitored if the participants are inexperienced.

Active Stretching

Also known as static-active stretching, this stretches muscles without external assistance, using the power of antagonist (opposing) muscles to stretch the agonist (target) muscles. An example would be stretching the triceps by placing one arm behind the head, then flexing the biceps. It is a more complex version of stretching, requiring a little more knowledge to begin the process.

Dynamic Stretching

This form of stretch uses slow and focused movement to stretch the muscles, swinging, rotating or gently moving body parts to the limit of their range of motion, without sustaining the stretch. Joints or other body elements are never forced past their usual movement range, as this potentially causes damage. Used properly, these stretches are an extremely effective preparation for the work, particularly if the movements echo the planned form of exercise.

PNF Stretching

Proprioceptive neuromuscular facilitation is also sometimes known as contract-relax, or hold-relax stretching. It is effective for increased muscle strength and flexibility. It primarily involves precipitating the inverse myotatic reflex, otherwise known as the golgi tendon reflex, which relaxes the muscle to prevent it tearing. Usually done with a partner, it is an efficient tool, but it does require advanced knowledge. It should not be attempted without a qualified instructor to guide the process.

Isometric Stretching

This complex form of static stretching utilizes contraction of the stretched muscle and resistance without movement, placing the affected muscle under intense tension for the recommended period of time. This must be used with a level of caution and knowledge, as it places significant demands on the affected muscles. If it is not carefully monitored, there is an increased risk of injury.

Ballistic Stretching

This form utilizes energetic movement and body momentum to force joints and muscles beyond their natural range of motion. This alone can cause injury. In addition, if the stretched muscles are not allowed time to adjust to the state of stretch, the rapid bounce of the muscle can also trigger the myotatic reflex, commonly known as the stretch reflex. This causes the muscle to tighten involuntarily to protect it from tearing, which in turn increases the risk of injury. Not only can the muscle or tendon tear, but in extreme cases an avulsion fracture may occur, with the torn tendon ripping

This lift requires the victim's negotiated consent, alongside a pre-lift check that the attacker is fit for the task. *Wind in The Willows*, courtesy of The New Vic Theatre, Stoke-on-Trent.
ANDREW BILLINGTON

free a small section of bone. This form of stretching is almost universally cited as being unsafe in practice (Stretchify, 2013).

TO STRETCH OR NOT TO STRETCH?

Current Thinking

There are a growing number of studies that seem to disprove the assertion that stretching prior to exercise reduces or prevents muscle soreness or injury (Henschke and Lin, 2011). According to these studies, there is little or no evidence that stretching for this purpose has any impact on injury statistics. However, there is also no evidence that, as long as it is performed correctly, it will cause any harm. There also seems to be a general perception that dynamic stretching is slightly more useful for a sustained period of general movement (Ferrara, 2019). As the science lacks clarity at the moment, some practitioners are advising a more nuanced approach to the applicability of static stretching based on context and need (Riecken, 2016). What does seem clear is that there is some evidence that this form of stretching does have a place when it comes to increasing range of motion and flexibility (Shoukat et al., 2017).

Studies have also been conducted into the efficiency of muscles after a period of stretching, showing that they can suffer a reduction in performance for a period of time, specifically in vertical leap and in power (Hough et al., 2009). In a loose analogy, muscles release power in a way that is rather similar to that of a coiled spring releasing energy. The increased flexibility gained from a sustained stretch can measurably diminish the ability to unleash the explosive power that the muscle might otherwise attain. This could result in a loss of performance in jumping or sprint-like movements. The science and rigour behind these studies are beyond the remit of this book, but all the studies are readily available online. Fight practitioners would be well advised to keep up to date with developments in this fast-changing field.

Is Stretching Necessary?

The majority of stage combat classes often do not involve exertion at the same level as a session of sport, because it is a learning environment and the application of technique starts slowly. In fact, it could be argued that the slow repetition of the physical movement whilst learning the technique mimics the form of dynamic stretching, and could therefore be considered preparation for the faster version, in and of itself. The same applies to the initial learning period for choreography. It is only when moving on to rehearsal and performance that performers really begin to pick up speed, expending energy in explosive bursts.

There is a school of thought that the human body is already prepared, in terms of muscle structure and internal capability, for almost all forms of daily physical exertion, by evolutionary design (Cordain et al., 1998). It is arguable that the bodily effort involved in a short fight falls within those parameters and therefore would not require a specific, focused stretch before starting.

Is It Right for You and Your Students?

So, do you need to stretch and, if so, when? Deciding whether or not to stretch is a matter of individual comfort. If stretching seems to help physically or with mental focus, or if it is an established part of your routine, then do it. Ensure that you are specifically targeting the physical actions in which you will engage, and that you are doing the stretches safely and correctly. If explosive force in the muscles is required, it may be worth leaving ten minutes between static stretch and performance (Riecken, 2016).

For the teacher, it will take time for the current state of scientific research and thought to

These performers will have carefully focused their pre-show warm-up to protect their backs from injury. *A Midsummer Night's Dream*, courtesy of The Storyhouse, Chester.
MARK CARLINE

filter down to the grass roots level of professional practitioners and educational establishments, and become accepted practice. If a teacher stops stretching students before each class and one of them suffers a muscle strain, then decides to raise a formal complaint, it might be difficult to convince all involved that their strategy was not at fault. If a decision is taken to continue using stretching as a preparation tool, it might be worth exploring dynamic stretching as a more focused tool than static stretching. As the levels and types of physical activity within sessions change over the arc of a course, the type and intensity of the warm-up and, if utilized, the stretch, will need to alter responsively.

Using Appropriate Forms

If the choice is made to stretch, it is important to adopt a form that is appropriate for the mobility range and muscle groups to be used. Apply stretches gently; they should cause no pain and remain in the performer's natural range of motion. Use a slow tempo, stretching to the point of tension and no further. When the exercise alters, adjust the stretch to fit the new parameters. Once rehearsing choreography, when the expenditure of energy is increased, and that energy release is more explosive, reassess how best to support the body's new requirements.

Designed for an end-on audience, masking the way in which the attacker is bracing to provide physical support. *As You Like It*, courtesy of the Guildford Shakespeare Company. STEVE PORTER

Alternative Reasons for Stretching

There are other reasons to stretch that could benefit the theatre practitioner. After a very physical session or performance, some practitioners stretch as part of a cooling-down process, while others use it as an element of reflective practice. Some simply harvest the maximum benefit from stretching when muscles are warm. As a general health gain, continued stretching as the body ages will certainly help with flexibility, mobility and balance (Page, 2012).

CONCLUSION

There are no specific stretching exercises in this book, as this information is available elsewhere and practitioners will make their own choices based on their circumstances and context. With a field that is in a mild state of flux, and under a certain level of scientific focus, it is perhaps wiser not to settle on explicit recommendations, which may be proven to be less effective in future.

To summarize, it is apparent that the most recent advice in this area is that any physical work should be preceded by a warm-up to prepare the body; the evidence is absolutely clear on the manifold benefits of this. Anyone who also chooses to stretch, despite the growing evidence that its positive impact may be minimal, should ensure that they choose forms that are safe and efficient, and focused on the specific work to be done.

PART III

THE ESSENTIAL TECHNIQUES

13
SLAPS

(Note: no one technique will work for every venue. Each space or staging configuration brings its own challenges, leading to a variety of slaps. The 'Works For' section beginning each technique indicates clearly what works where.)

REALITY

A slap is an attack made with an open hand to the victim's body, most commonly to their face. It can range from a gentle tap to a full-power blow. It is also one of the few techniques of real violence that is considered acceptable for the theatre. It is common to hear someone suggest slapping a fellow performer for real, instead of relying on technique.

SAFETY

The first fact to acknowledge is that a performer's face, at a basic level, is their career. Every contact made with the face and head will greatly increase the risk of career-altering damage. It is a part of the body that is fragile and easily injured in many shocking ways. The most common issue seems to be ruptured eardrums caused by contact slaps.

There are techniques to mitigate the dangers of a contact slap, many of which work some of the time – in ideal conditions. But when are conditions ever 'ideal' in the heat of performance? The performer may get caught in the character's energy, they may be tired, or lose focus momentarily, or simply misjudge their position. Only a small increase in energy takes a slap from resulting in a sting to causing an injury; it only takes one mistake to change the victim's life.

Contact slaps are also a poor story-telling choice. The performer will always have to dilute their character impulses down to something that can be performed safely. No risk-averse practitioner will suggest a contact slap when there are non-contact techniques that cover most performance eventualities. This is particularly the case with the legal and insurance ramifications that such a choice could entail for the fight director or teacher, the production company or the educational establishment concerned.

Non-contact slaps rely on being out of distance for upstage/downstage versions and displacing the target when in distance.

THE UPSTAGE/ DOWNSTAGE SLAP

Works For

Proscenium arch mid-sized performance spaces, and smaller.

Safety Principle

Out of distance – the attacker is not close enough to the victim to actually make contact without stepping or leaning in.

Position

Victim downstage, attacker upstage, so the victim can mask the knap. Can be modified to a slight diagonal, consequently adjusting the journey of the hand. Can be reversed if the knap can be located elsewhere, or if the victim has very fast hands. The attacker's slapping side foot is slightly back, but not too far, otherwise they cannot pivot as far and the slap stops short.

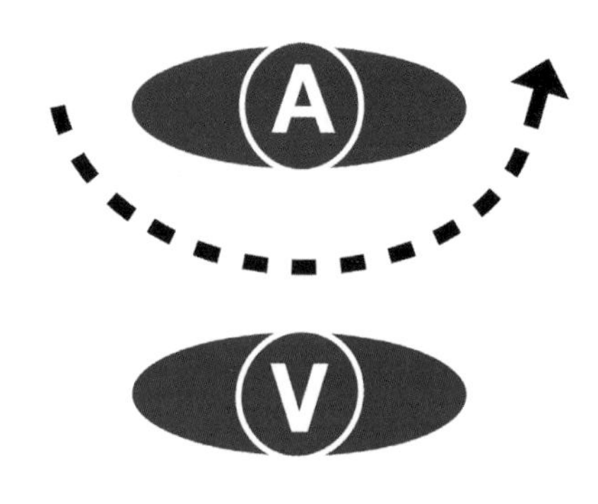

Figure 18: The staging of the upstage/downstage slap.

Eye Contact

The performers make eye contact, ensuring their partner is ready. If not, they attract their attention.

Preparation

The attacker's non-slapping hand ensures they are not close enough to hit the victim. This distance check can be masked as a pointing finger, a threatening fist, and so on.

Simultaneously the attacker raises their slapping hand beside them at the height of their partner's face. Performers often want to pull it back behind them as it feels more powerful. However, this instinctive action rarely reads well in the auditorium. It makes the attacking semi-circle smaller, reducing the illusion of contact. Craft and technique must create the illusion of instinctive action.

Performers often prepare lower than the target, only hitting the correct height as the hand crosses between them and their partner. This is perfectly acceptable if fighting for a single point of view (POV), such as a camera, but on stage the illusion of contact is drastically reduced. Make the preparation clear to the audience, giving them the opportunity to anticipate the moment just before it occurs, and engage more strongly with the story and character.

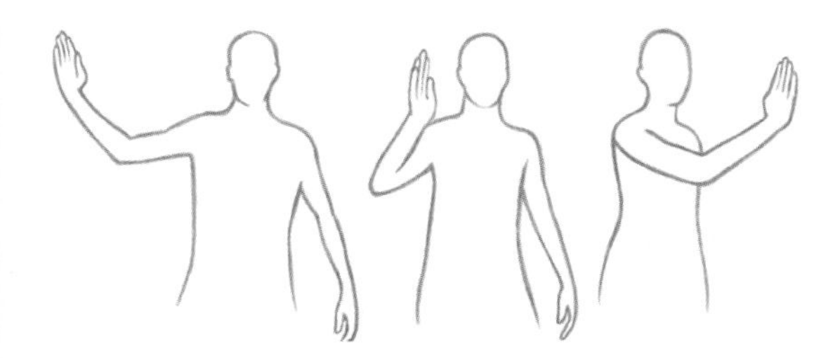

Figure 19: The upstage/downstage slap.

Action

Keeping their arm half-bent, the attacker sweeps their hand in a semi-circle crossing the victim's face. The hand remains at target height all the way. Crossing in front of their face, the hand rotates 90 degrees, facing the palm to the audience, as if jolting off the face. This fast hand adjustment subliminally cues the illusory moment of actual contact. The arm remains bent throughout, finishing beside the attacker's opposite shoulder.

Performers often instinctively use a fully extended arm; this movement can be successful with a straight arm but it weakens the illusion of the victim being in distance. It is also scarier for the victim, as the hand is almost always closer to their face, moving at speed.

Common Errors

Attacker

Preparing the hand behind them
Crossing the target at an angle instead of horizontal from beginning to end
Fully extending the arm
Stepping forwards as they slap
Standing too close

Victim

Reacting at an angle that does not match the path of the slap
Mistiming the reaction
Knapping slowly enough that the audience can see
Knapping to their side, or turning their body before their hands release contact

Reaction

The victim's head turns sharply sideways as the hand crosses their nose, matching the attack's energy and speed. They clap their hands as fast as they can, making the knap and creating the auditory illusion of contact. The knap must have no element of preparation, and should be as fast and surprising as possible.

OPPOSITE RIGHT: Four stages of the upstage/downstage slap with a slightly late reaction.
TOM ZIEBELL

BELOW: A flowing image of the upstage/downstage slap.
TOM ZIEBELL

THE BACKHAND UPSTAGE/ DOWNSTAGE SLAP

Works For

Proscenium arch performance spaces.

Safety Principle

Out of distance – the attacker is not close enough to the victim to actually make contact without stepping or leaning in.

Position

Victim downstage, attacker upstage, so the victim can mask the knap. Can be modified to a slight diagonal, consequently adjusting the journey of the hand. Can be reversed if the knap can be located elsewhere, or if the victim has very fast hands.

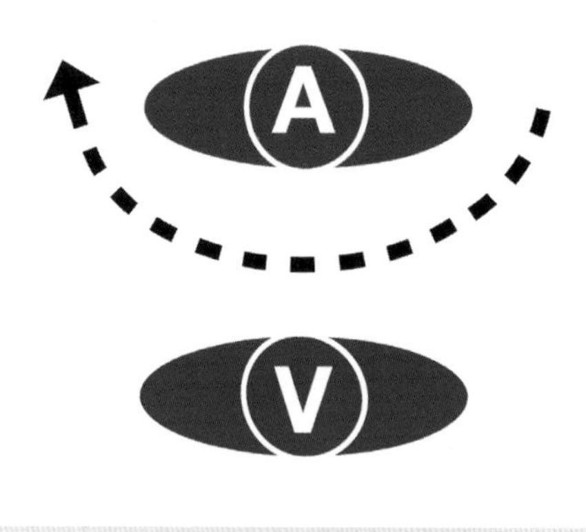

Figure 20: The staging of the backhand upstage/downstage slap with dropped elbow.

Eye Contact

The performers make eye contact, ensuring their partner is ready. If not, they attract their attention.

Preparation

As a standalone moment distance is checked with the slapping hand, either with a gesture or a small negotiated push. Following a previous technique where distance has been established, and the position is unchanged, there is no need to re-check distance.

The attacker's slapping hand raises across their body, at the height of the victim's face, elbow bent, anywhere between straight down, to horizontal, pointing in the direction of travel, pivoting their hips and shifting their weight to that side.

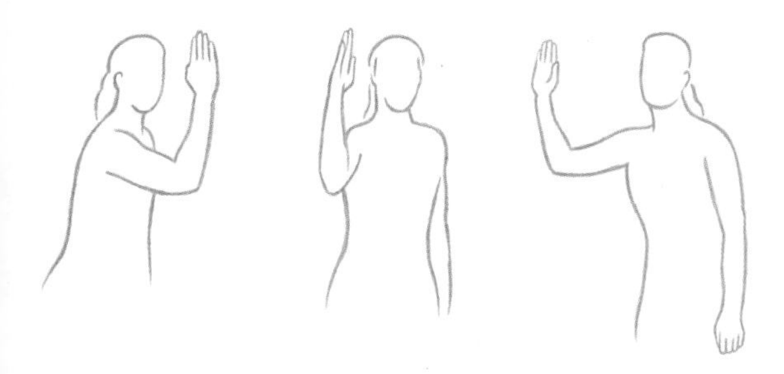

Figure 21: The backhand upstage/downstage slap with dropped elbow.

Action

Keeping their arm half-bent, the attacker sweeps their hand past the victim's face, as they pivot their hips, shifting their weight to the opposite foot. The hand remains at target height all the way around. The more horizontal the arm, the more it opens out into an extended position on the front diagonal. The lower the elbow, the less extended the end of the technique. Avoid over-extending the elbow at speed; keep it slightly bent to protect it as the arm stops. Note that the arm does not fully extend until the hand passes the victim's face.

Reaction

The victim's head turns sharply sideways as the hand crosses their nose, matching the attack's energy and speed. They clap their hands as fast as they can, making the knap, creating the auditory illusion of contact. The knap must have no element of preparation, and should be as fast and surprising as possible.

Common Errors

Attacker

Preparing the hand at the wrong height
Crossing the target at an angle instead of horizontal from beginning to end
Extending the arm towards the victim during the slap
Misjudging the distance

Victim

Reacting at an angle that does not match the path of the slap
Mistiming the reaction
Knapping too slowly, so that the audience can see
Knapping to their side, or turning their body before their hands release contact, allowing the audience to see

OPPOSITE RIGHT: Four stages of the backhand upstage/downstage slap with dropped elbow.
TOM ZIEBELL

BELOW: A flowing image of the backhand upstage/downstage slap with dropped elbow.
TOM ZIEBELL

THE WIDE-ANGLE UPSTAGE/ DOWNSTAGE SLAP

Works For

Proscenium arch mid-sized performance spaces, and smaller.

Safety Principle

Out of distance – the attacker is not close enough to the victim to actually make contact without stepping or leaning in.

Position

Victim downstage; attacker upstage, so the victim can mask the knap. Can be reversed if the knap can be located elsewhere, or if the victim has very fast hands. The attacker is slightly further out of distance than in the previous slaps, as they step forwards on a front diagonal as they prepare.

A more advanced technique, this is a less instinctive action and requires stronger conscious control of the path of the hand. It can omit the distance check.

AUDIENCE

Figure 22: The staging of the wide-angle upstage/downstage slap.

Eye Contact

The performers make eye contact, ensuring their partner is ready. If not, they attract their attention.

Preparation

The attacker steps on the front diagonal, reaching forwards on that front 45-degree diagonal, shifting their weight to that side. Imagining a glass wall between the performers, the attacker places the little finger of their hand on it approximately a metre to the side of the victim.

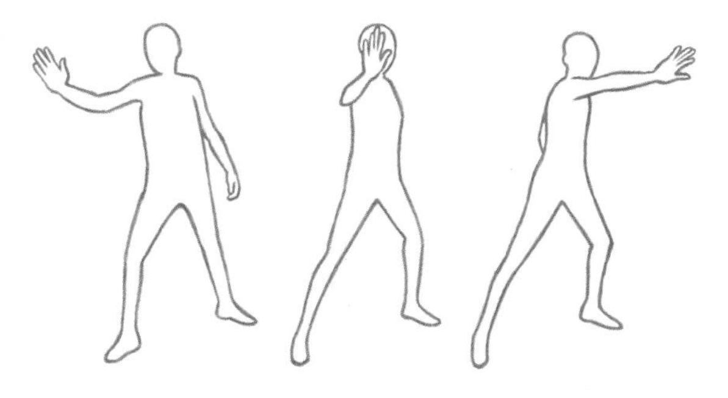

Figure 23: The wide-angle upstage/downstage slap.

Common Errors

Attacker

Preparing the hand behind or to the side, rather than on a front diagonal from the shoulder
Crossing the target at an angle instead of horizontal from beginning to end
Allowing the path of the hand to become semi-circular rather than straight
Stepping forwards as they slap
Starting too far back

Victim

Reacting at an angle that does not match the path of the slap
Mistiming the reaction
Knapping too slowly, so that the audience can see
Knapping to their side, or turning their body before their hands release contact, allowing the audience to see

Action

The attacker shifts their weight to the other side, traversing or stepping as far as possible, their hand crossing the victim's face to the opposite side. The hand remains in contact with the 'wall' throughout. The arm starts fully extended, bends as it travels and finishes fully extended. Seen from above, the path of the hand would seem to be a straight line. Crossing the face, it rotates 90 degrees, creating the illusory moment of contact. The path of the hand most closely resembles that of a cross punch, travelling in a straight line from one side to the other, relative to the victim's position. It is possible to use a crossing rather than a sliding step, although it can adversely affect the safety distance, and encourages the attacker to slap in a semi-circular action.

Reaction

The victim's head turns sharply sideways as the hand crosses their nose, matching the attack's energy and speed. They clap their hands as fast as they can, making the knap, creating the auditory illusion of contact. The knap must have no element of preparation, and should be as fast and surprising as possible.

OPPOSITE RIGHT: Four stages of the wide-angle upstage/downstage slap with a slightly late reaction.
TOM ZIEBELL

BELOW: A flowing image of the wide-angle upstage/downstage slap.
TOM ZIEBELL

THE PROFILE SLAP

Works For

Proscenium arch spaces of all sizes; can work in traverse, and variations work for thrust and in-the-round staging.

Safety Principle

Displace the target to the parrot space – relies on the hand obscuring the line of sight from audience to target, creating the illusion of contact. Used when performers are in distance and, of necessity, must move the target to a safe position.

Position

Both performers are in profile to the audience, meaning that they are in distance and must pay particular attention to the risk that this creates.

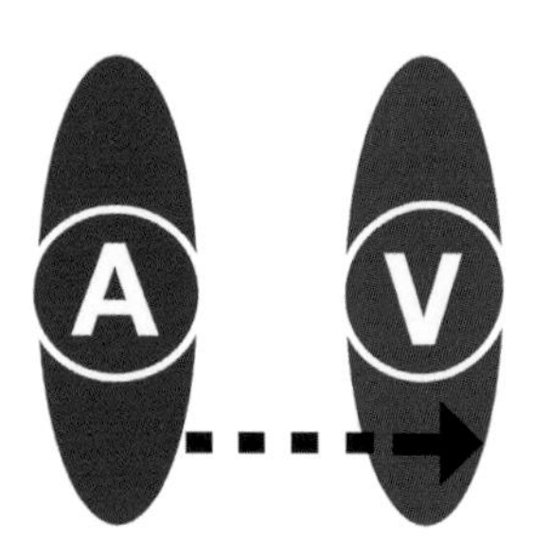

Figure 24: The staging of the profile slap.

Eye Contact

The performers make eye contact, ensuring their partner is ready. If not, they attract their attention. They then shift focus to the target over the victim's shoulder; if they do not do this, the risk of actual contact is increased.

Preparation

The attacker's hand lifts up beside them, hip slightly back, elbow back, palm out towards the audience. This position creates the illusion of a more full-powered slap.

A less complex version lifts the hand up, back towards the audience. This position creates the illusion of a lighter slap.

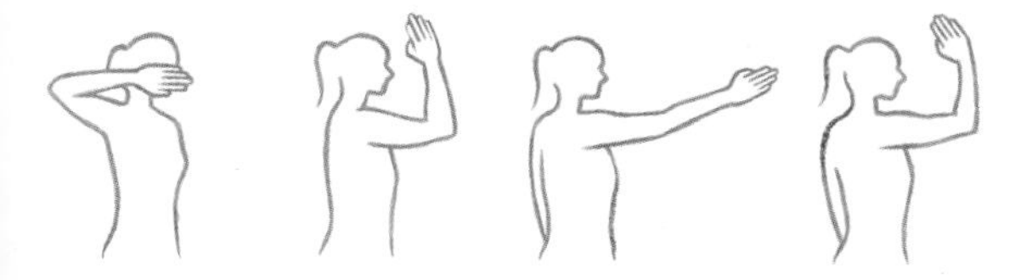

Figure 25: The profile slap.

Action

The hip moves forwards and the elbow drops inwards, rotating the palm away from the audience, as the hand travels in a straight line towards the target zone. The hand flicks into that space, fingers loosely spaced, then recoils halfway back, pausing briefly, fingers up, giving the audience time to catch up with the story before dropping. This is described as a 'smoking gun' moment.

The hand does not move laterally. The illusion of a circular path is created by the journey of the elbow. The hand aims straight for the outside edge of the shoulder space, far from the victim's head.

The less complex version sees the hand travel in a straight line, finishing as described above.

Variation: The V Slap

After the illusion of contact, the attacker increases the illusion of circularity by dropping the elbow, pulling the hand from the target zone and bringing it back so their fingers point over their upstage shoulder, palm facing upstage. The hand must travel in a vertical plane created by bending the elbow, and not a horizontal sweep, otherwise the attacker will hit the victim in the face. It may help to imagine a shallow rainbow from the victim's downstage shoulder to the attacker's upstage shoulder, and wipe the palm of the hand along that arc.

Reaction

The victim begins their reaction a beat later than expected, as the hand starts to withdraw from the target zone, pulling back into the victim's peripheral vision. If the reaction is any earlier, the illusion does not work.

The victim's head turns sharply to the side in a reaction matching the attack's energy and speed. They clap their hands together as fast as they can, making the knap, creating the auditory illusion of contact. The head reacts upstage, then back.

Alternatively, the victim or the attacker can knap off their upstage thigh.

Common Errors

Attacker

Does not reach far enough to create the illusion of contact

The hand is too low or too high at the moment of illusory impact

Allowing the path of the hand to become semi-circular rather than straight

The hand is too close to the victim's face

Victim

Mistiming the reaction

Knapping too slowly, so that the audience can see

Attempting to hide the knap, thus drawing attention to it

OPPOSITE RIGHT: Four stages of the profile slap.
TOM ZIEBELL

BELOW: A flowing image of the profile slap.
TOM ZIEBELL

THE BACKHAND PROFILE SLAP

Works For

Proscenium arch spaces of all sizes; can work in traverse, and variations work for thrust and in-the-round staging.

Safety Principle

Displace the target to the parrot space – this relies on the hand obscuring the line of sight from audience to target, creating the illusion of contact. Used when performers are in distance and, of necessity, must move the target to a safe position.

Position

The victim is profile to the audience; the attacker is usually in profile, but often with the non-slapping side slightly stepped back and hips on a slight diagonal. They are offset from the victim so their slapping-side shoulder lines up with the target zone. Usually they are slightly downstage of the victim, profile to the audience. The attacking shoulder must line up on the target shoulder or the line from attacking shoulder to target will be a diagonal between the two bodies, increasing the risk of hitting the victim in the face. They are in distance and must pay particular attention to the potential hazard this creates.

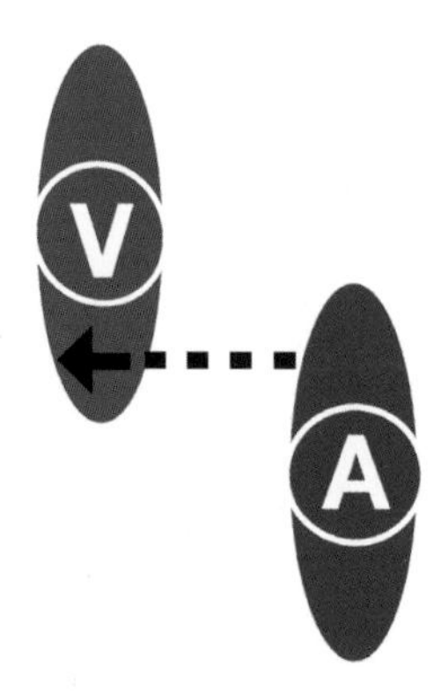

Figure 26: The staging of the backhand profile slap.

Eye Contact

The performers make eye contact, ensuring their partner is ready. If not, they attract their attention. They then shift focus to the target over the victim's shoulder; if they do not do this, the risk of actual contact is increased.

Preparation

The attacker reaches across their body, elbow pointing towards the target zone and fingers back over their downstage shoulder.

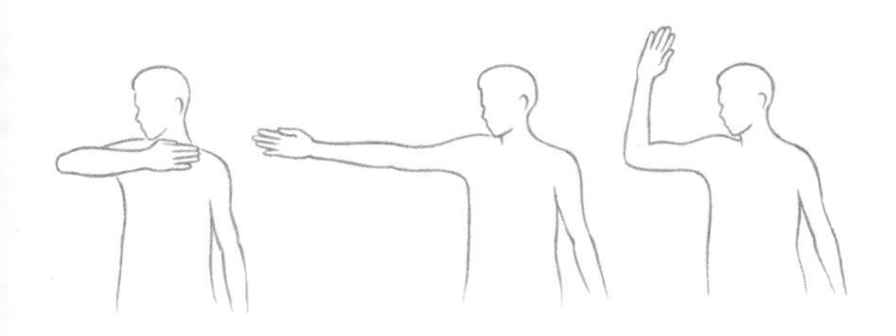

Figure 27: The backhand profile slap.

Action

The attacker's arm straightens, opening the elbow horizontally, the hand flicking sideways into the target zone, then the elbow is bent, bringing the hand halfway back towards themselves. There are two common versions of this: in one, the elbow drops, pulling the hand back; in the other, the hand lifts up past the victim's ear, creating a flick-up moment. The choice is dictated primarily by the audience height.

In both versions, the horizontal and vertical elements must not be allowed to blur into an ill-defined angular sweep, because the rotational bend of the elbow will almost certainly ensure that, from the audience's perspective, the attacker misses the victim entirely. The horizontal action must be crisp, and then join seamlessly into the vertical action, creating the sharp illusion of bouncing off their face.

It is possible to make this technique work in the round, by slightly extending the reach of the arm, relaxing the fingers and allowing the wrist to flick open more, just before lifting the hand clear, thus closing the sightlines from all angles. This is achieved by creating an 'L' shape with the wrist.

Common Errors

Attacker

Does not reach far enough to create the illusion of contact
Does not clearly define the horizontal and vertical elements of the technique
The hand is too close to the victim's face
Stands too square to the victim

Victim

Mistiming the reaction
Knapping too slowly, so that the audience can see
Attempting to hide the knap, thus drawing attention to it

Occasionally, the back of the fingers may brush the back of the victim's head, but the physical position of the arm and shoulder mean that this should never be more than the lightest of contacts. It is to be avoided if possible.

Reaction

The victim's head turns sharply to the side, then back in a reaction matching the attack's energy and speed. They knap as fast as they can, creating the auditory illusion of contact.

Alternatively, the victim or the attacker can knap off their upstage thigh.

OPPOSITE RIGHT: Four stages of the backhand profile slap. TOM ZIEBELL

BELOW: A flowing image of the backhand profile slap. TOM ZIEBELL

THE PROFILE SWEEP SLAP

Works For

Proscenium arch spaces of all sizes; can work in traverse, and variations work for thrust and in-the-round staging.

Safety Principle

Displace the target – this relies on the hand obscuring the line of sight from the audience to the target, creating the illusion of contact.

Position

Both performers are in profile to the audience, meaning that they are in distance and must pay particular attention to the risk that this creates. This technique is customizable according to the height of the audience. For a lower audience, the slap reaches the height of the victim's face, then the elbow bends and the hand flicks slightly back. The higher the audience, the higher the hand reaches before the elbow bends.

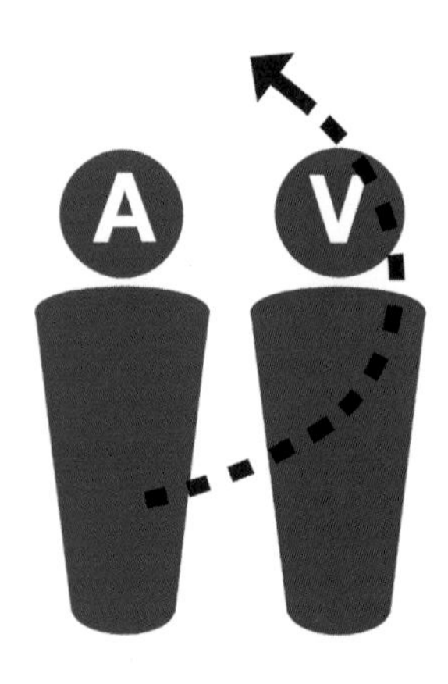

Figure 28: The staging of the profile sweep slap.

Eye Contact

The performers make eye contact, ensuring their partner is ready. If not, they attract their attention. They then shift focus to the target over the victim's shoulder; if they do not do this, the risk of actual contact is increased.

Preparation

The attacker steps slightly forward and downstage of the victim as they prepare their hand low by their side; like a discus thrower preparing to throw. It is necessary to be close for this technique to work.

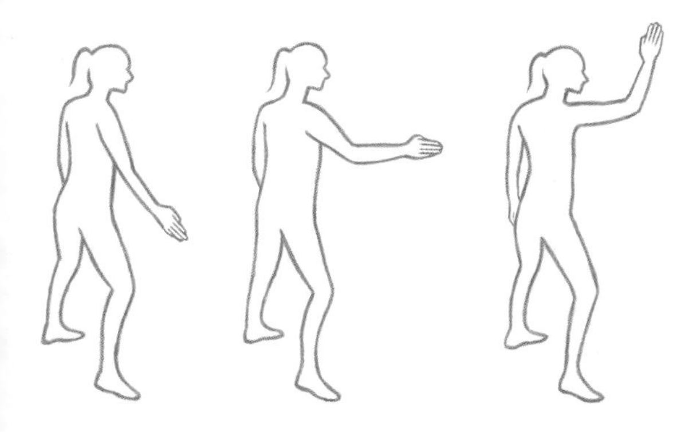

Figure 29: The profile sweep slap.

Action

The attacker sweeps their hand, arcing up past the victim's head on a rising diagonal. Imagine sliding a hand up a pyramid that encloses the victim. As the hand passes the victim's head, the elbow bends and the hand pulls slightly back.

The attacker's wrist lines up on the victim's shoulder with the arm at full extension; this ensures the hand will seem to strike the target, although it will feel as though the performers are too close. As the shoulder is a ball and socket joint, once the arm passes its full horizontal extension it starts to arc back, causing the distance to shorten. Inevitably, if the attacker's hand lines up on the victim's shoulder, which feels more natural, there is no illusion of contact for most of the audience.

Keep the elbow pointing at the victim's target zone as the technique finishes. If it travels between attacker and victim, there is an increased risk of hitting them with the elbow.

Reaction

The victim's head turns sharply to the side in a reaction matching the attack's energy and speed. They clap their hands together as fast as they can, making the knap, creating the auditory illusion of contact. The head reacts upstage, then back.

If performed with a high sweep it can work to corkscrew the reaction to the side and down, as if the strike were higher on the side of the head.

Alternatively, the victim or the attacker can knap off their upstage thigh.

Common Errors

Attacker

Does not reach far enough to create the illusion of contact

Misjudges how the height difference between attacker and victim will affect the distance for the illusion of contact

Travels the elbow across the victim

Victim

Mistiming the reaction

Knapping too slowly, so that the audience can see

Attempting to hide the knap, thus drawing attention to it

OPPOSITE RIGHT: Four stages of the profile sweep slap.
TOM ZIEBELL

BELOW: A flowing image of the profile sweep slap.
TOM ZIEBELL

THE BACKHAND PROFILE SWEEP SLAP

Works For

Proscenium arch spaces of all sizes; can work in traverse, and variations work for thrust and in-the-round staging.

Safety Principle

Displace the target – this relies on the hand or foot obscuring the line of sight from the audience to the target, creating the illusion of contact.

Position

The victim is in profile to the audience; the attacker is usually in profile, but often with the non-slapping side foot stepped back and the hips on a slight diagonal. They are offset from the victim so their slapping-side shoulder is lined up with the victim's target zone. They are, of course, in distance and must pay particular attention to the risk that this creates.

This technique is customizable according to the height of the audience. For a lower audience, the slap reaches the height of the victim's face, then the elbow bends and the hand flicks slightly back. The higher the audience, the higher the hand reaches before the elbow bends.

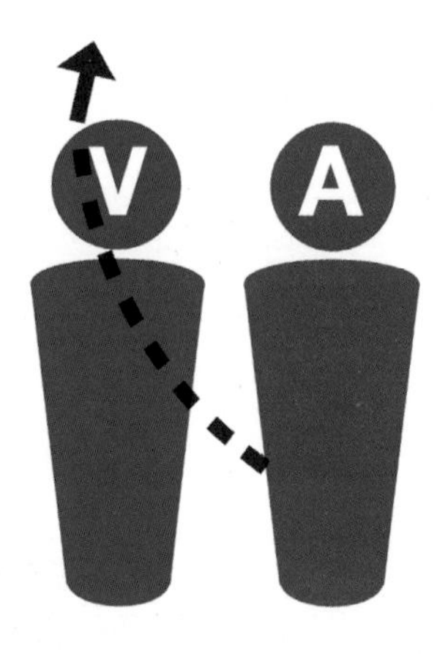

Figure 30: The staging of the backhand profile sweep slap.

Eye Contact
The performers make eye contact, ensuring their partner is ready. If not, they attract their attention. They then shift focus to the target over the victim's shoulder; if they do not do this, the risk of actual contact is increased.

Preparation
The attacker steps slightly forward and downstage of the victim as they prepare their hand low across their body. It is necessary to be close for this technique to work.

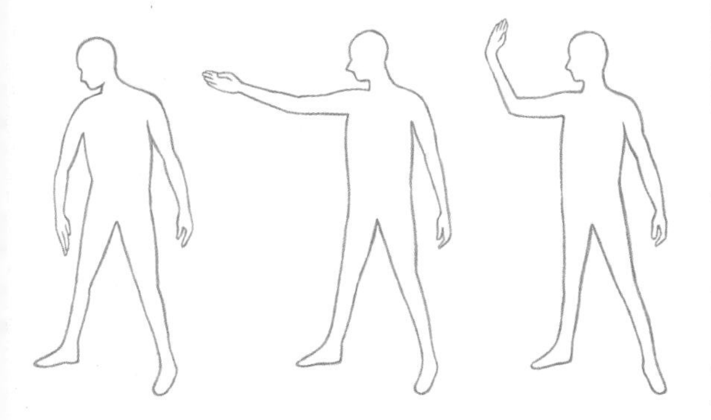

Figure 31: The backhand profile sweep slap.

Action
The attacker sweeps their back hand arcing up past the victim's head on a rising diagonal. Imagine sliding a back hand up a pyramid that encloses the victim. As the hand passes the victim's head, the elbow bends and the hand pulls slightly back.

The attacker's wrist lines up on the victim's shoulder with the arm at full extension; this ensures the hand will seem to strike the target, although it will feel as though the performers are too close. As the shoulder is a ball and socket joint, once the arm passes its full horizontal extension it starts to arc back, causing the distance to shorten. Inevitably, if the attacker's hand lines up on the victim's shoulder, which feels more natural, there is no illusion of contact for most of the audience.

Reaction
The victim's head turns sharply to the side in a reaction matching the attack's energy and speed.

Common Errors

Attacker

Does not reach far enough to create the illusion of contact

Misjudges how the height difference between attacker and victim will affect the distance for the illusion of contact

Forgets to offset shoulder to shoulder to reduce the risk of accidental contact

Victim

Mistiming the reaction

Knapping too slowly, so that the audience can see

Attempting to hide the knap, thus drawing attention to it

They clap their hands together as fast as they can, making the knap, creating the auditory illusion of contact. The head reacts upstage, then back.

If performed with a high sweep it can work to corkscrew the reaction to the side and down as if the strike were higher on the side of the head.

Alternatively, the victim can knap off their upstage thigh.

OPPOSITE RIGHT: Four stages of the backhand profile sweep slap. TOM ZIEBELL

BELOW: A flowing image of the backhand profile sweep slap. TOM ZIEBELL

14
PUNCHES (NON-CONTACT)

(Note: no one technique will work for every venue. Each space or staging configuration brings its own challenges, leading to a variety of punches. The 'Works For' section beginning each technique indicates clearly what works where.)

REALITY

A punch is an attack made with a closed hand to the victim's body. It can be either trained or untrained. If trained, there are a number of different styles available for research.

In a real fight, no participant wishes to telegraph their intention before committing to an attack, for obvious tactical reasons. Therefore, most trained punching styles are extremely efficient, delivering maximum effect for minimum expenditure of energy, without revealing their intention prior to the attack. With live performance, this can create issues of visibility and of story-telling clarity. Without allowing the audience to anticipate the attack a beat early, there is a risk of creating a situation where they either miss vital elements of the physical narrative, or are left playing mental catch-up as they struggle to work out what has just happened.

The situation is different for the camera, where the ability to be closer to the action, and the technical need to bring as much truth as possible to each physical choice, positively encourages the use of real boxing styles. Even then, certain styles need to be subtly adjusted to focus the story-telling aspects.

Whether using a trained punching style or not, it is vital to adhere to the fundamental physical truth of how to punch. When committing energy to the illusion of a punch, performers can find their brain has fooled them. Because it recognizes that there will be no contact, in its never-ending quest to minimize the body's output of energy, it can trick the performer into punching with their arm only instead of fully engaging the body. Without that illusion of body weight in the strike, the impact of the violence on the audience is reduced.

SAFETY

It is possible safely to create contact punches (*see* Chapter 17). For obvious reasons, there must be no contact punches to the face or other sensitive areas of the body.

Non-contact punches rely on the performers being out of distance for upstage/downstage versions and displacing the target when in distance.

For live performance, punches should be made with a hollow fist to reduce damage in case of accidental contact. This relaxed form of a real fist will sustain the visual illusion of a punch, but the softer hand will transmit far less energy if it does make contact. The wrist must also remain aligned with the forearm. If it is slightly bent during an actual contact, its unsupported position will leave it prone to injury.

WHAT WORKS?

These techniques are a mixed bag. Some of the upstage/downstage versions do not work well in large auditoriums. Techniques in this orientation moving down the target line rather than across it are better for smaller venues with narrower audience sightlines, or for the single POV of a camera. Others, mostly the profile variants, are designed for larger, wider performance spaces.

THE HOOK PUNCH

Works For
Proscenium arch staging in mid-sized performance spaces and smaller.

Safety Principle
Out of distance – the attacker is not close enough to the victim to actually make contact without stepping or leaning in.

Position
Victim upstage; attacker downstage. This position, or a modified version of it, allows the attacker to mask the knap. It can be reversed if the victim makes the knap, or if it can be located elsewhere.

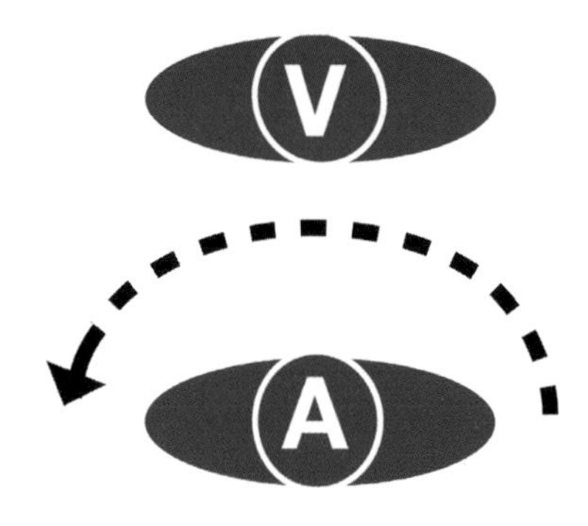

Figure 32: The staging of the hook punch.

Eye Contact
The performers make eye contact, ensuring their partner is ready. If not, they attract their attention.

Preparation
The attacker's punching-side foot is slightly back, enabling them to pivot easily on the balls of their feet. They extend their non-punching fist to ensure they are not close enough to hit their partner.

Simultaneously, the other fist lifts to the height of the victim's face, the elbow bent at a right-angle, preparing to punch, the hip rotating slightly back. The elbow is lower than the fist, for safety: if it is

Figure 33: The hook punch.

level and the distance is misjudged, it is possible to miss with the fist, but make accidental contact with the elbow to the face. If it is lower, any inadvertent contact is likely to be to the torso, with less serious ramifications for the victim.

Action

The attacker pivots, sweeping the fist in a semicircle crossing the target. The punching hand remains at target height all the way. The arm does not move independently of the body, but remains fixed in its relationship to the torso; the hip rotation moves the fist past the target. The other hand opens to make a chest knap, then closes again.

Reaction

The victim's head then shoulders turn sharply to the side as the fist crosses their face, creating a reaction matching the attack's energy and speed. Separating the movement of the head and shoulders is important for the clarity of the visual story-telling. Releasing the shoulders a fraction of a second after the head moves can also help to relieve stress in the neck at its fullest rotation.

If knapping, the victim keeps the hands close to their chest, creating a simple chest knap.

Common Errors

Attacker

Preparing the fist too low and crossing the target at an angle
Standing too deep to pivot easily
Moving the arm independently of the body
Knapping too slowly and turning their body while their hand is still on their chest, allowing the audience to see
Straightening the arm at the end of the punch

Victim

Mistiming the reaction
Reacting at an angle that does not match the path of the punch

OPPOSITE RIGHT: Four stages of the hook punch.
TOM ZIEBELL

A flowing image of the hook punch.
TOM ZIEBELL

THE UPSTAGE/DOWNSTAGE BACKFIST

Works For

Proscenium arch staging in mid-sized performance spaces, and smaller.

Safety Principle

Out of distance – the attacker is not close enough to the victim to actually make contact without stepping or leaning in.

Position

Victim upstage; attacker downstage. This position, or a modified version of it, allows the attacker to mask the knap. It can be reversed if the victim makes the knap, or if it can be located elsewhere.

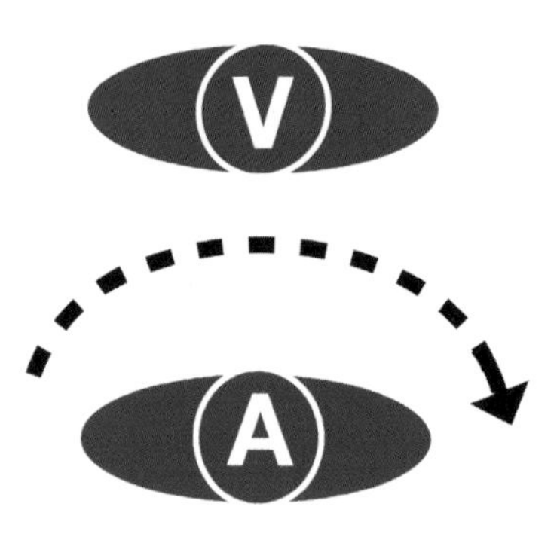

Figure 34: The staging of the upstage/downstage backfist with dropped elbow.

Eye Contact

The performers make eye contact, ensuring their partner is ready. If not, they attract their attention.

Preparation

As a standalone moment distance is checked with the punching hand, either with a gesture or a small negotiated push. Following a previous technique where distance has been established, and the position is unchanged, there is no need to re-check distance.

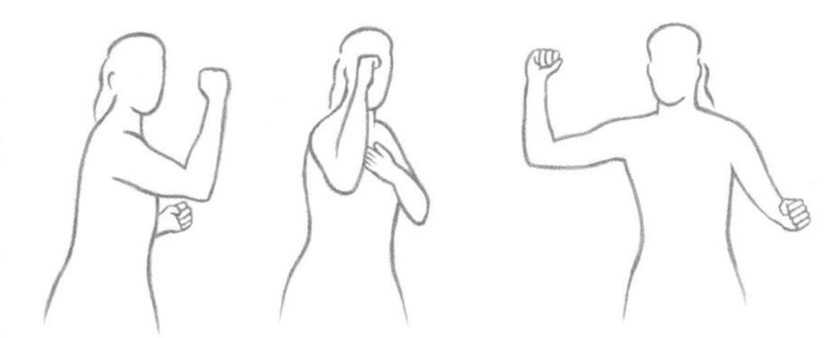

Figure 35: The upstage/downstage backfist with dropped elbow.

The attacker's fist raises across their body, at the height of the victim's face, elbow bent, anywhere between straight down, to horizontal, pointing in the direction of travel, pivoting their hips and shifting their weight to that side. Their other fist tucks in close to the centre of their chest.

Action

The attacker sweeps their fist past the victim's face, shifting their weight to the opposite foot. The punching hand remains at target height all the way across. The more horizontal the arm, the more it opens out into an extended position on the front diagonal. The lower the elbow, the less extended the end of the technique. Avoid over-extending the elbow at speed; keep it slightly bent to protect it as the arm stops.

Most chest knaps are made by moving the knapping hand to the chest. There are two upper-body knaps for this technique. One keeps the non-punching fist close to the chest, popping it open for a knap then closing it. The other uses the opposite principle: as the chest rotates, the fist opens into a cupped shape, and the moving chest makes contact with the fixed hand on the edge of the upper pec. A thigh knap can also work.

Reaction

The victim's head then shoulders turn sharply to the side as the fist crosses their face, creating a reaction matching the attack's energy and speed. Separating the movement of the head and shoulders is important for the clarity of the visual story-telling. Releasing the shoulders a fraction of a second after the head moves can also help to relieve stress in the neck at its fullest rotation.

If knapping, the victim keeps their hands close to their chest, creating a simple chest knap.

COMMON ERRORS

Attacker

Preparing the fist too low and crossing the target at an angle
Standing too deep to easily pivot or shift weight
Extending the arm towards the victim during the punch
Misjudging the distance

Victim

Reacting at an angle that does not match the path of the punch
Mistiming the reaction

OPPOSITE RIGHT: Four stages of the upstage/downstage backfist with dropped elbow.
TOM ZIEBELL

BELOW: A flowing image of the upstage/downstage backfist with dropped elbow.
TOM ZIEBELL

THE ROUNDHOUSE PUNCH

Works For

Proscenium arch staging in spaces of all sizes. With an avoidance rather than illusion of contact, it works in all formats.

Safety Principles

- Illusion of contact and avoided: out of distance.
- Avoided: displace the target to the hairline.
- Avoidance: red light/green light.

With illusory contact, the attacker is not close enough to the victim to actually make contact without stepping or leaning in. If the attack is avoided, all three safety principles will apply.

Position

With illusion of contact, the victim is upstage and the attacker is downstage. This position, or a modified version of it, allows the attacker to mask the knap. It can be reversed if the victim makes the knap, or if it can be located elsewhere.

With avoidance, any orientation works relative to the audience.

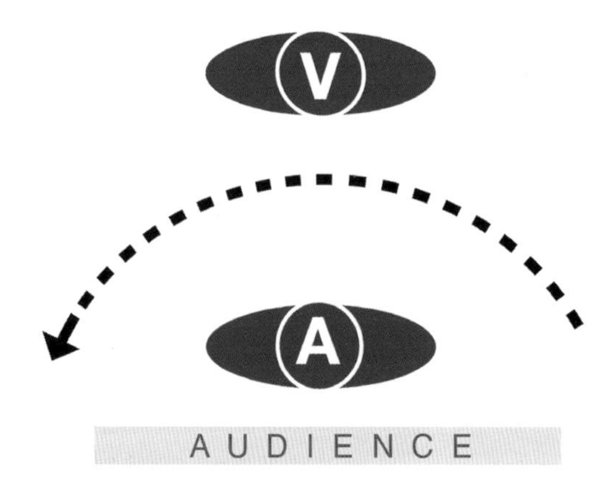

Figure 36: The staging of the roundhouse punch.

Eye Contact

The performers make eye contact, ensuring their partner is ready. If not, they attract their attention.

Preparation

Step wide to the side, lifting a fist out wide to the height of the target. The arm is fractionally bent and weight is shifted towards that side. The fist can be in a vertical or a horizontal orientation.

In a real fight, an untrained fighter generally prepares the roundhouse low, then sweeps it up to the victim's face, finishing on a downward swing. However, although this is the real body impulse, it looks poor on stage: not from a story-telling, character perspective, but because it makes the performer look bad. Although it is exactly what happens in a real, untrained confrontation, on stage the parabola of the attack looks as though the performer is deliberately missing, therefore undermining the story they are creating.

Figure 37: The roundhouse punch.

Figure 38: The bob and weave avoidance.

Action

The attacker shifts their weight to the other side, pivoting as they go, sweeping their fist across the victim's face to the opposite side, keeping their arm almost fully extended.

Using a sliding step to the side increases the coverage and sense of power. A cross step could be used, but with a bob and weave avoidance this greatly increases the risk of accidental contact between their head and the attacker's leg.

Common Errors

Attacker

Preparing the fist too low and/or behind, and crossing the target at an angle
Making eye contact throughout the punch
Tightening into a hook punch
Standing too deep to easily pivot or shift weight

Victim

Mistiming the reaction or avoidance
Making eye contact throughout the punch
Leaning too far forward in the avoidance

A wide punch such as this can cause hyperextension of the elbow at speed, or the apparent centrifugal force can cause a rush of blood into the fist. Both issues can be avoided by tightening the muscles of the arm when releasing the punch. The same shape must be maintained, without allowing the tightening to alter it into a hook punch.

If there is illusory contact, the attacker (or victim) makes a chest knap.

If it is avoided, the attacker ensures the victim has begun to avoid (giving the green light) before they release the punch, keeping their eye-line fixed where the target was, as they punch. If they follow the victim with their eyes they greatly increase the risk of accidental contact.

OPPOSITE RIGHT: Four stages of the roundhouse punch with avoidance.
TOM ZIEBELL

BELOW: A flowing image of the roundhouse punch with avoidance.
TOM ZIEBELL

Reaction

With the illusion of contact, the victim's head then shoulders turn sharply to the side as the fist crosses their face, creating a reaction matching the attack's energy and speed. Separating the movement of the head and shoulders is important for the clarity of the visual story-telling. Releasing the shoulders a fraction of a second after the head moves can also help to relieve stress in the neck at its fullest rotation.

With a powerful punch and a big reaction, it is important for the victim to look into the space, spotting any hazards, before reacting into it at speed. Balance must be maintained throughout.

Avoidance

Many avoidances can be performed with this technique. The most complex, and therefore the most useful to elucidate, is the bob and weave.

Timing is vital. If the victim waits until the end of the preparation, for safety the attacker will wait for the victim to begin to move, introducing a moment of stasis mid-fight, which disrupts the story-telling. Conversely, the avoidance must not start so early as to seem illogical. The avoidance begins two-thirds of the way through the attacker's preparation; at speed this is late enough to seem logical, but early enough that the safety principle does not stop the attack. Once the performers have rehearsed together for long enough to develop trust, the timing of this can be squeezed so that it begins later. However, this requires a stringent focus on the safety of the moment.

The victim leans their head away from the attack, shifting their weight to that side, sliding the opposite foot under the punch. They bob their head under the attack (ensuring that they do not lean too far forwards as they do so, in case the attacker moves forwards), and completing the sliding step to the side. A slight lean forward creates the illusion for thrust or in-the-round staging, as the head travels under the fist. If it is too far forward, the move becomes risky. The victim looks at the attacker's belt, their peripheral vision ensuring that they can judge when it is safe to stand upright.

THE JAB PUNCH (THE STRAIGHT PUNCH)

The name of this punch is dependent upon which hand punches. If the lead hand punches, it is a jab; if the back hand punches, it is a straight.

Works For

Smaller, intimate proscenium arch staging.

Safety Principle

Out of distance – the attacker is not close enough to the victim to actually make contact without stepping or leaning in.

Position

Victim upstage, attacker downstage, offset right shoulder to right shoulder, or vice versa to reveal the victim's face, and to allow the attacker to mask the knap. It has most impact in this orientation, but can be reversed if the victim makes the knap, or if the knap can be located elsewhere.

To the attacker it will always look as if they have missed. This punch forces them to place their mental eyes out into the auditorium. They visualize a line from the target out to the centre of the audience. For the illusion of contact their fist must momentarily spike into that line, obscuring the target, before it drops back again. The distance between fist and face is a variable that depends on the position of the audience and the skill of the performers. In reality, the performer should imagine a target line out to every set of eyes in the audience. However, the wider the cone of target lines is, the closer the attacker needs to punch to the victim, to convince the majority of the audience contact that was made. The closer the fist is to the victim's face, the better the illusion, but the greater the risk of accidental contact. The further away it is, the safer the technique, but the less effective it is for a rapidly narrowing section of the audience. Ideally, the attacker needs to leave at least 6 inches (15cm) between their fist and the victim's face. It is difficult to be accurate and the attacker will initially require feedback from the victim in order to achieve consistency.

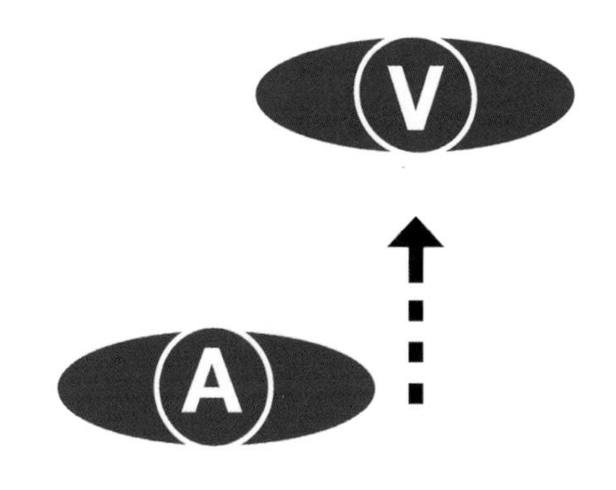

Figure 39: The staging of the jab punch.

RIGHT: Four stages of the jab punch.
TOM ZIEBELL

Eye Contact

The performers make eye contact, ensuring their partner is ready. If not, they attract their attention.

Preparation

The attacker makes a fist below the target height, rotating their hip slightly back. With the performers offset, this fist will already be lined up on the victim's centreline, which means that the attacker need worry only about finding the right height for the attack.

Action

The attacker pulses their hip slightly forward, pistoning their fist up to the height of the target, then dropping it back slightly. It might help to visualize Pinocchio's long nose, to create the safe distance, and then aim to punch the end of it. The fist can be either vertical or horizontal at the moment of illusory impact; the latter provides wider coverage of the target and convinces more members of the audience. The arm should not be fully straightened during the punch as this reveals to

Figure 40: The jab punch.

Common Errors

Attacker
Preparing the hand too high and obscuring the target early
Fully extending the arm
Missing the target

Victim
Throwing their head back at risk of whiplash
Mistiming the reaction
Making the reaction too physically stiff

the audience how far away the victim is; keeping the arm slightly bent as it stops creates the illusion of being in distance. The attacker's other hand makes a chest knap.

Reaction

The victim must avoid the body's instinctive reaction of throwing the head backwards and looking up. This move done at speed, and repetitively, leads to whiplash.

The face must move backwards and then bounce forwards again in a jarring reaction, but in such a way as to minimize the impact on the soft tissue of the neck. The reaction can be small yet still be effective.

It is difficult to bounce the face backwards at speed independent of the torso; the head wants to roll back over the top of the spine. To counter this, the victim slightly drops their chin as they move the face back and then lets it rock forwards again with an appropriate vocal. Allowing the upper chest to move back slightly relieves pressure on the neck. To clarify visually, the victim might imagine a bad smell under their nose that makes them immediately vomit.

A flowing image of the jab punch.
TOM ZIEBELL

THE PARROT PUNCH

Works For

All staging variations.

Safety Principles

- Displace the target to the parrot space.
- Red light/green light.

The illusion is of a punch that misses or is avoided. The fist is aimed at the parrot space over the victim's shoulders. Performed fast with an avoidance, it minimizes the chance that the audience will spot the deception. It can be straight or hooked to the same-side target, or can cross to the opposite target.

Performers instinctively want to punch as far from the victim as possible. After enough rehearsal, they should punch right into the space over their shoulder. If red light/green light is used, the partner will be safe, but the illusion will be as tight as possible.

Because this is an avoided punch, it is easy for the performer to forget to attack with full energy. Remember, the attacking character hopes that this will be the last punch of the fight, so it needs to be released with fully physicalized intention.

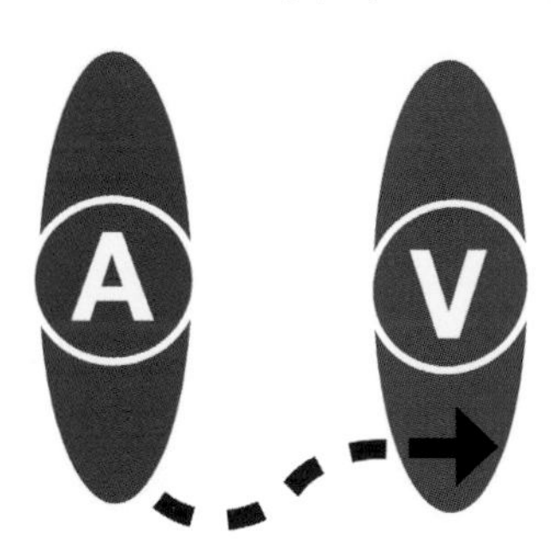

Figure 41: The staging of the semi-circular into a straight path parrot punch.

RIGHT: Four stages of the parrot punch.
TOM ZIEBELL

Position

Any angle will work, except straight upstage/downstage, which would invite the audience to look directly into the trick at the heart of the illusion.

Eye Contact

The performers make eye contact, ensuring their partner is ready. If not, they attract their attention. They then shift focus to the target; if this is not done, the risk of actual contact is increased.

Preparation

The attacker must give a clear preparation otherwise the victim will not be able to time the avoidance correctly. Lift the fist up and slightly back as the hip rotates back.

Common Errors

Attacker

Not waiting for the victim to avoid – red light
Following the victim's head with their fist
Not retracting the arm immediately
Punching too wide
Not giving a clear preparation cue
Wrong fist orientation if the punch is blocked
Not punching into distance
Cross parrot – not straightening the arm

Victim

Mistiming the avoidance
Making an off-balance avoidance

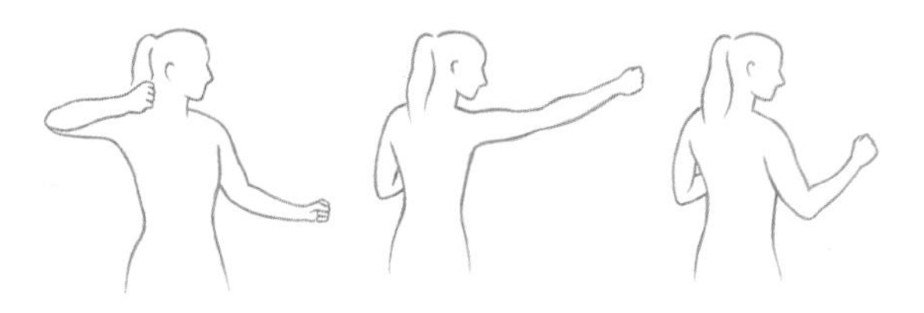

Figure 42: The parrot punch.

Action

Ensure the victim has already begun to avoid (green light) before releasing the punch. (If they do not move, the punch is not thrown.) Keep the

A flowing image of the parrot punch.
TOM ZIEBELL

eye-line fixed where the target was when punching. Looking at the victim's moving head greatly increases the risk of accidental contact, as the fist follows the eyes.

Extend the punch straight into the target zone and immediately retract. The fist is in a vertical orientation to facilitate soft on soft safety if it is blocked. Step into distance as you punch, with whichever foot fits the logic of the choreography.

The punch can be hooked, using the hook punch preparation; when released, the punch travels roughly a third of a circle before straightening at the last moment, finishing exactly as the straight form described above.

If the punch crosses to the opposite side, it is vital for the arm to be fully straight when extended. Any bend to the arm there heightens the risk of a forearm smash to the victim's face.

Reaction

The avoidance begins before the end of the attacker's preparation; late enough at speed to seem logical, but early enough so that red light/ green light does not stop the attack.

The reaction may be as simple as a lean of the head away from the fist, but more commonly the head lean is combined with a small sidestep. Moving both feet usually creates better visual storytelling. Do not look away as you avoid; watch the attacker.

With a hooked punch, the avoidance should be made slightly circular, rather than to the side, for visual story-telling. With a crossing parrot punch, the avoidance is to the outside of the arm.

The avoidance is often linked to a block: *see* 'Blocks' in Chapter 17.

THE CROSS PUNCH

Works For

Proscenium arch staging in all size spaces; can work in traverse.

Safety Principle

Out of distance, or displace the target.

In a high auditorium, for the illusion of contact, the fist needs to pass closer to the face. This technique must be learned out of distance, but, through diligent rehearsal, it can move closer to the target, displacing the target, until it is at an appropriate, but still safe, distance for the venue.

Position

The attacker can be upstage or downstage as they can create a masked knap either way round. Alternatively, the victim can make the knap, or it can be located elsewhere.

When performed in distance, the fist crosses roughly 8 inches (20cm) in front of the victim's face. If in doubt, always increase the safety distance between fist and face. The movement of the bodies relative to each other must be carefully and continuously monitored.

This punch can travel diagonally in relation to the victim, angled over one shoulder, rather than parallel. Pay close attention to audience sightlines and the path of the victim's reaction.

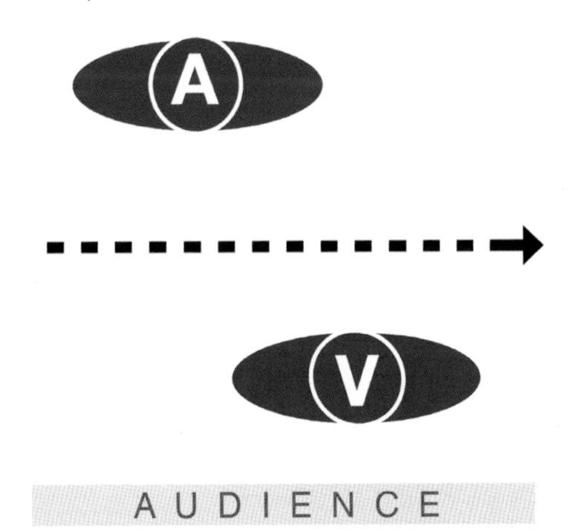

Figure 43: The staging of the cross punch.

Eye Contact

The performers make eye contact, ensuring their partner is ready. If not, they attract their attention. They then shift focus to the target; if this is not done, the risk of actual contact is increased.

Preparation

The attacker steps wide to the side, lifting their elbow out to the side with their fist by their shoulder. This is known as the archer's prep, as it is similar to the action of drawing a bow. The other fist extends slightly ahead of the attacker.

A variant has the attacker rotate their fist back, then swing it around, finishing in a straight line crossing the target. Whilst entirely valid, this punch can cover less distance, consequently impacting sightlines. With less physically able performers, activating the ball and socket shoulder joint can send the fist on a semi-circular path with higher risk of accidental contact.

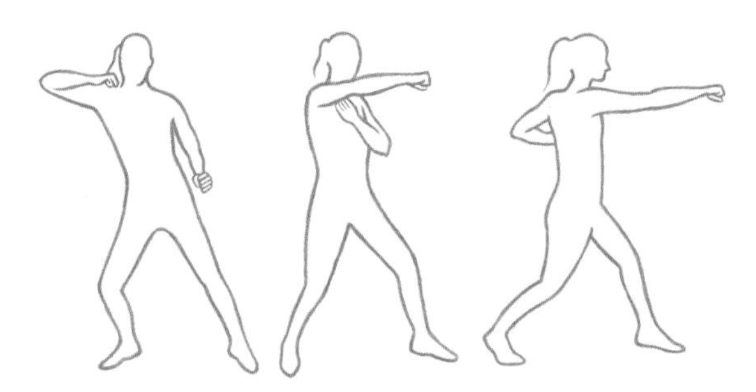

Figure 44: The cross punch.

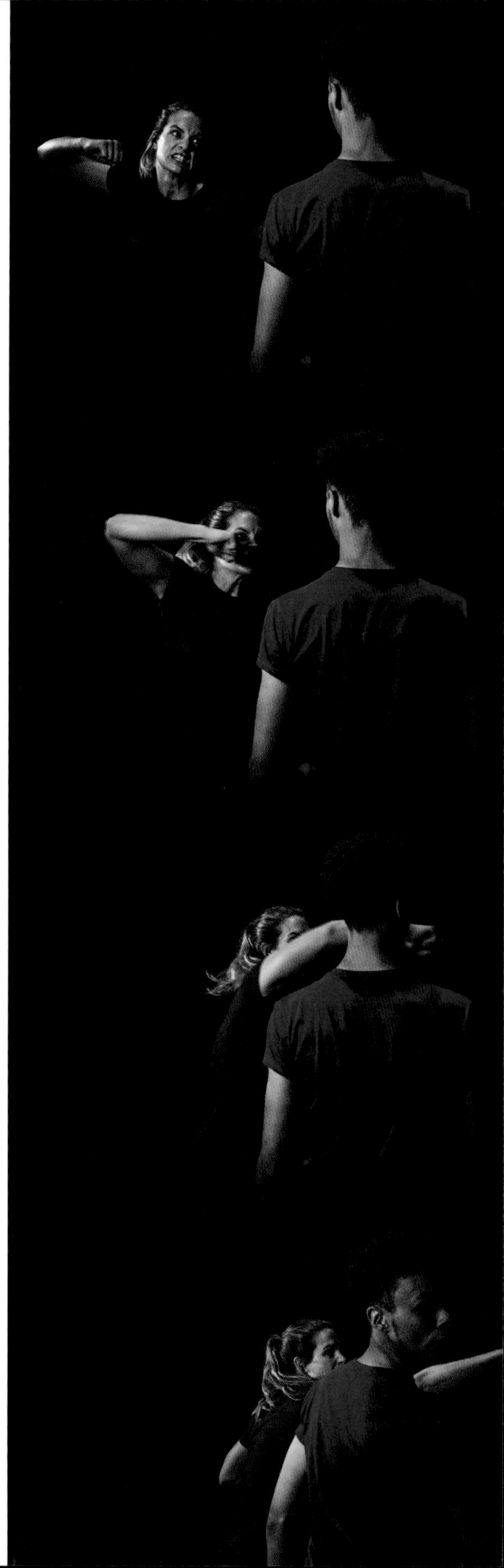

RIGHT: Four stages of the cross punch.
TOM ZIEBELL

Action

If the attacker is upstage, they pivot their downstage hip towards the victim, only extending their arm once their downstage shoulder masks their upstage chest. The fist extends through the target zone as the other hand knaps across the upstage chest, closing back to a fist. The attacker steps to cover the sightlines for both sides of the audience, with care taken to keep a safe distance from the victim.

If the attacker is downstage, they shift their weight towards the victim, close enough to drive their fist through the target zone whilst the downstage shoulder masks the upstage chest. The other hand knaps the upper pectoral next to the punching-side shoulder, immediately closing into a fist as the hips finally rotate allowing the arm to fully extend, covering the sightlines for both sides of the audience.

There is no circular action; the fist travels in a straight line to ensure maximum sightline coverage.

Reaction

The victim's head then shoulders turn sharply to the side as the fist crosses their face, creating a reaction matching the attack's energy and speed. Separating the movement of the head and shoulders is important for the clarity of the visual story-telling. Releasing the shoulders a fraction of a second after the head moves can also help to relieve stress in the neck at its fullest rotation. It is important for the victim to look into the space, to spot hazards, before reacting into it at speed. It is vital that the victim does not lean into the target zone as they begin their reaction, but reacts to the side and away from the line of the punch.

If knapping, the victim keeps their hands close to their chest, creating a simple chest knap.

Common Errors

Attacker
Not preparing at the height of the target
Punching in an arc not a straight line
Not masking the knap adequately

Victim
Reacting into the target zone
Mistiming the reaction

A flowing image of the cross punch.
TOM ZIEBELL

THE STRAIGHT PUNCH IN PROFILE

Works For

Proscenium arch staging in spaces of all sizes; can work in traverse.

Safety Principle

Displace the target to the parrot space.

Position

Both performers are in profile to the audience. They can be on a diagonal, but the illusion is harder the steeper the angle. The attacker is offset to the victim, punching-side shoulder in line with their target-side shoulder, reducing the risk of accidental contact, and increasing the chances of the illusion working.

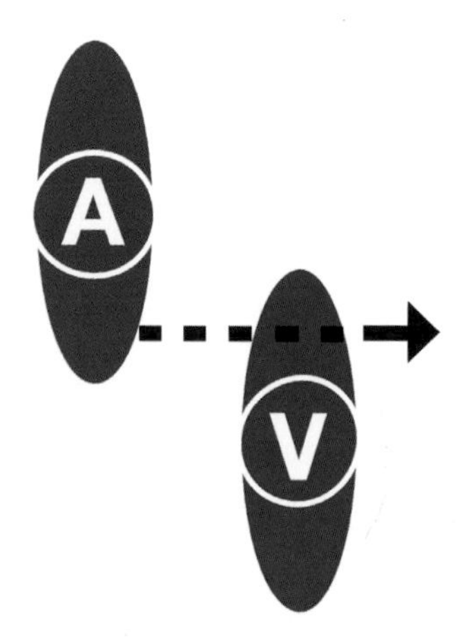

Figure 45: The staging of the straight punch in profile.

Eye Contact

The performers make eye contact, ensuring their partner is ready. If not, they attract their attention. They then shift focus to the target; if this is not done, the risk of actual contact is increased.

Preparation

The attacker lifts the fist up and slightly back as the hip rotates back.

Figure 46: The straight punch in profile.

COMMON ERRORS

Attacker
Misaligning the two bodies
Not punching far enough
Not straightening the arm
Not retracting the arm immediately
Not masking the knap adequately

Victim
Reacting into the target zone
Mistiming the reaction

Action

Stepping in if necessary, extend the punch straight into the target zone and immediately retract. The fist needs to extend far enough to cover all sight-lines for the audience.

The other hand knaps the upstage chest as its masked by the downstage shoulder. Alternatively, a thigh knap can be made on the upstage leg, by either attacker or victim.

Reaction

The victim's head turns sharply to the side of the attack as the fist passes their ear, creating a reaction that matches the energy and speed of the attack. If they simply turn their head over their shoulder there is a high risk that they will hit, or be hit by, the attacker's arm. To avoid this, the victim's head must remain over the column of their neck as it rotates. This is achieved by subtly shifting their weight to the downstage hip as they begin the reaction.

OPPOSITE RIGHT: Four stages of the straight punch in profile. TOM ZIEBELL

BELOW: A flowing image of the straight punch in profile. TOM ZIEBELL

THE UPPERCUT PUNCH

Works For
Smaller, intimate proscenium arch staging.

Safety Principle
Out of distance – the attacker is not close enough to the victim to actually make contact without stepping or leaning in.

Position
Victim downstage, attacker upstage, offset right shoulder to right shoulder, or vice versa to reveal the victim's face. This is the position if the performers use a shared knap, but it can be either way round if one performer alone knaps.

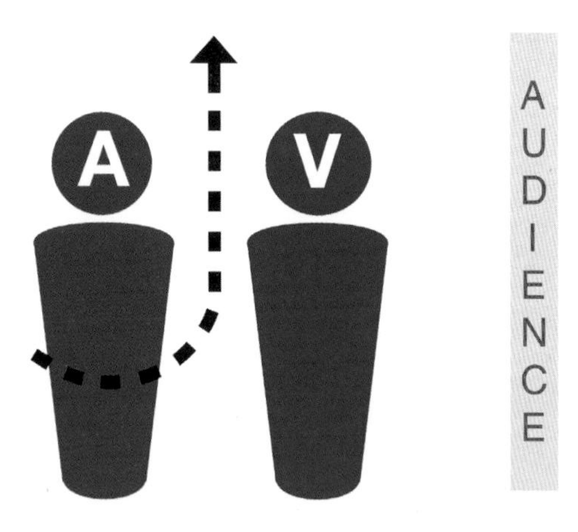

Figure 47: The staging of the uppercut punch.

Eye Contact
The performers make eye contact, ensuring their partner is ready. If not, they attract their attention.

Preparation
For a shared knap, the victim floats a stiff knapping hand 8 inches (20cm) from the centre of their chest. The thumb must be tucked to the side of the hand; a protruding thumb or relaxed fingers are at risk of injury.

In the case of both a shared or a solo knap, the attacker prepares a fist high enough to be seen by the audience behind the victim.

Figure 48: The uppercut punch.

COMMON ERRORS

Attacker
Not offset
Punching on an angle
Shared knap – full hand contact

Victim
Throwing their head back at risk of whiplash
Forgetting to lift their shoulders
Mistiming the reaction

Action

In the case of a shared knap, the attacker sweeps the fist in a circle down then up towards the knapping hand. Masked by the victim's body, it opens for a shared clap knap, then immediately closes and continues up their centreline before dropping back. Make the knap contact fingers to fingers, as full hand contact can be painful.

For a solo knap, whoever makes the knap is downstage. The action is the same, but the fist does not open; it travels up the victim's centreline through the target in front of their face, at safe distance. The other hand makes a chest knap.

Reaction

The victim must avoid the body's instinctive reaction of throwing the head backwards and looking up. This move done at speed, and repetitively, leads to whiplash. It is very similar to the jab, but, because it is bigger, it is more extreme in the energized bounce of the head backwards.

Although the end of both jab and uppercut reactions in reality is for the head to drop back down towards the shoulder blades, the initiating actions are on different vectors: forwards and upwards. Therefore, the illusions and techniques must be different.

The victim lifts on to the balls of their feet, as if the blow drives them upwards, and, most importantly, the shoulders hunch up as high as possible. Lifting the shoulders bunches the trapezius muscles, creating a supportive cushion behind the neck. The head must be rocked back only when the shoulders are up – the extra support will make it less likely that the neck will suffer whiplash. The head then immediately rocks forward to its natural position.

Some performers find that their neck still feels unsupported during this move. In that case, it might help to imagine something flying towards them, passing over their shoulder and on behind them. They look up and watch it fly over and past, stepping back on that side and turning back. The head reacts up and around at speed, but remains comfortably balanced on the extended column of the neck all the way through. This creates the illusion of a fast, reactive movement of the head up and back, pulling the body up and around, with none of the neck muscles in a position of strain.

If required, the victim chest knaps as the fist passes their face.

OPPOSITE RIGHT: Four stages of the uppercut punch.
TOM ZIEBELL

BELOW: A flowing image of the uppercut punch.
TOM ZIEBELL

THE NON-CONTACT STOMACH PUNCH

Works For

Proscenium arch staging in spaces of all sizes; can work in traverse or shallow thrust staging.

Safety Principle

Displace the target. (Note: the fist can finish very close to the target.)

Position

Upstage/downstage with the attacker in either position. The fist stops roughly 6 inches (15cm) from the victim's stomach. That distance can be reduced, but the closer it finishes, the greater the risk of contact. The victim should tighten their abdominal muscles in case of contact.

Either performer can make a chest knap or the victim can make a vocal knap.

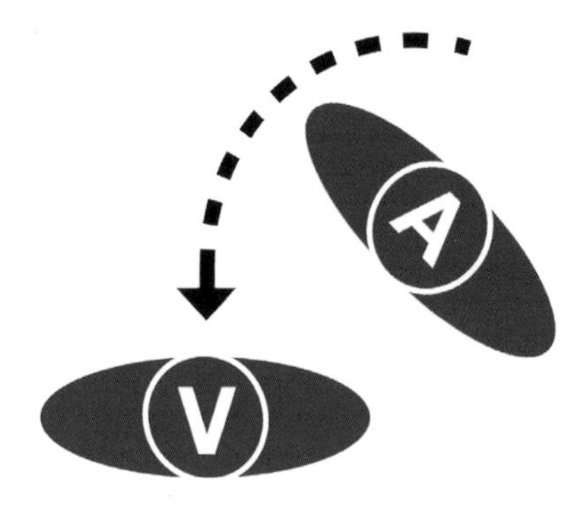

Figure 49: The staging of the non-contact stomach punch.

Eye Contact

The performers make eye contact, ensuring their partner is ready. If not, they attract their attention. They then shift focus to the target; if this is not done, the risk of actual contact is increased.

Preparation

The victim tightens their abdominals in case of contact.

The attacker prepares a relaxed fist at the height of the target, rotating their hip slightly back. The wrist aligns with the forearm, to avoid injury from an accidental contact.

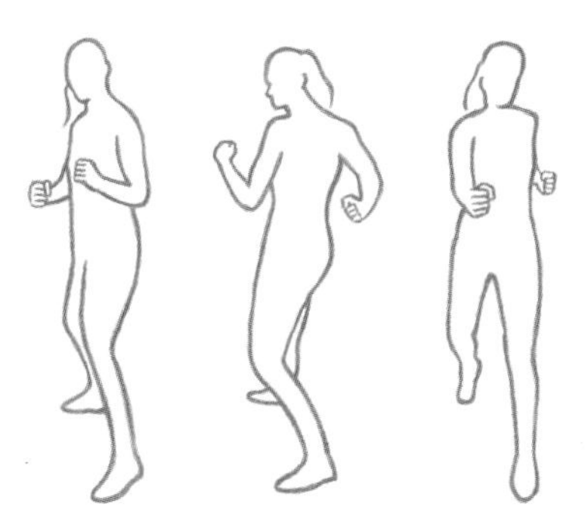

Figure 50: The non-contact stomach punch.

Action

The attacker rotates their hip forwards, moving the fist to the target at speed. Because it is close, the movement must be rehearsed before attempting it fast.

To avoid accidental contact, do not lean in or duck forward when punching. The illusion of power is in the hip, not the shoulder.

COMMON ERRORS

Attacker
Not engaging the hips
Misjudging the distance
Leaning in

Victim
Bending over as they react
Vocal knap lacking clarity
Mistiming the reaction

It is possible to punch with a piston arm only, without engaging the body, but it does not look as powerful or as aggressive.

Reaction

The stomach pulls back, the chest collapses slightly, the head stays up. The instinct is to fold over, head down: but dropping the face into the target zone greatly increases the risk of contact. The victim must avoid head-butting the attacker's shoulder.

The vocal reaction is dictated by the reality of an abdominal strike, combined with specific pain, the emotional response to it, and the technical needs of the auditorium.

OPPOSITE RIGHT: Four stages of the non-contact stomach punch. TOM ZIEBELL

A flowing image of the non-contact stomach punch. TOM ZIEBELL

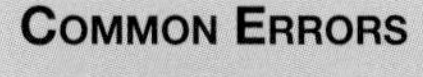

15
KICKS (NON-CONTACT)

(Note: no one technique will work for every venue. Each space or staging configuration brings its own challenges, leading to a variety of kicks. The 'Works For' section beginning each technique indicates clearly what works where.)

REALITY

A kick can be both trained or untrained. If trained, there are a number of different styles available for research. The different areas of the foot that can be used are the toes, heel, ball or either edge. There are a number of different styles of preparation, from simple to complex.

Kick injuries run the full gamut, from bruises through broken bones and unconsciousness, ultimately all the way to death. The outcome depends on who is kicking, exactly where, with what, and how many times, as well as the position of the victim. The attacker can also be injured by the kick, although such damage is rarely as traumatic as that of the victim.

The performer must fully engage the body behind the blow. Without that illusion of body weight, the impact of the story on the audience is reduced.

SAFETY

Upstage/downstage kicks use out of distance and in distance kicks displace the target.

Performers find it harder to judge distance for a kick – judging how far to reach with the hands is far more common in everyday life than assessing how far something is from the feet. The first time a kick is rehearsed, the distance should be set, then one small step taken further back, just to be sure. After some rehearsal, the performer's judgement of distance will be more accurate and they will be able to adjust.

Some kicks require the performer to pivot the standing foot. It is absolutely vital always to check that their footwear pivots easily on the performance surface, before they attempt the action. If the foot sticks as they pivot, the knee will continue to rotate and potentially tear itself apart. If in doubt, pivot the foot in the air, dropping it into position. Always check first.

There are kicking techniques for the stage that utilize shared knaps, whereby the victim cups one or two hands, and the attacker kicks them, making contact with the top of their foot. These techniques can greatly increase the risk of injury, as any misjudgement exposes the fragile bones of hands and wrists to a strong kick. For that reason, they are not discussed here.

WHAT WORKS?

Upstage/downstage kicks do not work well in large auditoriums, for the same sightline reasons that limit the effectiveness of the jab punch. Techniques in this orientation that move down the target line rather than across it are much better for a single POV such as a camera.

That said, it is possible to increase their effectiveness fractionally by kicking on a slight offset diagonal, crossing the target line at a sharp angle rather than spiking it. Aiming the kick along a line towards the partner's opposite shoulder, intersecting the target line, slightly widens the sightline availability to the audience.

There are three basic formats to use: snap kicks, prepared by lifting the knee, then snapping the kick, horizontally or vertically; swing kicks, prepared by stepping the foot back, then swinging from the hip, horizontally or vertically; and push kicks, prepared by lifting the knee, foot flexed, then pushing the foot forwards. Most performers find it easier to be more accurate with a snap than with a swing.

With kicks to the head, it can be problematic to actually reach the target. It is possible to achieve a measurable increase in the height of a kick by leaning back slightly. This is to be used with caution, however. If the kicker arches too far back, they will inevitably lose their footing and fall on their back, with the consequent risk of injury.

THE UPSTAGE/DOWNSTAGE KICK TO THE HEAD

Works For

Smaller, intimate proscenium arch staging.

Safety Principle

Out of distance – the attacker is not close enough to the victim to actually make contact without stepping or leaning in.

Position

Victim downstage, attacker upstage, diagonally offset right shoulder to right shoulder, or vice versa. This position, or a modified version, allows the victim to mask the knap. Can be reversed if the

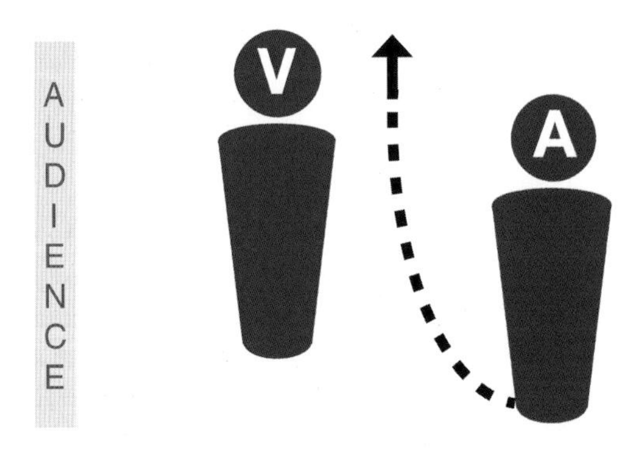

Figure 51: The staging of the upstage/downstage kick to the head.

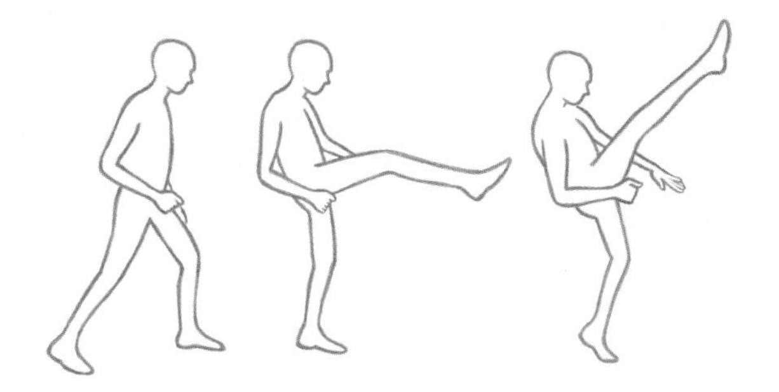

Figure 52: The upstage/downstage kick to the head.

COMMON ERRORS

Attacker
Not offset
Not kicking high enough
Not crossing the target line
Revealing the knap (if attacker's)

Victim
Throwing their head back, at risk of whiplash
Forgetting to lift their shoulders
Mistiming the reaction or knap
Knapping too high (if victim's)

attacker knaps, or if it can be located elsewhere. The kick is made with the foot closest to the victim's centreline.

For the illusion of contact, the attacker visualizes a line from the centre of the audience passing through, and upstage of, the target. Their foot swings up through that line and drops back. The closer the foot is to the victim's face, the larger the proportion of the audience who will believe the illusion, but the greater the risk of accidental contact. The further away it is, the safer the technique, but the less effective it is for the audience. The attacker should leave at least 8 inches (20cm) between their foot and the target. The victim will tell the attacker if they are too close.

Eye Contact

The performers make eye contact, ensuring their partner is ready. If not, they attract their attention. They then shift focus to the target, their partner's opposite shoulder; if this is not done, the risk of actual contact is increased.

Preparation

If they are performing a snap kick, the attacker lifts their knee vertically. For a swing kick, they step their kicking foot back.

OPPOSITE RIGHT: Four stages of the upstage/downstage kick to the head. TOM ZIEBELL

A flowing image of the upstage/ downstage kick to the head. TOM ZIEBELL

Action

The attacker kicks up through the line just passing the target, then drops back down. They aim to finish where the kick started – if they step forward there is an increased risk of inadvertent contact – and must remain balanced throughout.

If knapping, the attacker brushes their hand past their thigh. This knap on the upstage side is hidden within the natural movement of the arms to maintain balance.

Reaction

The illusion is that the foot makes contact with the chin or nose. The body's instinctive reaction is to throw the head backwards but, done at speed and, in particular, repetitively, this will lead to whiplash.

The victim lifts on to the balls of their feet, as if the blow drives them upwards, and, most importantly, the shoulders hunch up, high as possible. Lifting the shoulders bunches the trapezius muscles, creating a supportive cushion behind the neck. The head should be rocked back only once the shoulders are up, when the extra support makes it less likely that the neck will suffer whiplash. The head then immediately rocks forward to its natural position.

Some performers find that their neck still feels unsupported during this move. In this instance, it might help to imagine something flying towards them, passing over their shoulder and on behind them. They look up and watch it fly over and past, stepping back on that side and turning back. The head reacts up and around at speed, but remains comfortably balanced on the extended column of the neck all the way through. This creates the illusion of a fast reactive movement of the head up and back, pulling the body up and around, with none of the neck muscles in a position of strain.

The victim makes a clap knap as the foot passes their face. Relaxed hands clap together with no preparation, remaining low, then separating to allow the foot to safely drop down. If the knap is mistimed or too high, there is a greater risk of the hands being kicked.

THE UPSTAGE/DOWNSTAGE KICK TO THE STOMACH

Works For

Smaller, intimate proscenium arch staging.

Safety Principle

Out of distance – the attacker is not close enough to the victim to actually make contact without stepping or leaning in. If pivoting, check that footwear allows easy turning on the performance surface before attempting the action.

Position

This technique works best with the attacker upstage, victim downstage, diagonally offset, right shoulder to right shoulder, but can work to some degree the opposite way round. This position, or a modified version, allows the victim to mask the knap. The kick is made with the foot closest to the victim's centreline.

For the illusion of contact, the attacker visualizes a line from the centre of the audience passing through, and upstage of, the target. Their foot kicks up to that line and drops back. The closer the foot is to the victim's stomach, the larger the proportion of the audience who will believe the illusion, but the greater the risk of accidental contact. The further away it is, the safer the technique, but the less effective it is for the audience.

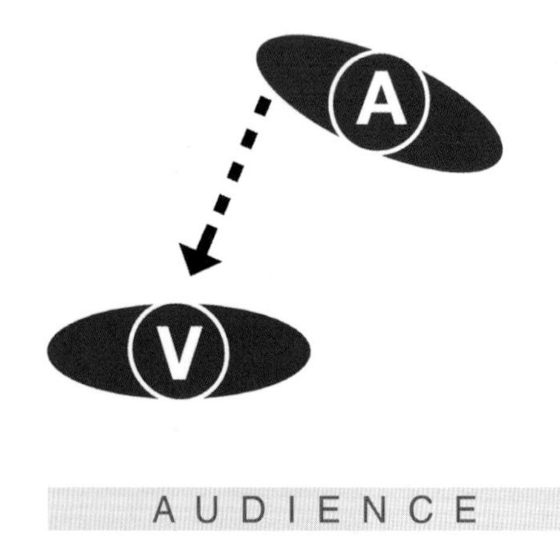

Figure 53: The staging of the upstage/downstage kick to the stomach.

The attacker should leave at least 8 inches (20cm) between their foot and the target.

There are three basic kicks for this technique:

- toes; the illusion is contact with the boot toes
- blade of foot; the illusion is of contact with the outside edge of the foot
- heel; the illusion is of a push kick towards the stomach.

This kick is performed with a vocal or a body knap. It can be a victim's chest knap or an attacker's upstage thigh knap, masked by the diagonal offset.

Eye Contact

The performers make eye contact, ensuring their partner is ready. If not, they attract their attention. They then shift focus to the target; if this is not done, the risk of actual contact is increased.

Preparation

- Toes: for a snap kick, lifting the knee vertically; for a swing kick, stepping the kicking foot back.
- Blade of foot: pivot the standing foot 90 degrees away from the victim, lean back as the knee lifts, angling the ankle to present the edge of the foot.
- Push kick: lift knee vertically, flexing the foot up.

The victim tightens their abdominals, in case of contact.

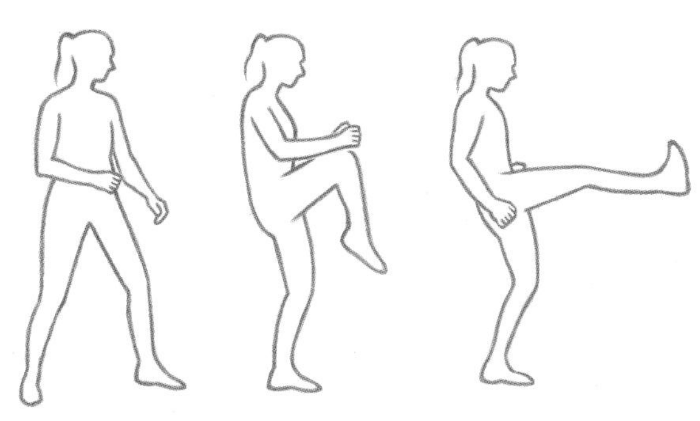

Figure 54: The upstage/downstage kick to the stomach, as a push kick.

RIGHT: Four stages of the upstage/downstage kick to the stomach, as a push kick.
TOM ZIEBELL

Action

The attacker kicks into the target zone then drops back down, aiming to finish where the kick started. If they step forwards, there is an increased risk of inadvertent contact. The attacker needs to remain balanced throughout.

For an attacker knap, the hand is brushed past their upstage thigh or gluteus. This knap is hidden within the body's natural movement of the arms to maintain balance.

Common Errors

Attacker
Not offset
Not targeting accurately

Victim
Bending over as they react
Vocal knap lacking clarity
Mistiming the reaction

Reaction

The stomach pulls back, the chest collapses slightly, the head stays up. The instinct is to fold over, with the head down, but dropping the face into the target zone greatly increases the risk of contact. The victim can make a chest knap.

The vocal reaction is dictated by the reality of an abdominal strike, combined with specific pain, the emotional response to it, and the technical needs of the auditorium.

BELOW: A flowing image of the upstage/downstage kick to the stomach, as a push kick.
TOM ZIEBELL

THE UPSTAGE/DOWNSTAGE CRESCENT KICK

Works For

Proscenium arch staging in mid-sized performance spaces, and smaller.

Safety Principle

Out of distance – the attacker is not close enough to the victim to actually make contact without stepping or leaning in. If pivoting, check that footwear allows easy turning on the performance surface, before attempting the action.

Position

Victim upstage, attacker downstage. This position, or a modified version of it, allows the attacker to mask the knap. It can be reversed if the attacker has fast hands, the victim knaps, or the knap can be located elsewhere.

For the illusion of contact, the attacker visualizes a line from the centre of the audience passing through, and upstage of, the target. Their foot sweeps up through that line and drops back. The closer the foot is to the victim's face, the larger the proportion of the audience who will believe

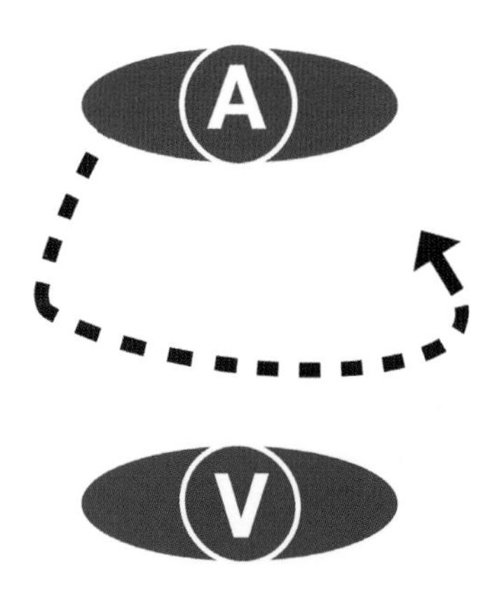

Figure 55: The staging of the upstage/downstage crescent kick.

RIGHT: Four stages of the upstage/downstage crescent kick.
TOM ZIEBELL

Figure 56: The upstage/downstage crescent kick.

the illusion, but the greater the risk of accidental contact. The further away it is, the safer the technique, but the less effective it is for the audience. The attacker should leave at least 8 inches (20cm) between their foot and the target. The victim will tell the attacker if they are too close.

This kick can work in both directions, forward or reverse, known as the inside or outside crescent kick, depending on which edge of the foot makes illusory contact with the victim's face.

COMMON ERRORS

Attacker
Not kicking high enough
Not crossing the target line with a wide fanning action
Revealing the knap (if attacker's)

Victim
Mistiming the reaction or the knap
Revealing the knap (if victim's)

Eye Contact

The performers make eye contact, ensuring their partner is ready. If not, they attract their attention.

Preparation

- Inside crescent kick: the attacker pivots their hips back, stepping their foot behind them on a slight diagonal, facing their dominant-side front 45-degree diagonal. Their hands prepare across their body to help counterbalance during the kick.
- Outside crescent kick: the attacker faces their hips towards their non-dominant-side front 45-degree diagonal, stepping their foot back.

A flowing image of the upstage/downstage crescent kick.
TOM ZIEBELL

Their hands prepare across the dominant side of their body to help counterbalance during the kick.

Action

- Inside crescent kick: kick up the front 45-degree diagonal line, pivot the standing foot, fanning the kick past the victim's face, through the target line, dropping down the opposite 45-degree diagonal. Remain balanced throughout.
- Outside crescent kick: kick up the opposite front 45-degree diagonal line, pivot the standing foot to fan the kick past the victim's face, through the target line, dropping down the original 45-degree diagonal. Remain balanced throughout.

The counterbalancing arms move in the opposite direction from the kick, brushing the dominant hand over the thigh, hiding the knap within the body's natural movement. Make contact with the fingers of a stiff hand for the brightest-sounding knap.

Reaction

The victim's head then shoulders turn sharply to the side as the foot crosses their face, creating a reaction matching the attack's energy and speed. Separating the movement of the head and shoulders is important for the clarity of the visual story-telling. Releasing the shoulders a fraction of a second after the head moves can also help to relieve stress in the neck at its fullest rotation. It is important that the victim looks into the space, to spot hazards, before reacting to the kick at speed. They must not lean into the target zone as they begin their reaction, but react to the side and away from the line of the kick.

If knapping, the victim clap knaps as the foot passes their face. The knap has no preparation, and it remains low.

THE PROFILE KICK TO THE HEAD

Works For

Proscenium arch staging in spaces of all sizes; can work in traverse.

Safety Principle

Displace the target.

Position

Victim downstage if knapping, back to the audience, with the attacker one step further upstage, in profile to the audience. If the attacker knaps, these positions reverse: victim upstage facing the audience, attacker one step downstage in profile.

For the illusion of contact, the attacker visualizes a line from the centre of the audience passing through, and upstage of, the target. Their foot swings up through that line and drops back. The attacker must leave at least 8 inches (20cm) between their foot and the target. If in doubt, they should always increase the safety distance between foot and face. The distance the foot travels past the target is a variable, dependent on the relative positions of the audience and the performers. The wider the audience, the further the attacker needs to kick past the victim, to convince most of them that contact has been made. The further the

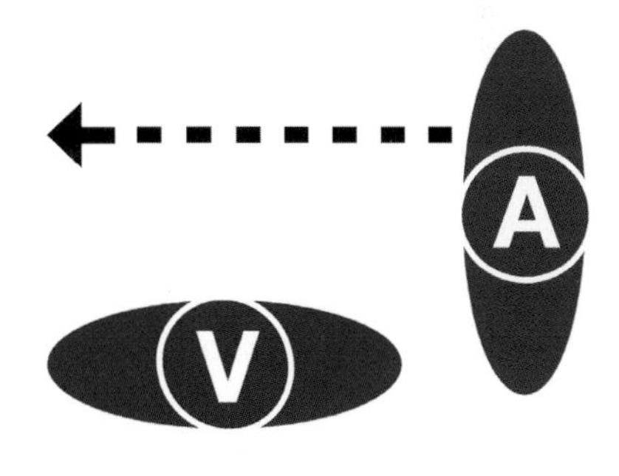

Figure 57: The staging of the profile kick to the head.

foot travels for the illusion of contact, the more it begins to look like a strike with the shin.

Eye Contact

The performers make eye contact, ensuring their partner is ready. If not, they attract their attention. They then shift focus to the target; if this is not done, the risk of actual contact is increased.

Preparation

If a snap kick the attacker lifts their knee vertically, if a swing kick they step their kicking foot back.

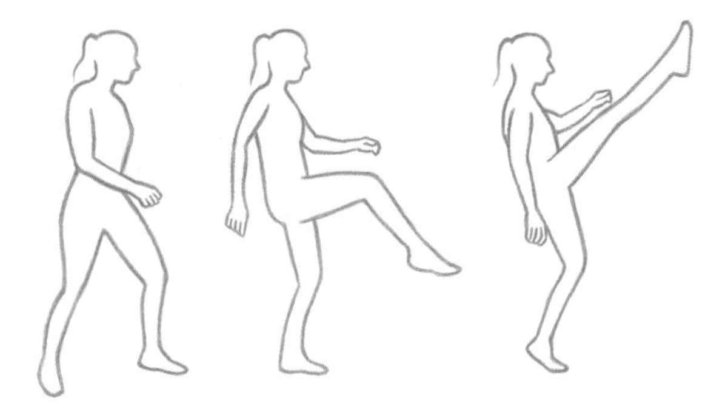

Figure 58: The profile kick to the head.

Action

The attacker kicks up through the line just passing the target, then drops back down. Finish where the kick started: if they step forward there is an increased risk of inadvertent contact. Remain balanced throughout.

The attacker's leg is at its fullest extension when held out horizontal from the hip. Once it lifts higher it draws back closer to their vertical centreline, meaning they need to be closer to the victim than they think, for the audience to see the foot cross the target.

Attacker knap; they brush their hand past their upstage thigh. This knap is hidden within the body's natural movement of the arms to maintain balance.

Reaction

The illusion is that the foot makes contact with the chin or nose. Avoid the body's instinctive reaction

Common Errors

Attacker

Not enough safe distance
Looking at the eyes not the target zone
Not kicking high enough
Not close enough to cross the target line
Revealing the knap (if attacker's)

Victim

Throwing their head back, risking whiplash
Forgetting to lift their shoulders
Mistiming the reaction or the knap
Knapping too high (if victim's)

of throwing the head backwards. Done at speed, and, in particular, repetitively, this will lead to whiplash.

The victim lifts on to the balls of their feet, as if the blow drives them upwards, and, most importantly, the shoulders hunch up as high as possible. Lifting the shoulders bunches the trapezius muscles, creating a supportive cushion behind the neck. The head should be rocked back only when the shoulders are up, when it is less likely that the neck will suffer whiplash. The head then immediately rocks forward to its natural position.

Some performers find that their neck still feels unsupported during this move. In that case, it might help to imagine something flying towards them, passing over their shoulder and on behind them. They look up and watch it fly over and past, stepping back on that side and turning back. The head reacts up and around at speed, but remains comfortably balanced on the extended column of the neck all the way through. This creates the illusion of a fast reactive movement of the head up and back, pulling the body up and around, with none of the neck muscles in a position of strain.

The victim makes a clap knap as the foot passes their face. Relaxed hands clap together with no preparation, remaining low, then separating to allow the foot to safely drop down. If the knap is mistimed or too high, there is a greater risk of the attacker kicking their hands as the foot drops. If the knap is early, there is also an increased risk of contact.

OPPOSITE RIGHT: Four stages of the profile kick to the head.
TOM ZIEBELL

A flowing image of the profile kick to the head.
TOM ZIEBELL

THE PROFILE KICK TO THE HEAD (KNEELING)

Works For

Proscenium arch staging in spaces of all sizes; can work in traverse.

Safety Principle

Displace the target.

Position

Victim downstage if knapping, kneeling, back to the audience, the attacker one step further upstage, in profile to the audience. If the attacker knaps, these positions can be reversed: victim kneeling upstage facing the audience, attacker one step downstage in profile.

For the illusion of contact, the attacker visualizes a line from the centre of the audience passing through, and upstage of, the target. Their foot swings up through that line and drops back. The attacker should leave at least 8 inches (20cm) between their foot and the target. If in doubt, they should always increase the safety distance between foot and face. The distance the foot travels past the target is a variable, dependent on the relative positions of the audience and the performers. The wider the audience, the further the attacker needs to kick past the victim, to convince most of them that contact has been made. The

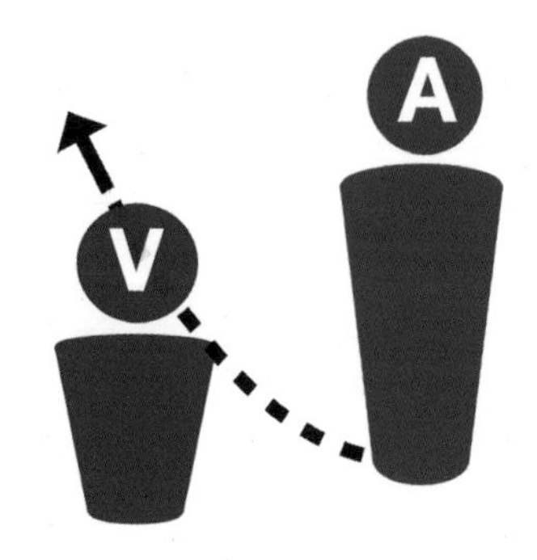

Figure 59: The staging of the profile kick to the head (kneeling).

further the foot travels for the illusion of contact, the more it begins to look like a strike with the shin.

Eye Contact

The performers make eye contact, ensuring their partner is ready. If not, they attract their attention. They then shift focus to the target; if this is not done, the risk of actual contact is increased.

Preparation

For a snap kick, the attacker lifts their knee vertically. For a swing kick, they step their kicking foot back, and for a push kick, they lift their knee vertically, foot flexed.

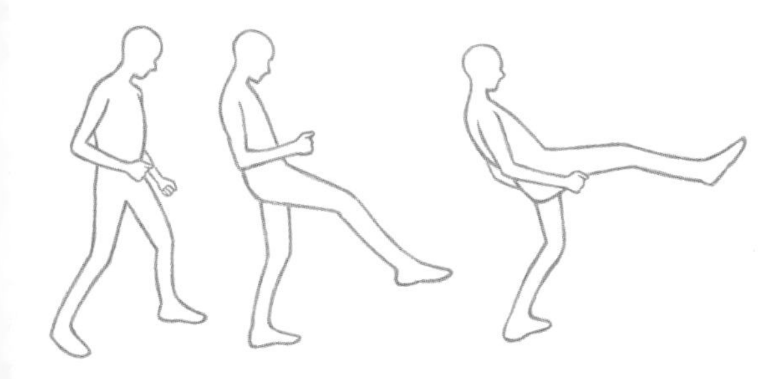

Figure 60: The profile kick to the head (kneeling).

COMMON ERRORS

Attacker
Not enough safe distance
Looking at the eyes not the target zone
Not kicking far enough past the target (push)
Revealing the knap (if attacker's)

Victim
Wrong reaction
Mistiming the reaction or the knap
Collapsing too hard
Knapping too high (if victim's)

Action

- Snap or swing kick: the attacker kicks up through the line just passing the target, then drops back down, aiming to finish where the kick started. If they step forward there is an increased risk of inadvertent contact. They must remain balanced throughout.
- Push: the attacker pushes the sole of their foot forwards in a straight line crossing through the target line, at least 8 inches (20cm) in front of the face. The foot covers all sightlines before dropping. This usually means stepping

OPPOSITE RIGHT: Four stages of the profile kick to the head (kneeling).
TOM ZIEBELL

A flowing image of the profile kick to the head (kneeling).
TOM ZIEBELL

forward on to that foot, taking great care to avoid the victim.

The attacker knaps by brushing their hand past their upstage thigh. This knap is hidden within the body's natural movement of the arms to maintain balance.

Reaction

- Snap or swing kick: the illusion is that the foot makes contact with the chin, on a rising diagonal. It is important that the victim looks into the space, to spot hazards, before reacting into it at speed. The victim looks up and to the side, slightly lifting the body, briefly hanging suspended. They collapse to the side, sitting on to their thigh and rolling out along their side, flopping their arm out as a cushion for their face. (Contact with the floor must be made with areas of muscle, avoiding areas of bone. Before attempting this move, *see* Chapter 18 for the safety principles relating to side descents.)
- Push kick: the illusion is that the foot makes contact with the side of the victim's face. Their head then shoulders turn sharply to the side as the foot crosses their face, creating a reaction matching the attack's energy and speed. Separating the movement of the head and shoulders is important for the clarity of the visual storytelling. Releasing the shoulders a fraction of a second after the head moves can also help to relieve stress in the neck at its fullest rotation. The victim must look into the space, to spot hazards, before reacting into it at speed. They must not lean into the target zone as they begin their reaction, but react to the side and away from the line of the kick. They then perform a side descent, as with the snap or swing kick (*see* Chapter 18 for the safety principles).

If knapping, the victim claps as the foot passes their face. Relaxed hands clap together with no preparation, remaining low, then separating to allow the foot to safely drop down. If the knap is mistimed, or too high, there is a greater risk of the hands being kicked.

THE ROUNDHOUSE KICK TO THE STOMACH

Works For

Proscenium arch staging in spaces of all sizes; can work in traverse and, with a variation, in all other staging formats.

Safety Principle

Displace the target. If pivoting, check that footwear allows easy turning on the performance surface, before attempting the action.

Position

Works best with the victim downstage, back to the audience, the attacker one step upstage, profile to the audience. It can work to some degree with these positions reversed: victim upstage facing the audience, attacker one step downstage in profile.

For the illusion of contact, the attacker visualizes a line from the centre of the audience passing through, and upstage of, the target. Their foot swings up through that line and drops back. The attacker must leave at least 6 inches (15cm) between their foot and the target. If in doubt, they should always increase the safety distance between foot and stomach. The distance the foot travels past the target is a variable dependent on

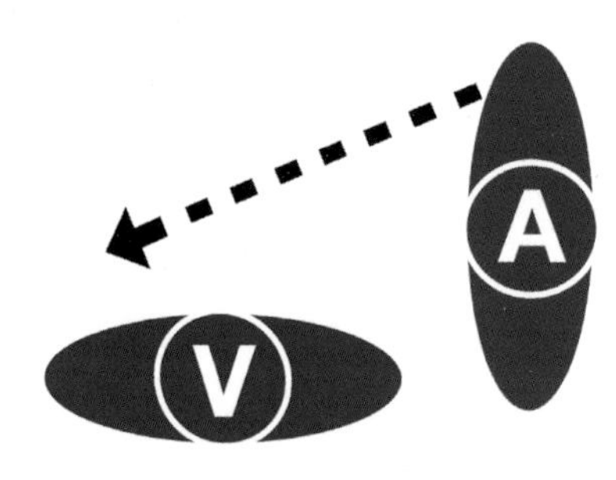

Figure 61: The staging of the roundhouse kick to the stomach.

the relative positions of the audience and the performers. The wider the audience, the further the attacker needs to kick past the victim, to convince most of them that contact has been made. The further the foot travels for the illusion of contact, the more it begins to look like a strike with the shin; which of course is an entirely valid technique.

Can be made to work in the round by allowing the toes to curl around the side of the victim, momentarily closing off sightlines on all sides. Due to the proximity this entails, this is considered a more advanced technique, with a higher risk of accidental contact, which demands greater skill.

This kick is often performed with a vocal knap, or with a chest knap created by whichever partner is facing upstage, or an attacker thigh knap if staging allows.

Eye Contact

The performers make eye contact, ensuring their partner is ready. If not, they attract their attention. They then shift focus to the target; if this is not done, the risk of actual contact is increased.

Preparation

The attacker pivots 90 degrees on their standing foot as they lift their knee horizontally, parallel to the ground, foot pointed.

The victim tightens their abdominals in preparation for unexpected contact.

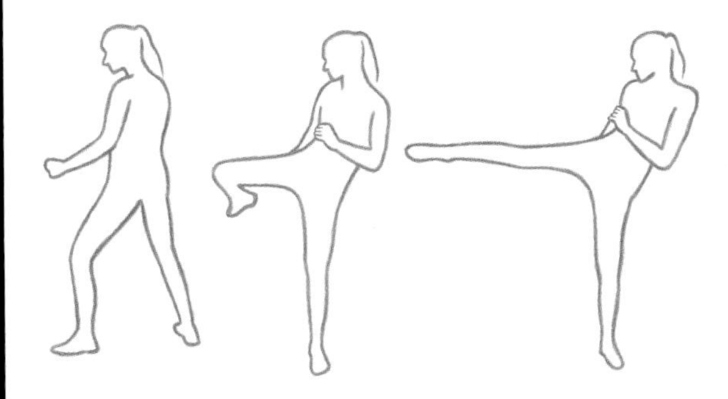

Figure 62: The roundhouse kick to the stomach.

RIGHT: Four stages of the roundhouse kick to the stomach.
TOM ZIEBELL

COMMON ERRORS

Attacker
Not close enough to cross the target line
Not targeting accurately
Flexing the foot instead of extending
Kicking up on an angle instead of horizontally

Victim
Bending over as they react
Lack of clarity in the vocal knap
Mistiming the reaction

Action

The attacker kicks sideways across the target line, pointing the foot, then retracting it. It may help to imagine the shin is sliding flat along a tabletop. The kick should finish where it started. Stepping forward on to the descending foot increases the risk of accidental contact. The attacker must remain balanced throughout.

Reaction

The stomach pulls back, the chest collapses slightly and the head stays up. The instinct is to fold over, with the head down: but dropping the face into the target zone greatly increases the risk of contact. The victim can make a chest knap.

The vocal reaction is dictated by the reality of an abdominal strike, combined with specific pain, the emotional response to it, and the technical needs of the auditorium.

A flowing image of the roundhouse kick to the stomach.
TOM ZIEBELL

The upstage/downstage kick to the head.
TOM ZIEBELL

16
CHOKES AND RELEASES

(Note: no one technique will work for every venue. Each space or staging configuration brings its own challenges, leading to a variety of chokes and releases. The 'Works For' section beginning each description indicates clearly what works where.)

REALITY

When is a choke not a choke but a strangle? According to medical professionals, choking is an internal blockage of the airway, while strangling is an external restriction of oxygen flow to the brain, through tracheal or vascular pressure (Brouhard, 2019). Within sports and martial communities, the technical consensus appears to be that strangulation involves pressure on the flow of oxygenated blood to the brain and the term 'choking' refers to pressure on the airway (BJJEE, 2018). However, for the general public there seems to be a great deal of synonymity in the common usage of both terms (Merriam-Webster, 2019; Collins, 2019).

Experience shows that the public commonly assume that the term 'strangulation' refers to the use of hands to compress the trachea, and that 'choking' refers to holds applied with the arm around the neck. Those assumptions are adopted here, with the caveat that every performer will encounter different terminology applied to the same techniques by different practitioners.

All pressure across the airway leads to extreme physical distress, the inability to breathe, the eventual de-oxygenation of the blood supply, and a lot of pain. Depending on variables such as the relative strength of the opponents, it can take two minutes or more before unconsciousness is achieved and up to four minutes or more before death occurs (FJCA, n.d.). Should the victim survive, the soft tissue of the throat will be bruised and swollen, leading to continued difficulty in breathing (Dunn, Lopez, 2019). It will hurt to talk and eat, and their vocal delivery and the sound of their breathing will be affected for an appreciable time (FJCA, n.d.).

Pressure on the carotid arteries leads to loss of consciousness after 7 to 15 seconds (Worthington, n.d.). If pressure is sustained once the victim is unconscious, permanent brain damage begins after approximately 60 seconds, with death occurring within minutes (Villines, 2016). Should the victim survive, they would probably suffer a headache, but few issues with breathing or speaking. However, with both techniques, there is a high risk of complications arising over the following days, which could easily lead to death (Utley, 2014).

It is clear that creating the illusion of a chokehold must be approached with extreme caution and a strong focus on safety. The performers are dealing directly with the location of a colleague's vocal instrument with potentially devastating consequences for their career.

Regarding releases, there are many different techniques to choose from. Each attack described here is followed by a single version of many possibilities.

SAFETY

The first priority in terms of safety is consent. Without the explicit permission of your partner, you can go no further. Once it has been given – explicitly – and the parameters of what is acceptable have been established, the illusion may be constructed. The safety principles in the following techniques rely on allowing the victim to control the illusion as much as possible, and the attacker sustaining a flow of energy that impacts the victim as little as possible.

Any technique touching the victim's neck involves serious risk. It may restrict their ability to speak and, consequently, their ability to ask their partner to stop if necessary. Performers must not only agree on a safe word, which will instantly stop the action, but also on a safe gesture, which will do the same. The word they choose must be something that the character would never say in that situation; equally, the gesture must be one that absolutely cannot be mistaken for anything else. Martial arts practitioners commonly use a 'double tap' for this purpose, but this is not recommended, as it can easily be mistaken in the struggle, or missed entirely. Alternatively, it may inadvertently trigger an unnecessary emergency release. Instead, one example (there are many more) might be the hands clasped above the head. Both the safe word and safe gesture must be rehearsed regularly and randomly thrown into rehearsals and fight calls to ensure compliance and training.

WHAT WORKS?

The joy of these techniques is that they work in any orientation; the tricks that are hidden from the audience are internal to the technique and thus invisible. The potential for struggle within them allows the performers to manipulate sightlines and share with all of the audience.

THE STRANGLE

Works For

All staging.

Safety Principles

- Victim control: the victim can end the technique by letting go of the attacker's arms.
- Reversal of energy: the energy flow within the technique is redirected into a safe direction.
- Dove of peace: the overlapping of the attacker's hands to keep the thumbs away from the vocal instrument.
- Negotiation: the victim dictates where contact is made and how much energy is used.

If wrongly applied, these techniques could prevent the victim from breathing or speaking, so a safe gesture must be created and practised regularly, with the victim randomly choosing when in rehearsal to use it.

Position

The performers face each other in any position on stage. The hands must not be driven directly to the victim's throat as a misjudgement of energy or position can lead to an accidental hand strike on the vocal instrument. They should be placed on the chest first, releasing the aggressive energy before sliding up to the neck.

Eye Contact

The performers make eye contact ensuring their partner's ready. If not, they attract their attention.

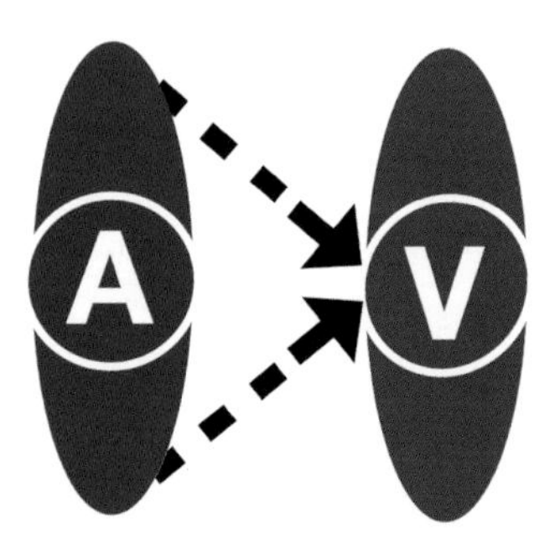

Figure 63: The staging of the strangle.

They then shift focus to the target, the upper chest.

Preparation

Clap hands flat on to the victim's chest. Negotiate the hand placement and how hard it should be with the victim. Some practitioners use a scale of 1–10 to judge the impact, but the victim always has final say on both aspects.

Make contact with a loud knap. The victim starts a back bend, lifting their chin, neck relaxed but straight, taking one step back. The slight lean back exposes the throat without stressing the neck.

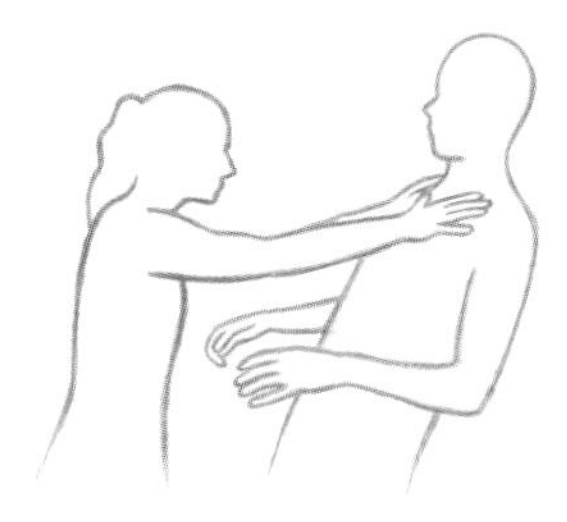

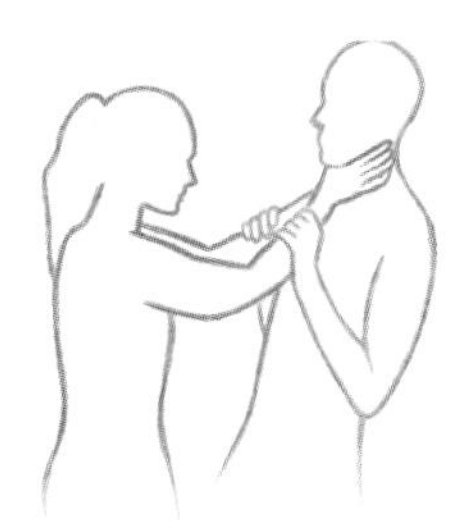

Figure 64: The strangle.

RIGHT: Four stages of the strangle.
TOM ZIEBELL

Action

The attacker knaps all aggressive character energy to the victim's chest, then slides gentle hands up to the neck, forming a dove of peace. One hand sits atop the other, thumb on top of opposite forefinger, and vice versa, the fingers creating a vertical collar hugging the victim's neck. The thumbs curl around the sides of the neck, not pressing against the trachea. The top of the hands sit right underneath the victim's jaw: the natural concavity of the palms protects their vocal instrument. The hands sit horizontally around the neck, like a collar, not angled upwards behind the ears.

The victim drops their chin atop the hands, lifting their shoulders enough to mask any gaps, but not so much that the hands are compressed, or cannot fit.

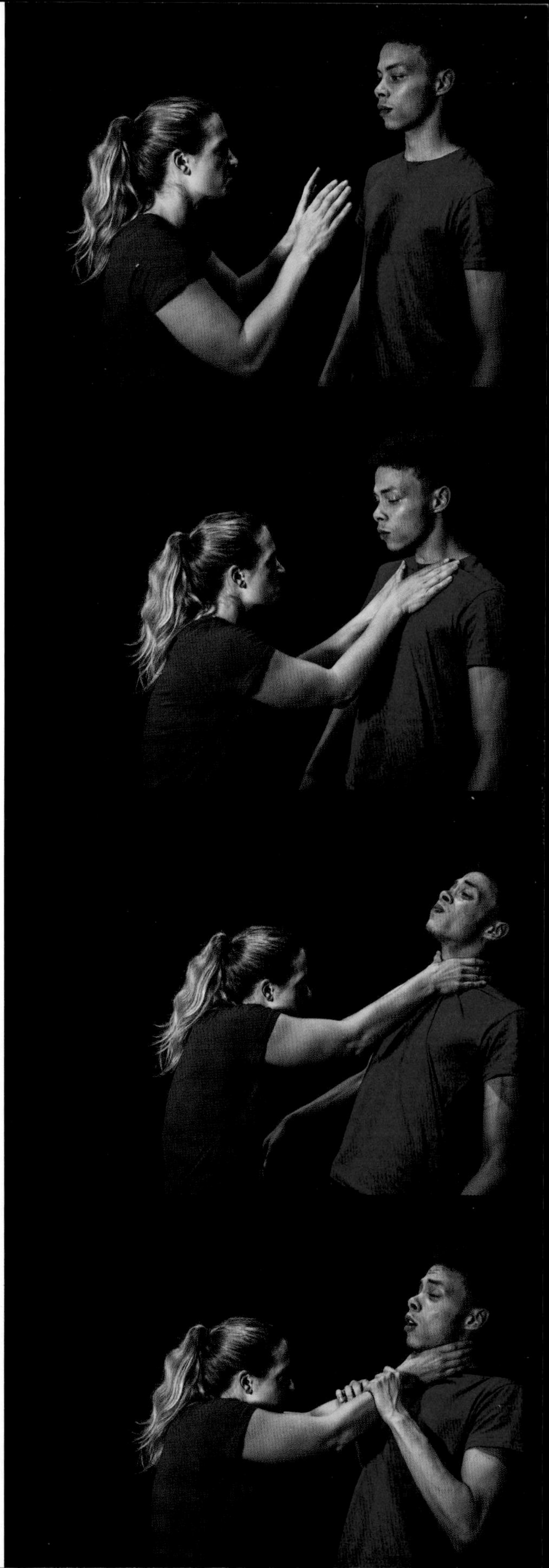

COMMON ERRORS

Attacker
Misjudges contact
Hands in wrong position on neck
Pulls too hard or with body
Grips neck too tight

Victim
Fails to rock back and lift chin
Grabs arms too early
Misjudges pull energy
Lifts chin to reveal gap

Reaction

The victim grabs the attacker's forearms just below the wrists (avoiding the wrists themselves, because they are fragile and can be damaged by a strong grip), using a C clamp grip (fingers on top, thumbs underneath). They should avoid cupping the hands over the top of the arms because it encourages them to pull downwards rather than out. This can pull the hands down from the neck, revealing the illusion. Often, in trying to keep the gap closed, the victim brings their face down, ending up looking at the floor not the audience.

The victim should avoid actively pulling the hands up to their neck. The risk is that the hands are pulled into the jaw harder than expected, because the victim is working by feel. If the attacker controls that moment, they can judge exactly where to stop their hands.

The victim locks the attacker's hands into position by actively pulling them towards their own throat. The attacker pulls away, using fractionally less energy than the victim, otherwise the hands start to bounce on the neck, with all of the attendant risks. Both partners must pull with their arms only. If the back or hips are engaged in the pull, the partner will be dragged off-balance. Both performers must focus actively on remaining balanced. This reversal of energy allows victim control (they can let go and it stops), making the audience believe that the attacker is pushing forward instead of pulling back. The advantage is that the tension in all four arms reinforces the perception of aggressive intent.

The victim must avoid stressing their vocal instrument by tightening the vocal folds, shifting the focus into the mouth and using the articulators – tongue, soft palate and lips – to produce a random, fractured series of pops, hisses and clicks. These sounds can be interspersed with silence, creating the character's struggle for air, and enriched with a subtle application of various consonantal sounds: sibilants, fricatives and plosives.

Strangles almost inevitably contain some element of struggle. For safety, that struggle must be as clearly choreographed as every other element. It is entirely dependent upon character, context and environment, so it is impossible to cover all the potentialities within a learning situation. However, it is worth considering that any struggle will contain the principles of negotiation, shared energy and victim control.

A flowing image of the strangle.
TOM ZIEBELL

THE SWEEP BREAK

Works With

The strangle.

Safety Principles

Negotiation – the victim dictates where contact is made and how much energy is used.

Position

Facing each other, engaged in the strangle.

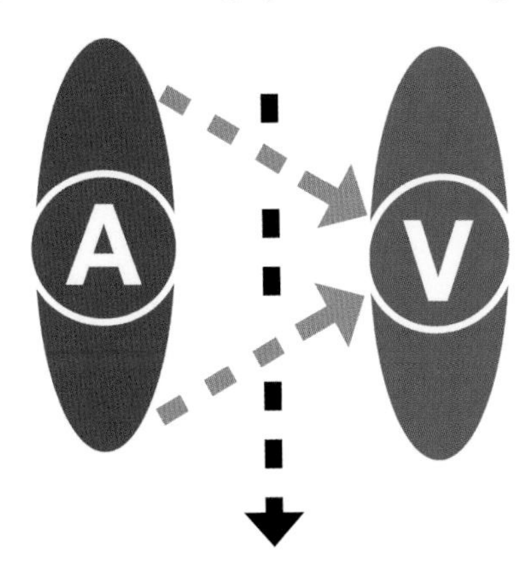

Figure 65: The staging of the sweep break.

RIGHT: Four stages of the sweep break.
TOM ZIEBELL

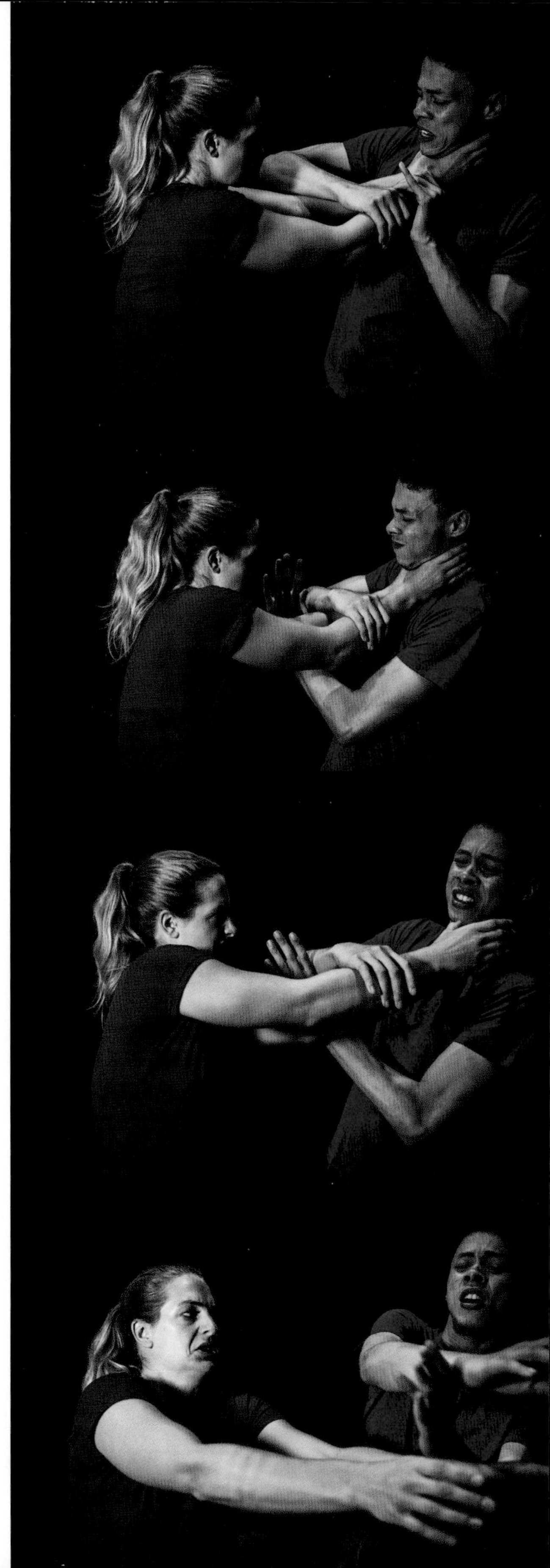

Eye Contact

The performers make eye contact, ensuring their partner is ready. If not, they attract their attention. The victim of the strangle then shifts their focus to the strangler's arms.

Preparation

The victim gradually relaxes the energy of their grip, the attacker matching that energy, sustaining the illusion of the strangle. Eventually, the victim completely releases their grip and the attacker continues to strangle with relaxed hands.

The victim places one arm on top of the strangler's arms (to prevent them lifting into the victim's face). They reach their other arm under the strangler's arms, placing the edge of their thumb against the front of their own elbow, fingers pointing up.

The strangler ensures their arms are relaxed and ready to release.

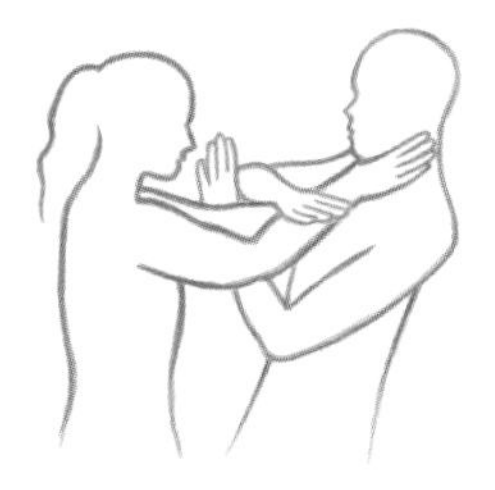

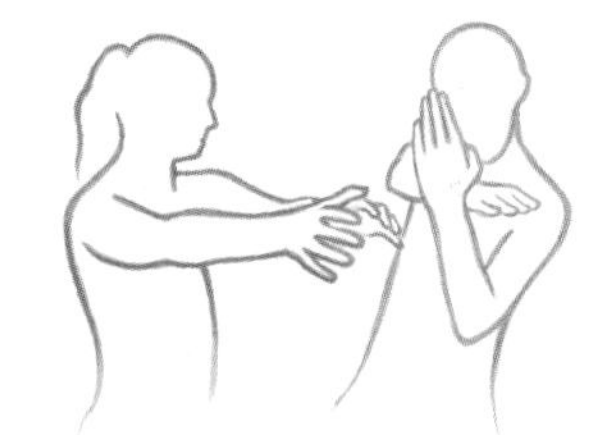

Figure 66: The sweep break.

Common Errors

Victim of strangle
Misjudges contact
Vertical hand inside elbow, not in front
Steps back on the wrong side
Forgets to step back

Strangler
Misjudges energy release
Fails to relax arms

Action

The victim of the strangle steps back on the side of the sweeping arm, pivoting their hips, and sliding their vertical hand along their horizontal forearm (moving hand moves towards moving leg), sweeping the strangler's arms away to the side.

Make the contact with the strangler's arms soft, and avoid contact with their elbow. Keeping contact between the hand and the forearm greatly reduces the risk of hitting their face. If the victim does not step back, but does pivot their hips, there is a strong risk of their elbow hitting their partner's face.

Reaction

The strangler allows their arms to be pushed to the side, keeping them below the victim's face. Their hands remain relaxed as they release the neck and they stay balanced throughout.

A flowing image of the sweep break.
TOM ZIEBELL

THE CHOKE

Works For

All staging.

Safety Principles

- Reversal of energy: the circle of life, the flow of energy within the technique, is redirected into a safe direction.
- Negotiation: the victim dictates where contact is made and how much energy is used.

If wrongly applied, this technique could prevent the victim from breathing or speaking, so a safe gesture must be created for them (*see* page 178). This must be practised regularly, with the victim randomly choosing when in rehearsal to use it.

Position

The attacker is behind the victim.

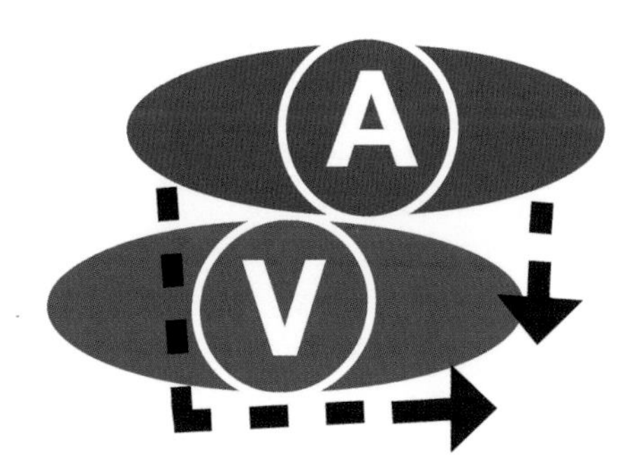

Figure 67: The staging of the choke.

RIGHT: Four stages of the choke.
TOM ZIEBELL

Eye Contact

Eye contact is replaced by hands on the victim's shoulders, cueing them as to the timing of the technique, and the attacker's position.

Preparation

The attacker places their hands on top of the victim's shoulders. This contact is negotiated. The attacking hand's thumb is tucked to the side of the hand to avoid catching in costume or jewellery.

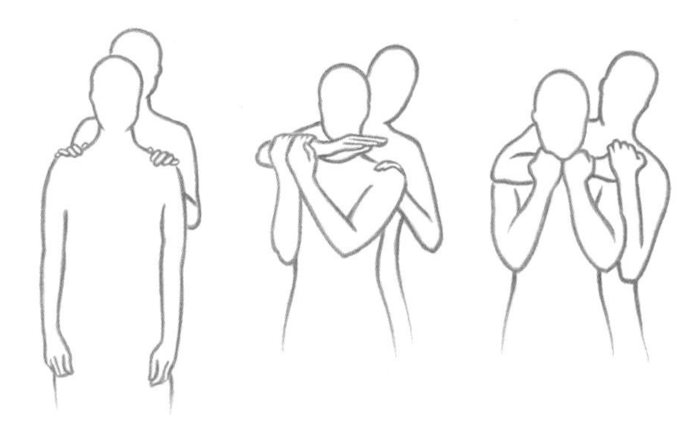

Figure 68: The choke.

Common Errors

Attacker
Pats the victim's shoulders before choke
Fails to place hands on shoulders
Arm on neck not chest
Fails to reverse energy
Does not move enough to the side to be seen

Victim
Grabs the arm too late
Does not hook over far enough to protect throat
Hands separated
Does not stretch chin far enough over
Does not lift shoulders to place arm
Pushes hips forwards
Leans to the side

Action

The attacker steps in, sliding their choking arm across the victim's chest to grip the side of their opposite shoulder, the forearm resting horizontally across the top of the chest. Contact with the neck must be avoided throughout this section.

The victim takes one step back with the opposite foot from the attacker, as if pulled, reaching up, creating the illusion of attempting to stop the attack. In reality, they make hook hands on top of the arm. Once in position, these hands relax; there is no need to grip or pull in any direction. They are however ready to pull down with enough force to gain breathing space if the attacker begins to choke them for real. They should also remain side by side, protecting their vocal instrument.

If the victim is taller, they can use the surprise of being pulled back as an opportunity to take a wider base, dropping their centre and bringing themselves to the right height.

The attacker repositions themselves slightly, revealing their head over the victim's shoulder. This reduces the risk of an accidental head-butt, allows the attacker to be seen and allows the choking arm to remain horizontal when energized. They then clasp their hands, vertical pulling hand in front, creating the illusion of applying pressure to the neck. The energy is reversed in this circle of life: the horizontal arm pulls out and the vertical arm pulls in. The energy circles through the arms around the victim; no energy enters the victim; they should feel no physical pressure at all.

A flowing image of the choke.
TOM ZIEBELL

Reaction

The victim hunches their shoulders, lifting the attacker's arm up in front of their throat, and leans back into the attacker's shoulder. Their chin rests atop their own hands. There is no contact with the front of the throat; if there is, the victim uses their hook hands to pull the arm down from their vocal instrument. At no point do the two heads line up, minimizing the risk of a head-butt.

The attacker must always lay their forearm across the top of the victim's chest in the first instance. If they habitually get this wrong, there is a high risk in performance that, with character energy, they will slam the forearm across the vocal instrument. The top of the victim's shoulder must be at armpit height on the attacker. If it is higher, the choking arm ends up on a diagonal across the victim, putting pressure across the muscle systems of the shoulders, with increased risk of injury.

The performers should remain in contact, with no gap between their bodies, upright and balanced and not leaning to one side.

Any struggle needs to be choreographed. The single most important issue when struggling is that both partners retain balance whilst playing the characters' intentions. If the victim shifts off their centre – forwards, back or to either side – there is a risk that they will pull the attacker off-balance, with consequent issues for safety and story-telling. The simplest solution is for the victim to struggle around their vertical axis, allowing the attacker to remain balanced.

The music for this technique is similar to that of the strangle. Technically, the performer avoids stressing their vocal instrument by shifting the focus into the mouth and using the articulators – tongue, soft palate and lips – to produce a random, fractured series of pops, hisses and clicks, interspersed with silence, to create the character's struggle for air. These sounds may be subtly enriched with various consonantal sounds – sibilants, fricatives and plosives.

THE ELBOW STRIKE TO THE STOMACH

Works With

The choke from behind.

Safety Principles

Displace the target – in reality the victim drives their elbow straight back into the choker's abdominals. On stage they make contact on their own side, not the attacker's stomach.

Position

Attacker behind victim, actively engaged in the choke.

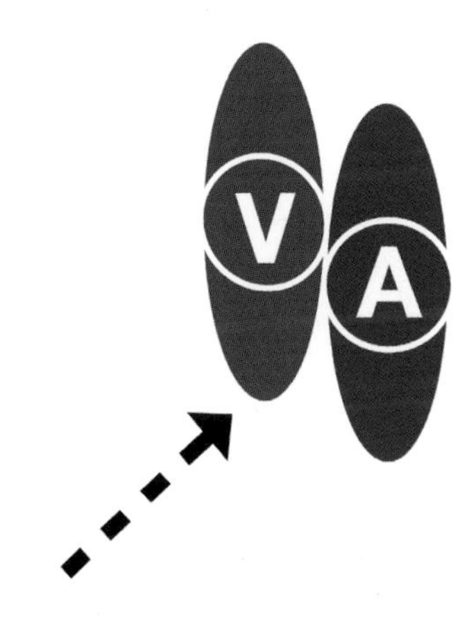

Figure 69: The staging of the elbow strike to the stomach.

Eye Contact

There is no eye contact. The choker is cued by the victim's preparation.

Preparation

The victim of the choke lifts up their arm on the side of the attacker's hands, on a front diagonal line. If it is difficult to lift high enough because of the circle of life, the attacker relaxes their grip as if it is forced up.

Action

They drop their elbow to their side at speed, making triceps contact to their own side, then dropping the fist forwards.

Common Errors

Victim of choke
Misjudges angle and makes accidental contact
Makes the action too small
Leaves the fist by their shoulder

Choker
Forgets to release victim of choke
Bends over in reaction
Misjudges the music required

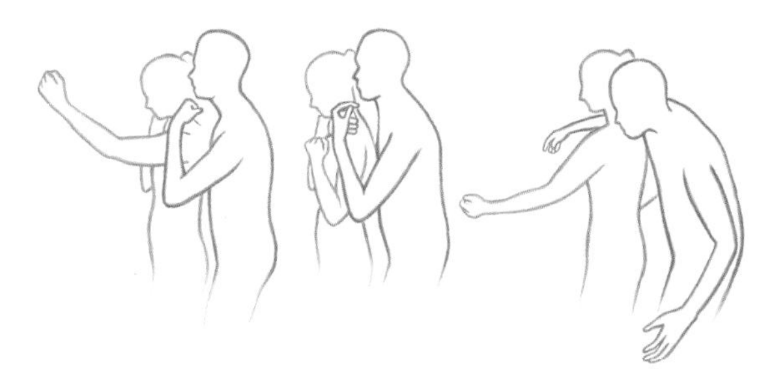

Figure 70: The elbow strike to the stomach.

RIGHT: Four stages of the elbow strike to the stomach.
TOM ZIEBELL

A flowing image of the elbow strike to the stomach.
TOM ZIEBELL

It is important to keep the fist close to the shoulder as the elbow drops, otherwise they will hit their hipbone. If the fist is not removed forwards, there is a risk the choker will head-butt it as they react.

Reaction

The choker releases the arm encircling the victim to avoid dragging them into the reaction. Their stomach moves back, the chest collapses slightly and the face remains up as they create a strong vocal knap.

A strike to the abdominals forces air out of the mouth. That gust of air is unstructured and less effective for story-telling purposes, so it is better to craft structured sounds that carry the story and character's emotional response to the back of the auditorium.

THE SLEEPER HOLD

Works For

All staging.

Safety Principles

- Victim control: they place the choking arm.
- Reversal of energy: the circle of life, the flow of energy within the technique, is redirected into a safe direction.
- Negotiation: the victim dictates where contact is made and how much energy is used.

If wrongly applied, this technique could prevent the victim from breathing or speaking, so a safe gesture must be created (*see* page 178) and practised regularly, with the victim randomly choosing when in rehearsal to use it.

Position

The attacker is behind the victim.

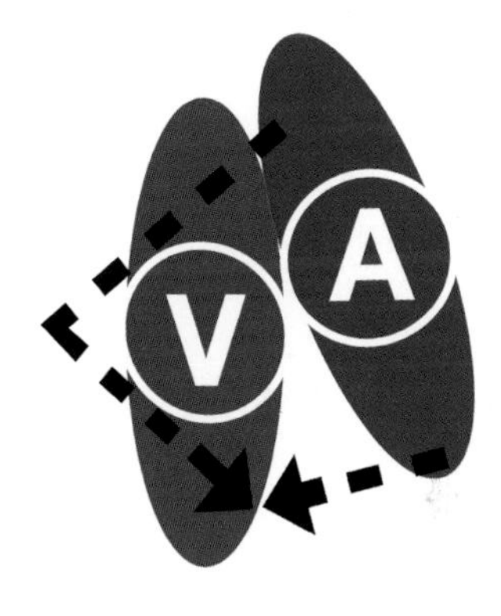

Figure 71: The staging of the sleeper hold.

Eye Contact

Eye contact is replaced by hands on the victim's shoulders, cueing them as to the timing of the technique and the attacker's position.

Preparation

The attacker places the hands on top of the victim's shoulders. This contact is negotiated. The attacking hand's thumb is tucked to the side of the hand to avoid catching in costume or jewellery.

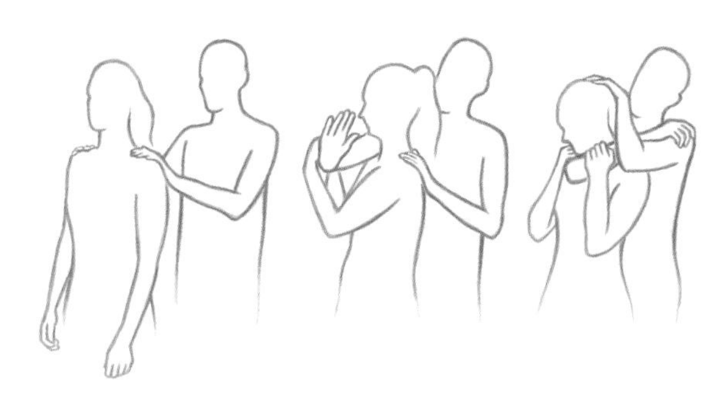

Figure 72: The sleeper hold.

RIGHT: Four stages of the sleeper hold.
TOM ZIEBELL

Action

The attacker gently pulls the victim back, stepping forward on the side of their choking arm, sliding it part way round them. The victim steps back on their opposite foot, reaching up as if to stop the attack: in reality, they make hook hands over the arm, either side of the elbow, guiding it into position. The victim controls this element. The attacker's elbow rests below the victim's chin, pointing forwards, fingers pointing back, up over their opposite shoulder. There may be gentle contact with the sides of the neck, but the hands should ensure the safety of the vocal instrument. The side of the attacker's chest makes firm contact with one side of the victim's back, ensuring the heads are not lined up. If the victim is taller than the attacker, they can use the surprise of being pulled back as an opportunity to take a wider base, dropping themselves to the right height.

The attacker creates a circle of life by placing the side of the wrist of the choking hand inside the bent elbow of the other arm. The choking arm pushes out, attempting to straighten, the other pulls inwards in opposition, creating the reversal of energy. The free hand rests like a relaxed cobra atop or behind the victim's head, creating the illusion of forcing the head forward into the hold. The victim feels no physical pressure in their neck.

The attacker must not complete the initial action bringing the arm around the victim's neck. If they habitually get this wrong, there is a high risk

Common Errors

Attacker
Pats their shoulders before choke
Fails to place hands on shoulders
Brings the arm all the way round themselves
Angle of arm incorrect
Fails to reverse energy

Victim
Grabs the arm too late
Does not hook over far enough to protect throat
Does not stretch chin far enough over
Does not extend upper chest to bring face up
Pushes hips forwards
Leans to the side

that in performance, with character energy, they will cause a serious injury. The top of the victim's shoulder should be at armpit height on the attacker; if it is higher, the choking arm will put pressure across the neck, with a high risk of damage.

Reaction

The victim grabs the attacker's arm with hook hands, fingers over the top, either side of the elbow, guiding it into position at the top of the chest, point of elbow forwards. They stretch their chin as far over the elbow as possible, face slightly down towards the ground. They then extend through the upper chest bringing their face back up to the audience without lifting their chin off their hands. They must not try to achieve this by pushing the hips forwards, as this would adversely affect both balance and visual story-telling.

Once in position, the hook hands are relaxed; there is no need to grip or pull. They are however in position to pull down with enough force to gain breathing space if the attacker inadvertently chokes them for real. It is also vital to ensure that there is no pressure on the victim's vocal instrument or the sides of the neck. The performers should remain in contact throughout, with no gap between their bodies; they should be upright and balanced, not leaning to one side.

Any struggle needs to be choreographed. The single most important issue when struggling is that both partners retain balance whilst playing the character's intentions. If the victim shifts off their centre, forwards, back or to either side, there is a risk that they will pull the attacker off-balance, with consequent issues for safety and story-telling. The simplest solution is for the victim to struggle around their vertical axis, allowing the attacker to remain balanced.

The music for this technique is similar to that of the strangle. Technically, the performer avoids stressing their vocal instrument by shifting the focus into the mouth and using the articulators – tongue, soft palate and lips – to produce a random, fractured series of pops, hisses, clicks, interspersed with silence, to create the character's struggle for air. Those sounds could be subtly enriched with various consonantal sounds – sibilants, fricatives and plosives.

BELOW: A flowing image of the sleeper hold.
TOM ZIEBELL

THE HORIZONTAL ELBOW STRIKE TO THE LATS

Works With

The sleeper hold.

Safety Principles

Displace the target – in reality, the victim would drive their elbow around horizontally, hammering it into the victim's ribs. On stage, the victim covers the target zone with their arm: if contact is made, it is light and with soft muscle.

Position

Attacker behind victim, actively engaged in the sleeper hold. The illusion is an elbow strike to the attacker's side ribs or lats.

Figure 73: The staging of the horizontal elbow strike to the lats.

Eye Contact

There is no eye contact. The choker takes their cue from the victim's preparation.

Preparation

The victim of the choke lifts the attacking arm parallel to the ground. This can be performed with either arm.

Action

They push their elbow out to the side, rotating the hips slightly, creating the illusion of striking the victim's ribs.

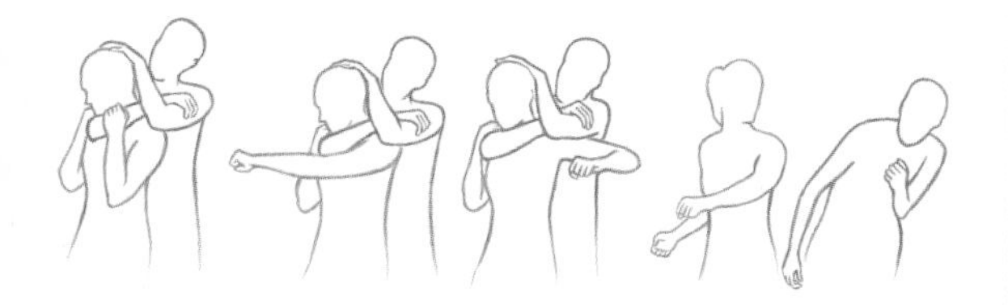

Figure 74: The horizontal elbow strike to the lats.

The fist is kept close to the front of their own shoulder as the elbow rotates, reducing the risk of overextending the shoulder joint. The arm is kept horizontal so that, if there is an accidental contact, it is with the muscle, not the elbow. This can be performed as a contact technique, utilizing all of the contact safety principles.

Reaction

The choker releases the arm encircling the victim and staggers clear.

If the attack is repeated a number of times with the release on the last one, the choker must avoid jerking on the victim's neck as they react to each strike, isolating the energy of the reaction from the victim.

Common Errors

Victim of choke
Elbow is low and makes accidental contact
Makes the action too small
Opens the fist out

Choker
Forgets to release victim of choke
Jerks victim's neck as reacting

OPPOSITE RIGHT: Four stages of the horizontal elbow strike to the lats.
TOM ZIEBELL

BELOW: A flowing image of the horizontal elbow strike to the lats.
TOM ZIEBELL

17
CONTACT

WHY AND WHEN

The guidelines about how to use this book – as a reference during or after a stage combat course, and *not* as a substitute for having an instructor in the room – are particularly relevant when looking at contact techniques. If these techniques are explored outside of a supervised class environment, extreme care must be taken.

It is difficult persuading an audience that performed violence is real, as they intellectually understand that this cannot be the case. This will be exacerbated by poorly performed non-contact strikes. With most contact techniques, the tricks supporting the illusion are internal to the move and the rehearsal process, so there are fewer opportunities to arouse a sense of disbelief in the audience. Most contact illusions can be examined from any angle and, if acted well, will persuade most audiences.

Convincing performers to use a contact technique can be problematic. This is unsurprising, as many will have experiences to recount of unsafe partners, and injuries borne and damage sustained. It is undoubtedly true that a poorly executed contact moment carries with it a higher risk of injury than the non-contact version.

So why might the fight director choose what is, on the face of it, a riskier set of techniques? The reality is that the exigencies of staging, and the demands of text or character, can often leave them with little choice. In-the-round, thrust or traverse staging can offer few options to a good fight director, beyond creating fights in which illusory contact between characters is minimal.

What are the ramifications of such a choice? How can a performer's understandable anxiety be alleviated? First, in order to gain confidence, they will need more dedicated rehearsal time, and perhaps longer fight calls before each show. They may be able to use padding, if it is possible within the constraints of the production. With some performers, contact techniques will never be feasible, due to an inability to retain physical information or a lack of consistent physical ability.

It should be acknowledged that with certain techniques the risks are simply too high to proceed (*see* Chapter 13). Each performer will, rightly, have their own line drawn in the sand, as they will know their own body and capabilities better than anyone else. However, it is to be hoped that, with good instruction and clarity of information, combined with a strong focus on specific safety, more performers will be encouraged to accept contact techniques into their toolkit.

SAFETY

The focus on safety is always paramount in stage combat, but it must be taken to an extreme degree when dealing with contact techniques. There are a number of principles that are relevant in this context; these are discussed in detail below.

Negotiation

Permission must be asked for, and granted, before a performer touches a partner's body. Without explicit consent it is not permissible to touch somebody. That consent should be renewed daily. If there is an element of force to the contact, the level of energy must also be negotiated. The accepted method is to start gently, gradually increasing the energy, with constant feedback from the victim, until an acceptable level is fixed. Some performers use a scale of one to ten, others use a more fluid sense of measurement. The victim's word is law in this situation. They can change their mind, alter the parameters, or even withdraw permission entirely. There are no egos involved with contact work. Everyone must simply collaborate to create the best illusion they can and whatever the victim requests is what happens, as it is potentially their body and career on the line.

Soft on Soft

Make contact on large areas of muscle and avoid areas where bone is prominent, or only lightly padded. Abdominals and hamstrings are strong choices for contact targets. Depending on the performer's individual physique, it is possible to use the latissimus dorsi, deltoids and calf muscles. It depends on the thickness of the natural padding and the performer's tolerance for energetic contact. A rugby player will respond less sensitively to a blow than a more sedentary person might. Not all muscle groups are good candidates for contact: for example, the glutei maximi, or buttocks, are well padded but between them lies the coccyx (tailbone), which can be easily damaged by misjudged contact.

Soften the Striking Implement

Whatever makes contact with a performer must be as soft as possible. If a character is struck with a prop, the company would have a soft version made, which visually convinces the audience but creates far less impact. For unarmed strikes, the softest aspect of the striking element is used: the most padded section, the widest/flattest area, or the most easily relaxed part. For the foot, this is usually the shoelace area, for a knee attack, the thigh muscle, and for a fist, the relaxed or hollow version.

Withdraw the Energy

The body is damaged when energy is transferred into it at speed, and the contact is sustained long enough for it to shock through to the interior of the body. However, it is possible to hit at speed and to stop the blow at the surface of the skin. Everyone experiences this regularly when they are clapping hands: every time they make contact with one hand against the other, they negotiate with themselves how hard that contact will be, and withdraw the energy as soon as their hands meet.

To support these techniques, a clear communication must be set up between all involved. The attacker and stage management must check in constantly with the victim during rehearsals to ensure they are happy with the positioning and energy of the techniques. There is also a check-in at fight calls and after performances. The victim should always feel free to comment without fear of giving offence.

The individual performer's physicality, and how it interacts with the partner's, will have a strong impact on the ways in which the following techniques are created and focused. Contact techniques are inherently customizable to the physical requirements of performers.

Constant repetition of most of these techniques leads to the potential for bruises. Padding reduces that risk and would almost certainly be used in performance.

WHAT WORKS?

Most of these techniques work in any orientation; the tricks that are hidden from the audience are internal to the technique and thus invisible. Other than a couple of the contact stomach strikes, all the other techniques work in the round.

THE ZERO ENERGY PUSH

Works With

All staging.

Safety Principles

- Negotiation: the victim dictates where contact is made.
- Push your partner to safety.

Position

Partners face each other.

It is easy to misjudge the timing of this technique and spoil the illusion. However, it is a useful technique for performers who wish to control their own movement. Negotiate where the hand is placed.

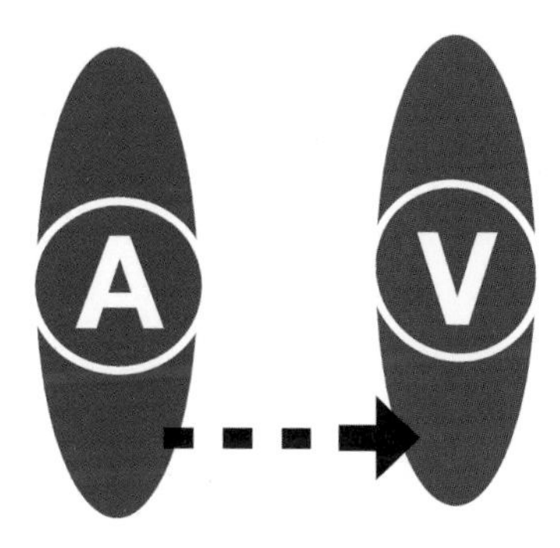

Figure 75: The staging of the zero energy push.

RIGHT: Four stages of the zero energy push.
TOM ZIEBELL

Eye Contact

The performers make eye contact, ensuring their partner is ready. If not, they attract their attention. The attacker shifts focus to the space behind the victim.

Preparation

The attacker places one hand on the negotiated target, the shoulder, with the arm bent. They scan the space behind the victim, ensuring it is safe for them to move into. This is a predictive check, not only looking for fixed hazards, but also checking that no one is about to move into the space. If there is a safety issue, the push stops at this point.

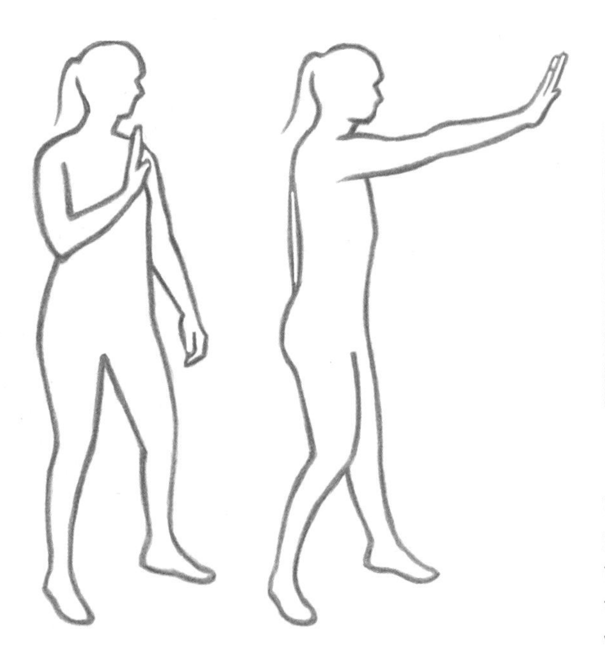

Figure 76: The zero energy push.

Common Errors

Attacker
Actually pushing victim
Lifting the hand near the face
Opening the thumb out
Not checking the space behind the victim

Victim
Mistiming the reaction
Misjudging the energy

Action

The attacker shifts their weight forwards sliding their hand over the victim's shoulder, creating the illusion of a push but putting no energy into the victim's body. The hand slides over in a realistic hand shape, fingers slightly upwards.

The pushing hand does not lift into the victim's reaction space, staying at shoulder height as it pushes through, to avoid accidentally hitting their face. The thumb is tucked to the side of the hand, to avoid it catching in costume or jewellery or inadvertently striking the base of the throat.

Reaction

The victim reacts back with their shoulder or chest as if they have just been pushed. If the timing and the energy of the reaction do not match that of the action, the illusion fails. The victim needs to remain balanced whilst creating the illusion of imbalance.

A flowing image of the zero energy push.
TOM ZIEBELL

THE SHARED ENERGY PUSH

Works With

All staging.

Safety Principles

- Negotiation: the victim dictates where contact can be made.
- Push your partner to safety.

Position

Partners face each other.

This is a real push, but with negotiated parameters to ensure it is safe.

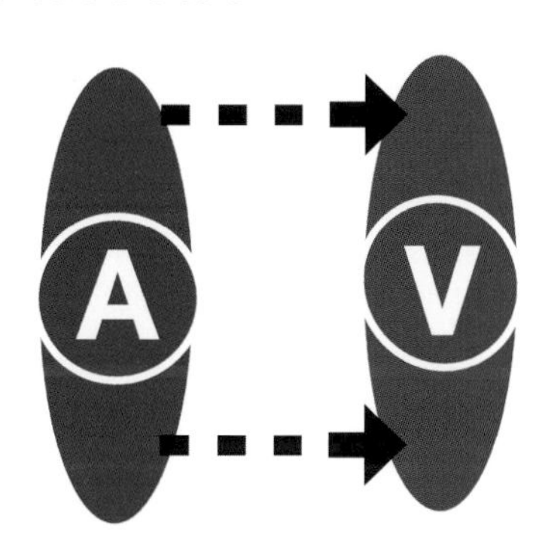

Figure 77: The staging of the shared energy push.

RIGHT: Four stages of the shared energy push.
TOM ZIEBELL

Eye Contact

The performers make eye contact, ensuring their partner is ready. If not, they attract their attention. The attacker shifts focus to the space behind the victim.

Preparation

The attacker places one or two hands on the negotiated target (shoulder or chest, for example), with a bent arm and feet braced. They scan the space behind the victim, ensuring it is safe for them to move into. This is a predictive check, not only looking for fixed hazards, but also checking that no one is about to move into the space. If there is a safety issue, the push stops at this point.

If it is a two-hand push the attacker slightly off-sets themselves, particularly if their partner is taller than them, so they can see the space behind the victim. They should not stand so far off-set, with feet lunged, that the move looks fake, but just far enough to check the safety.

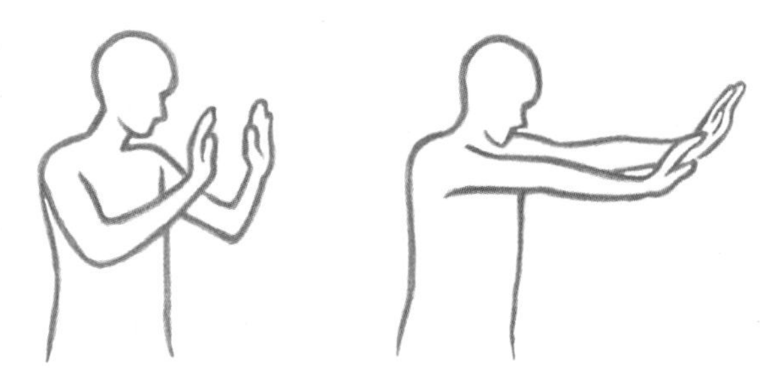

Figure 78: The shared energy push with two hands.

Action

The attacker shifts their weight forwards as they make a negotiated push through the target.

The pushing hand must not lift where the victim might react with their face, causing accidental contact; it pushes through it at the height of the shoulder. The thumb is tucked to the side of the hand to avoid it catching in costume or jewellery or inadvertently striking the base of the throat.

Common Errors

Attacker
Pushing victim too hard
Lifting the hand near the face
Opening the thumb out
Not checking the space behind the victim

Victim
Losing balance

Reaction

The victim reacts back, remaining balanced whilst creating the illusion of imbalance.

A loss of balance is common with a two-hand chest push, as the body's balance zone in the front-back axis is shallow; so the smallest push can have a significant effect. The victim should react as if one of the attacker's arms is stronger; they step back on one side, rotating their body anywhere up to 180 degrees and moving away from the push, reducing the risk of losing balance.

The victim should always give feedback to the attacker, helping them maintain the established parameters.

A flowing image of the shared energy push.
TOM ZIEBELL

THE COSTUME PULL

Works With

All staging.

Safety Principles

- Negotiation: the victim dictates where contact can be made.
- Victim control: they can let go to stop the technique.
- Pull your partner to safety: look before you pull.

Position

Partners face each other.

The simple version of this is a one- or two-hand costume grab, pulling the victim towards the attacker, or walking them around, keeping them safe as they move. A basic version of the energized technique involves grabbing with both hands (a lapel grab) and using them to move the victim, and at the same time to help them remain balanced, whilst creating the illusion of controlling them.

The more complex version is the fully energized one-hand pull through space (which can also be done with two hands).

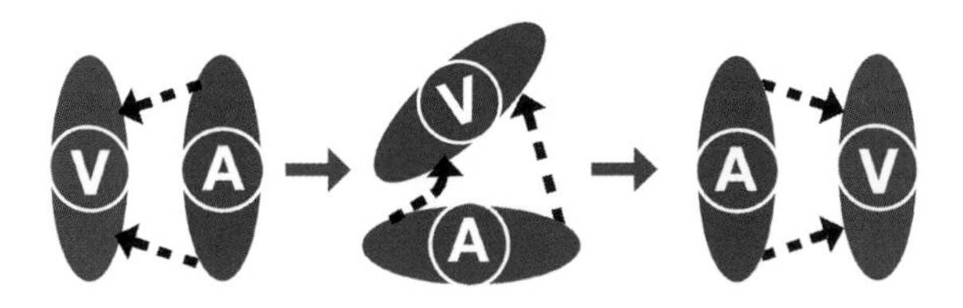

Figure 79: The staging of the two-hand costume pull.

RIGHT: Four stages of the one-hand costume pull.
TOM ZIEBELL

Eye Contact

The performers make eye contact, ensuring their partner is ready. If not, they attract their attention.

Preparation

The attacker grabs the negotiated area of costume with the pulling hand in a relaxed grip. (This ensures that the grip will release if the victim lets go.)

The grip forms a fist, with the front of the knuckles against the victim, wrist aligned with forearm. The victim grabs that forearm, just below the wrist, with both hands, as if to pull free but actually locking the fist into position. They grab with a C clamp grip, fingers on top, thumbs underneath and actively pull the fist towards them. They should not use a hook hand cupped over the top of the arm, as this would encourage them to pull downwards rather than inwards; this would begin to peel the attacker's hand down and their body inwards.

Simultaneously, the attacker hooks a cupped parachute hand behind one of the victim's elbows, thumb pointed vertically up the arm. Primarily it is there as a brake on the victim's momentum at the end of the pull, helping them remain upright, but it also visually engages the attacker's other hand in the violence. It does nothing and is purely cosmetic until it engages at the very end of the technique.

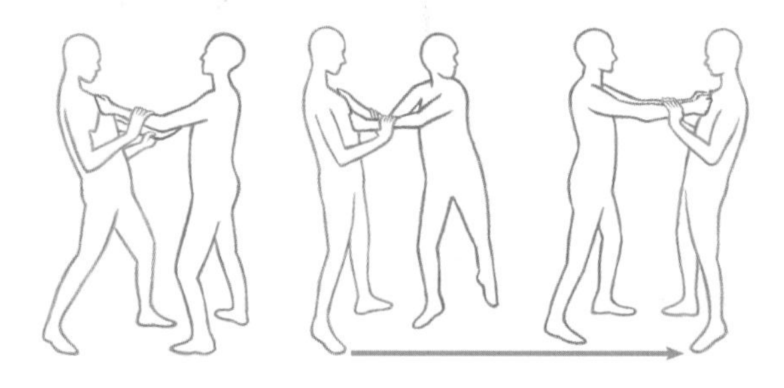

Figure 80: The two-hand costume pull.

Common Errors

Attacker
Angled gripping wrist
Forgets parachute hand
Forgets to look for partner's safety
Forgets to take the second step
Pulls down instead of across

Victim
Fails to lock arms tightly enough
Fails to relax into the pull
Jumps or hops into the pull
Lets go too soon at the end
Loses balance

In the two-hand version, the victim grabs hold of each forearm with one hand. There is of course no parachute hand.

Action

The attacker looks over their shoulder in the direction of the pull, specifically to ensure that the space is safe for the victim. This is a predictive check, not only looking for fixed hazards but also

A flowing image of the one-hand costume pull.
TOM ZIEBELL

checking that no one is about to move into the space. If there is a safety issue, the pull stops at this point.

Their eyes remain on the safe space. They must not look back to the victim, in case the space changes.

They step their foot out of the path of the victim, pivoting their hips and pulling the victim past themselves with energy. Once the victim has passed them, the attacker steps after them with their other foot. If they do not complete the pivot following the victim, the attacker's back will be misaligned while controlling the victim's energy, increasing the risk of injury.

This move does not rely on strength; it is purely a matter of geometry. If the attacker has stepped back and their hips have pivoted, the victim will have no choice but to move.

Reaction

Because the victim has locked their grip, the energy of the pull goes into their arms. They allow themselves to lose balance forwards, be pulled around and then regain their balance. Keeping the arms tight prevents the grip being lost. Jumping forward or tensing completely does not help the illusion. It is more effective to allow the victim to be pulled for real, and for both partners to work together to stay balanced. The attacker's parachute hand engages at this point, actively helping the victim to remain balanced and slow down.

The victim is in control because they can let go of the attacker's arm at any point up until the moment their body is committed to the action. Releasing the arm causes the attacker's relaxed grip to let go and the technique stops.

The victim must not let go after the pull until they have controlled their momentum, otherwise there is a risk of losing balance upon release.

THE HAIR PULL

Works With

All staging.

Safety Principles

- Negotiation: the victim dictates where contact can be made.
- Victim control: they can let go to stop the technique.
- Pull your partner to safety: look before you pull.
- Always pull away from the head.

Position

Partners face each other.

The simple version of this technique is a one-hand hair pull, struggling with the victim, or dragging them slowly through the space, keeping them safe as they move. The more complex version is a fully energized swing through space.

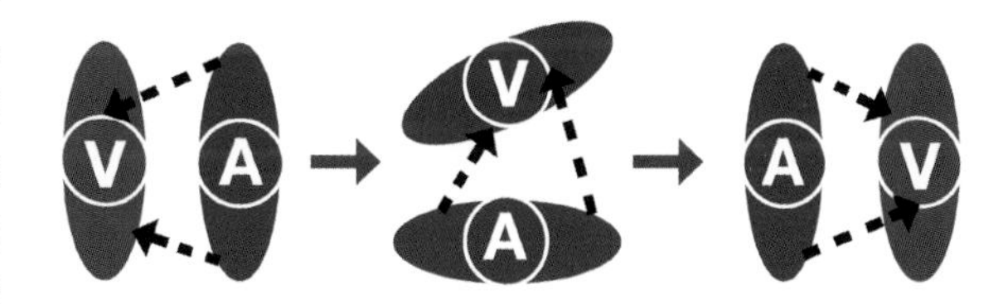

Figure 81: The staging of the hair pull.

Eye Contact

The performers make eye contact, ensuring their partner is ready. If not, they attract their attention.

Preparation

After negotiating the contact, the attacker grabs the victim's hair, allowing it to stick out between their fingers and closing their fist, strengthening the illusion of a real grab. This is a relaxed grip, so that, if the victim lets go, the attacker's hand slides free of the hair without catching. The fist must not be clenched.

The grab can be at the sides, top or back of the hair, but any potential stress in the victim's neck must be monitored as the pull engages. For example, gripping the top of the head encourages a downward pull, forcing the neck to bend, with heightened risk. Gripping the side of the head is less likely to introduce unwanted neck strain if used for a horizontal pull. Avoid the partner's ear and do not grab sideways into the hair, as this increases the risk of rupturing the ear drum. The direction of the grab should move alongside the head, not in towards it.

The victim cups one hand over the attacker's hand, placing the other hand on the forearm in a C clamp grip. It will look as if they are pulling free, but they are actually locking the hand into position by actively squeezing it between their head and hand.

Simultaneously, the attacker hooks a cupped parachute hand behind one of the victim's elbows, thumb pointed vertically up the arm. Primarily, it is there as a brake on the victim's momentum at the end of the pull, helping them remain upright, but it will also visually engage the attacker's other hand in the violence. It does nothing and is purely cosmetic until it engages at the very end of the technique.

There is an old version of this technique that is still often taught, in which a clenched fist is placed on the victim's head, without grabbing any hair, and is locked into position ready for the pull. The question the student should ask is, why use a technique that blatantly looks fake? Why stretch the belief of the audience to breaking point? Surely the remit of the performers is to make each moment look as real as possible – within the bounds of safety.

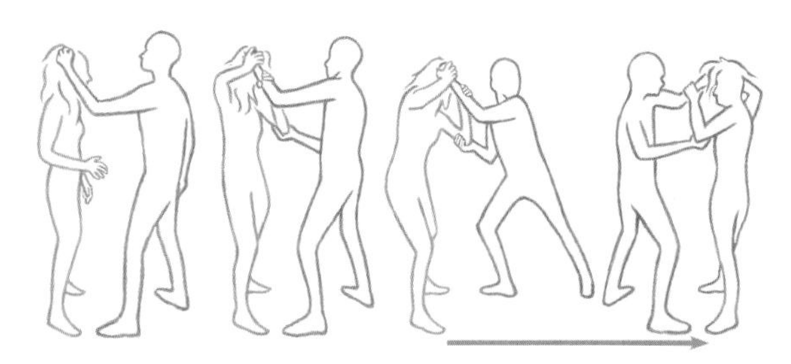

Figure 82: The hair pull.

Action

The attacker looks over their shoulder in the direction of the pull, specifically to ensure that the space

Common Errors

Attacker
Clenching the grip tight
Pushes against head instead of pulling
Forgets parachute hand
Forgets to look for partner's safety
Forgets to take the second step
Pulls down instead of across

Victim
Fails to lock arms tight enough
Fails to relax into the pull
Jumps or hops into the pull
Lets go too soon at the end
Loses balance

is safe for the victim. This is a predictive check, not only looking for fixed hazards, but also checking that no one is about to move into the space. If there is a safety issue, the pull stops at this point.

Their eyes remain on the safe space; they do not look back to the victim, in case the space changes.

They step their foot out of the path of the victim, pivoting their hips and pulling the victim past themselves with energy. Once the victim has passed them, the attacker steps after them with their other foot. If they do not complete the pivot following the victim, the attacker's back is misaligned while controlling the victim's energy, increasing the risk of injury.

Always pull away from the victim's head; never push against it. Pushing removes their ability to withdraw consent by letting go of the attacker's arm, and it risks damaging their neck.

This move does not rely on strength; it is purely a matter of geometry. If the attacker has stepped back and their hips have pivoted, the victim will have no choice but to move.

Reaction

Because the victim has locked their grip, the energy of the pull goes into their arms. They allow themselves to lose balance forwards, be pulled around and regain their balance. Keeping the arms tight prevents the grip being lost. Don't help by jumping forward, or tensing completely as this doesn't help the illusion. It's more effective allowing the victim to be pulled for real, and for both partners to work together to stay balanced. The attacker's parachute hand engages at this point actively helping the victim to remain balanced and slow down.

The victim is in control because they can let go of the attacker's arm at any point up until the moment their body is committed to the action. Releasing the arm causes the attacker's relaxed grip to let go and the technique stops.

The victim must not let go after the pull until they have controlled their momentum, otherwise there's a risk of losing balance upon release.

OPPOSITE RIGHT: Four stages of the hair pull.
TOM ZIEBELL

BELOW: A flowing image of the hair pull.
TOM ZIEBELL

THE EAR PULL

Works With

All staging.

Safety Principles

- Negotiation: the victim dictates where contact can be made.
- Victim control: they can let go to stop the technique.
- Pull your partner to safety: look before you pull.
- Always pull away from the head.

Position

Partners face each other.

The simple version of this technique is a one-hand ear pull, struggling with the victim or dragging them slowly through the space, keeping them safe as they move. The more complex version is a fully energized swing through space.

The technique is used for bald, short-haired or bewigged partners, or when the text specifically calls for an ear pull.

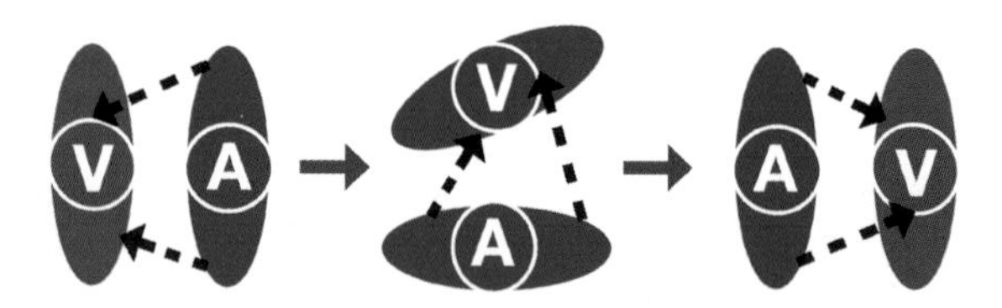

Figure 83: The staging of the ear pull.

Eye Contact

The performers make eye contact, ensuring their partner is ready. If not, they attract their attention.

Preparation

After negotiating the contact, the attacker cups their hand over the attacker's ear. The fingers curl behind the ear, fingernails flat on the mastoid bone, heel of the palm lightly resting on the cheekbone. This is a relaxed grip so that, if the victim lets go, the attacker's hand pulls free of the ear without catching.

The fist should not be clenched tight and the ear should not be really gripped. It is only skin and

cartilage and, given the wrong circumstances, it is possible to tear it. The ear should not be 'boxed' either; clapping the palm over the ear can rupture the eardrum.

The victim cups one hand over the attacker's hand, placing the other hand on the forearm in a C clamp grip, as if pulling free, but actually locking the hand into position by actively squeezing the hand between their head and hand.

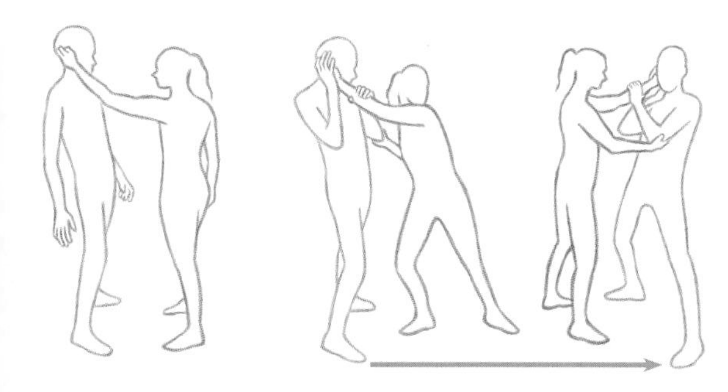

Figure 84: The ear pull.

Simultaneously the attacker hooks a cupped parachute hand behind one of the victim's elbows, thumb pointed vertically up the arm. Primarily it is there as a brake on the victim's momentum at the end of the pull, helping them remain upright. It also visually engages the attacker's other hand in the violence. It does nothing and is purely cosmetic until it engages at the very end of the technique.

Common Errors

Attacker
- Clenches the grip tight
- Pushes against head instead of pulling
- Forgets parachute hand
- Forgets to look for partner's safety
- Forgets to take the second step
- Pulls down instead of across

Victim
- Fails to lock arms tight enough
- Fails to relax into the pull
- Jumps or hops into the pull
- Lets go too soon at the end
- Loses balance

Action

The attacker looks over their shoulder in the direction of the pull, specifically to ensure that the space is safe for the victim. This is a predictive

OPPOSITE RIGHT: Four stages of the ear pull.
TOM ZIEBELL

A flowing image of the ear pull.
TOM ZIEBELL

check, not only looking for fixed hazards, but also checking that no one is about to move into the space. If there is a safety issue, the pull stops at this point.

Their eyes remain on the safe space; they do not look back to the victim, in case the space changes.

They step their foot out of the path of the victim, pivoting their hips and pulling the victim past themselves with energy. Once the victim has passed them, the attacker steps after them with their other foot. If they do not complete the pivot following the victim, the attacker's back is misaligned while controlling the victim's energy, increasing the risk of injury.

The pull should always be away from the victim's head, never pushing against it. Pushing removes the victim's ability to withdraw consent by letting go of the attacker's arm, and it risks damaging their neck. This move does not rely on strength; it is purely a matter of geometry. If the attacker has stepped back and their hips have pivoted, the victim will have no choice but to move.

Reaction

Because the victim has locked their grip, the energy of the pull goes into their arms. They allow themselves to lose balance forwards, be pulled around and regain their balance. Keep the arms tight, to prevent the grip being lost. Jumping forward or tensing completely will not help the illusion. It is more effective to allow the victim to be pulled for real, and for both partners to work together to stay balanced. The attacker's parachute hand engages at this point, actively helping the victim to remain balanced and slow down.

The victim is in control because they can let go of the attacker's arm at any point up until the moment their body is committed to the action. Releasing the arm causes the attacker's relaxed grip to let go and the technique to stop.

The victim must not let go after the pull until they have controlled their momentum, otherwise there is a risk of losing balance upon release.

THE KICK TO THE THIGH (STANDING)

Works With

All staging.

Safety Principles

- Negotiation: the victim dictates where and how hard contact can be made.
- Soft on soft: shoelaces to muscle.
- Withdraw the energy: as soon as contact is made, it bounces back.

In reality, this would be a kick with the toes of a boot to the target; theatrically, this is replaced with shoelaces contact.

Position

The attacker stands beside the victim, facing them, at kicking distance.

It is possible to make contact with both thighs when kicking. So the victim stands with their legs separated, and target leg back. The knee is slightly bent, to absorb the energy of the kick.

The target is the middle of the hamstring at the back of the thigh. The attacker avoids the gluteus because of the risk of hitting the coccyx. The back of the knee should also be avoided, because its structures are relatively fragile and easily damaged.

The victim keeps their nearest hand clear of the target zone. The contact must always be negotiated.

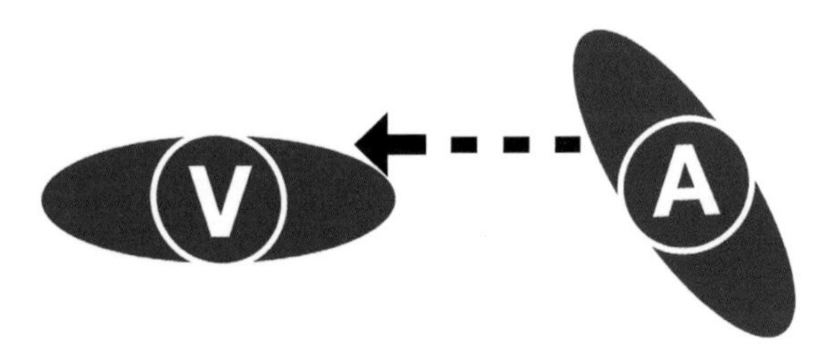

Figure 85: The staging of the kick to the thigh (standing).

OPPOSITE RIGHT: Four stages of the kick to the thigh (standing). TOM ZIEBELL

Common Errors

Attacker
Misjudges the target
Misjudges the energy of the contact
Misjudges the distance
Angles the foot down

Victim
Fails to leave enough distance between legs
Locks the knee back
Leaves the hand too close

Figure 86: The kick to the thigh (standing).

Eye Contact

The performers make eye contact, ensuring their partner is ready. If not, they attract their attention.

Preparation

The attacker pivots 90 degrees on their standing foot as they lift their knee horizontal, parallel to the ground, foot pointed.

Action

The attacker snaps the kick to the target, making negotiated contact with the shoelaces to the middle of the hamstring, then retracts the foot. The kick finishes where it started: stepping forward on to the descending foot increases the risk of accidental contact. The attacker must remain balanced throughout.

A flowing image of the kick to the thigh (standing).
TOM ZIEBELL

The foot should be horizontal: if the toes point downwards there is a risk of contact with the back of the knee.

This contact should always start light, gradually increasing until the victim confirms the level. As soon as contact is made, the foot withdraws, so there is minimal energy in the contact, but a clear knap.

Reaction

The victim bends the knee of the target leg, absorbing the energy of the kick. The ripple of energy moves through the entire body. It is possible to react to the ground, but care must be taken to protect the knees.

THE KICK TO THE THIGH (LYING DOWN)

Works With

All staging.

Safety Principles

- Negotiation: the victim dictates where and how hard contact can be made.
- Soft on soft: shoelaces to muscle.
- Withdraw the energy: as soon as contact is made, it bounces back.

In reality, this would be a kick with the toes of a boot to the target; theatrically, this is replaced with shoelaces contact.

Position

The victim lies on their side on the ground. The heel of the bottom leg is just under the knee of the top (target) leg, lifting that thigh off the ground. The target leg is slightly bent. The attacker stands behind the victim, where the angle of their kick is perpendicular to the target centre.

The attacker must be close to the victim, so that on impact the toes are pointing almost directly straight down from the knee. The further back they stand, the more the toes end up pointing under the thigh, increasing the risk of kicking a non-target area.

The target is the middle of the back of the thigh. The attacker avoids the gluteus because of the

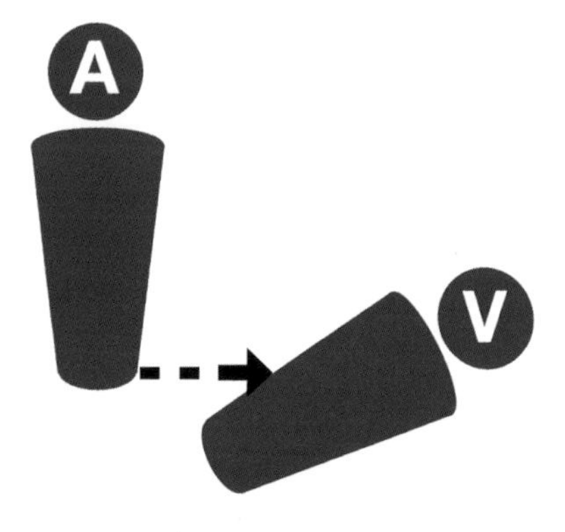

Figure 87: The staging of the kick to the thigh (lying down).

Common Errors

Attacker
Misjudges the target
Misjudges the energy of the contact
Misjudges the distance
Gets the angle of the kick wrong

Victim
Fails to leave enough distance between legs
Sticks bottom heel too far through
Locks the knee back

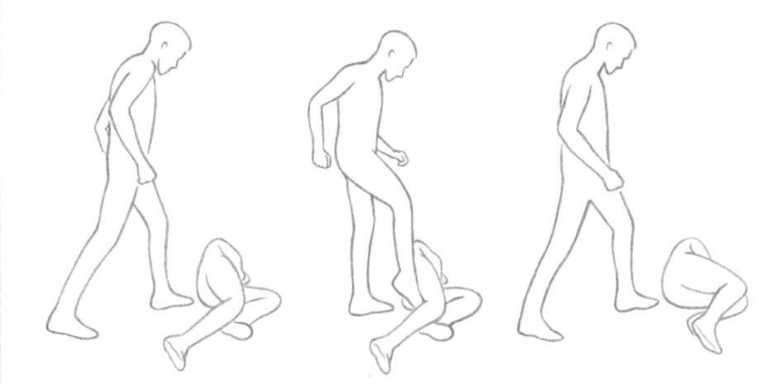

Figure 88: The kick to the thigh (lying down).

RIGHT: Four stages of the kick to the thigh (lying down).
TOM ZIEBELL

risk of hitting the coccyx, and the back of the knee because the structures there are easily damaged. The contact must always be negotiated.

Eye Contact

The performers make eye contact if possible, ensuring their partner is ready. If it's not possible they give a vocal cue.

Preparation

The attacker pulls their foot back, pointing their toes down.

Action

The attacker kicks the target, making negotiated contact with shoelaces to the middle of the hamstring, toes pointing down. The foot is then retracted and finishes in the starting position. The attacker must remain balanced throughout.

A flowing image of the kick to the thigh (lying down).
TOM ZIEBELL

This contact should always start light, gradually increasing until the victim confirms the level. As soon as contact is made, the foot withdraws, so there is minimal energy in the contact, but a clear knap. Because the hamstring is not load-bearing in this position, and therefore relaxed, the knap is usually louder.

Reaction

The victim bends the knee, pulling away from the kick, with appropriate pain reaction. They need to keep the muscle relaxed for the contact.

THE KNEE TO THE STOMACH

Works With

All staging.

Safety Principles

- Negotiation: the victim dictates where and how hard contact can be made.
- Soft on soft: thigh muscle to abdominals.
- Withdraw the energy: as soon as contact is made, it bounces back.

In reality, the knee would drive at speed into the abdominals. Because the knee is hard, it is replaced with a thigh contact.

Position

The attacker steps to the victim, placing their standing foot right next to the victim's foot. This ensures that, when the thigh is laid across the target, the dangerous knee is on the edge, or outside the line of the victim's body.

The target is the abdominals: the victim tells the attacker exactly where.

The victim's nearest hand must be kept clear of the target zone. So the attacker manages this arm by, in the most basic version, lifting it out of the way. In choreography this might be worked from a blocked punch or a disrupted costume grab.

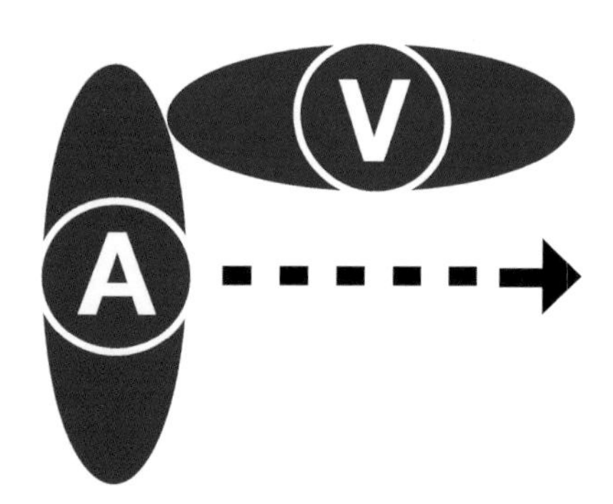

Figure 89: The staging of the knee to the stomach.

Eye Contact

The attacker makes eye contact, ensuring their partner is ready. If not, they attract their attention.

Preparation

The victim tightens their abdominals.

The attacker steps their foot right next to the victim's foot, heel to toe. If the feet are not aligned but have distance, front–back or sideways, it affects the balance and safe position of the attacker. Stepping in, they lift the victim's arm up, one hand on the shoulder, one on the forearm. They should take care not to lift the arm out to the victim's side, as there will be a risk of damaging the shoulder in their reaction to the attack.

The attacker lifts their thigh horizontal, parallel to the ground, heel pulled back towards the glutes. This ensures the thigh muscle rather than the knee reaches the target. This preparation flows directly into the action without pause.

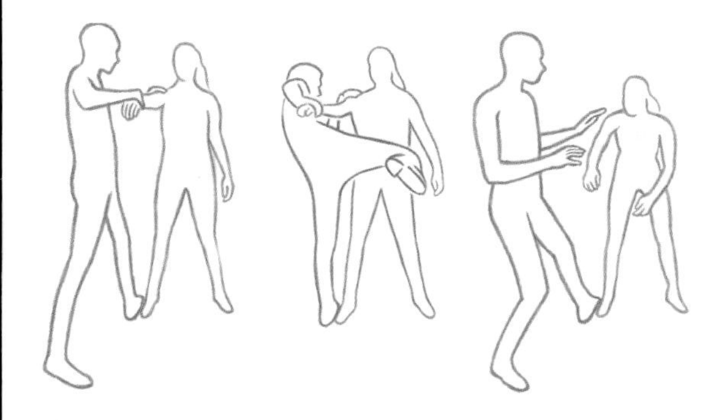

Figure 90: The knee to the stomach.

RIGHT: Four stages of the knee to the stomach.
TOM ZIEBELL

Action

The attacker pulses their hip forwards, making negotiated contact with the front of their thigh to the negotiated target, then withdraws back to the starting position. This initially feels awkward, but it is worth persevering. It has been described as a pelvic thrust, or a thigh bump. It is designed specifically to inhibit the brain from following its instinctive reaction to jerk the knee forwards, accidentally kneeing the victim for real.

The thigh lifts and rotates so the front moves horizontally towards the target. It might help to imagine lifting it up and over a table. If the attacker leaves their foot hanging down, making contact with the

Common Errors

Attacker
Stands in the wrong place
Makes contact with the knee
Foot dangling, not horizontal
Misjudges the energy of the contact
Gets the angle of the thigh wrong

Victim
Fails to tighten the abdominals
Reacts too early

inside of the thigh, the visual story-telling is poor, and there's a risk the foot hits the victim's knee.

The thigh must be horizontal, not diagonal, or there is a risk of hitting the hipbone or groin. If the target is too high, the attacker can lift up onto the ball of their foot, increasing their reach.

If the knee is used instead of the thigh, the contact is concentrated in a smaller area, increasing the impact and the risk to ribs if it is mis-targeted.

There is no pull: the attacker lifts their thigh, but does not pull the victim on to it.

Reaction

The victim's stomach moves back, chest dropping, face up. There is no knap; it is replaced with an explosive vocal knap. Keep hands clear of the target zone until the thigh has retracted. Do not bend fully over bringing the face close to the target, as this will increase the risk of being hit.

The reaction must be timed to the action: if it is early there is a risk the thigh will make contact with the base of the victim's rib cage, with a heightened possibility of injury.

A flowing image of the knee to the stomach.
TOM ZIEBELL

THE HOLLOW-FIST STOMACH PUNCH

Works With

All staging.

Safety Principles

- Negotiation: the victim dictates where and how hard contact can be made.
- Soft on soft: hollow fist to muscle.
- Withdraw the energy: as soon as contact is made, it bounces back.

In reality, a hard fist is driven at speed into the stomach. To avoid injury in a theatrical context, the hard fist relaxes into a hollow fist, which is completely soft.

Position

To line the fist on the victim's centreline, the attacker stands in distance, in front, but angled slightly to one side.

The target is the abdominals: the victim tells the attacker exactly where.

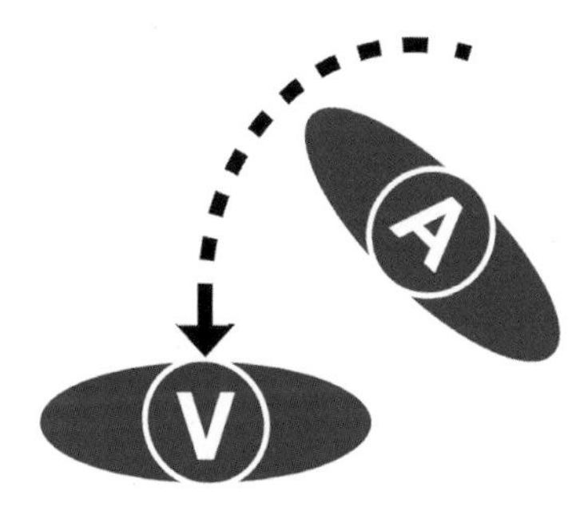

Figure 91: The staging of the hollow-fist stomach punch.

RIGHT: Four stages of the hollow-fist stomach punch.
TOM ZIEBELL

Eye Contact

The attacker makes eye contact, ensuring their partner is ready. If not, they attract their attention, before shifting their focus to the target.

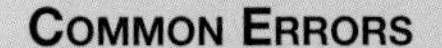

Preparation

The victim tightens their abdominals.

The attacker prepares a relaxed fist at the height of the target, rotating their hip slightly back. The wrist aligns with the forearm, to avoid injury from a hard contact. If there is any tension in the hand, there is a risk that the punch will hurt.

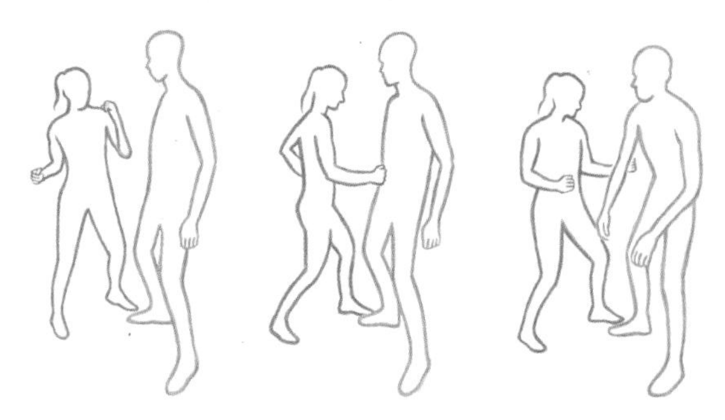

Figure 92: The hollow-fist stomach punch.

Action

The attacker rotates their hip forwards delivering the fist, making negotiated contact with the negotiated target, then withdraws. The more relaxed the fist and the briefer the contact, the clearer the knap.

The wrist is aligned with the forearm. The brain can be fooled by the rotation of the hip, and it will bend the wrist slightly. If hard contact is made with a bent wrist, there is a risk of it fracturing. Trust the rotation will place the fist dead centre of the target; keep the arm and fist in a straight line as they move.

Do not roll the shoulder or duck the head when punching, as this will increase the risk of accidental contact between heads and shoulders on both sides. Keep them relaxed back while punching.

It is possible to punch with a piston arm only, without engaging the body, but it does not look as powerful or as aggressive.

Common Errors

Attacker

Not relaxing the fist
Wrist bent when punching
Misjudging the target and the contact
Piston punching, not engaging the hips
Leaning in

Victim

Bending over as they react
Vocal knap lacking clarity
Mistiming the reaction

Reaction

The stomach pulls back, the chest collapses slightly and the head only drops slightly. The instinct is to fold over, head down, but dropping the face into the target zone greatly increases the risk of contact. The victim must be aware of the attacker's shoulder and avoid head-butting it accidentally.

The explosive vocal reaction is dictated by the reality of an abdominal strike, combined with specific pain, the emotional response to it and the technical needs of the auditorium.

A flowing image of the hollow-fist stomach punch.
TOM ZIEBELL

THE FLICK-HAND STOMACH PUNCH

Works For

Proscenium arch staging.

Safety Principles

- Negotiation: the victim dictates where and how hard contact can be made.
- Soft on soft: open hand to muscle.
- Withdraw the energy: as soon as contact is made, it bounces back.

Unlike other contact techniques, this one has something to hide. It is primarily an upstage/downstage technique, although it can be performed in profile if the attacker has fast hands. It is designed specifically to produce a sharper knap.

In reality, a hard fist is driven at speed into the stomach. To avoid injury in a theatrical context, the hard fist relaxes into a hollow fist, flicking open at the moment of contact.

This technique is 'old school' and, in the eyes of many practitioners, has been entirely superseded by the hollow-fist contact punch. However, it is still commonly encountered in the profession and therefore worth explaining.

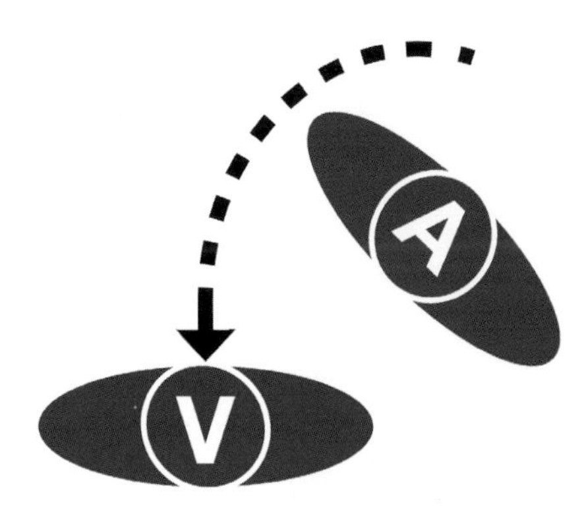

Figure 93: The staging of the flick-hand stomach punch.

RIGHT: Four stages of the flick-hand stomach punch.
TOM ZIEBELL

Position

The victim is downstage, masking the knap with the attacker upstage. It can be performed in profile, with the back of the attacker's fist towards the audience, but this requires a very fast knap to trick the audience.

To line the fist on the victim's centreline, the attacker stands in distance, in front, but angled slightly to one side.

The target is the abdominals: the victim tells the attacker exactly where.

Eye Contact

The attacker makes eye contact, ensuring their partner is ready. If not, they attract their attention, before shifting their focus to the target.

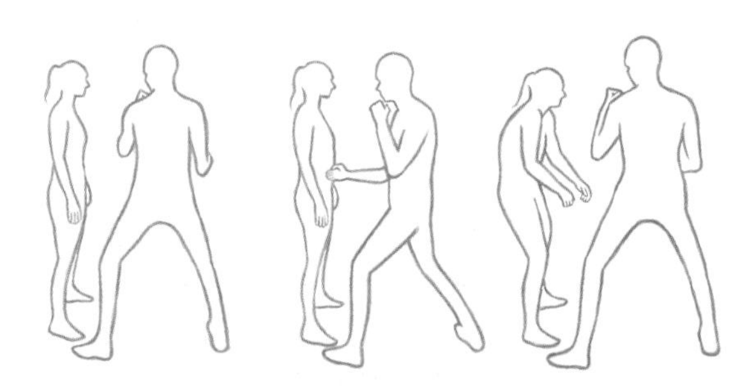

Figure 94: The flick-hand stomach punch.

Common Errors

Attacker

Not relaxing the fist
Wrist bent when punching
Knapping too slow
Knapping with the whole hand
Misjudging the target and the contact
Piston punching, not engaging the hips
Leaning in

Victim

Bending over in the reaction
Vocal knap lacking clarity
Mistiming the reaction

Preparation

The victim tightens their abdominals.

The attacker prepares a relaxed fist at the height of the target, rotating their hip slightly back. The wrist aligns with the forearm, to avoid injury from a hard contact. If there is any tension in the hand, there is a risk that the punch will hurt.

Action

The attacker rotates their hip forwards delivering the fist, making a negotiated contact with the negotiated target. At the moment of impact, the fist

A flowing image of the flick-hand stomach punch.
TOM ZIEBELL

opens and the fingers flick against the target, making a sharp knap, before closing and withdrawing. This knap only works if it is fast and light. For a brief moment, the fingers and the palm are at right-angles to each other. Do not bend the wrist, slapping with the back of the whole hand. At speed, this could break the wrist.

The wrist must still be aligned with the forearm. The brain can be fooled by the rotation of the hip, and it will bend the wrist slightly. If hard contact is made with a bent wrist, there is a risk of it fracturing. Trust the rotation will place the fist dead centre of the target and keep the arm and fist in a straight line as they move.

Do not roll the shoulder or duck the head when punching, as it risks accidental contact between heads and shoulders on both sides. Keep them relaxed back while punching.

It is possible to punch with a piston arm only, without engaging the body, but it does not look as powerful or as aggressive.

Reaction

The stomach pulls back, the chest collapses slightly and the head stays up. The instinct is to fold over, head down, but dropping the face into the target zone will greatly increase the risk of contact. The victim must also avoid head-butting the attacker's shoulder.

This knap stings more than a contact punch with a hollow fist.

The reality of an abdominal strike, combined with specific pain, the emotional response to it and the technical needs of the auditorium, dictate the explosive vocal reaction.

THE OPEN-PALM STRIKE TO THE STOMACH

Works For

Proscenium arch staging in mid-sized performance spaces.

Safety Principles

- Negotiation: the victim dictates where and how hard contact can be made.
- Soft on soft: open palm to muscle.
- Withdraw the energy: as soon as contact is made, it bounces back.
- Red light/green light: partner begins to avoid before the roundhouse punch is released.

This is another contact technique that has something to hide. It is an upstage/downstage technique creating the illusion of driving a fist into someone's stomach, usually whilst the victim attempts an attack. It is therefore an action into an interrupted action.

Position

The victim is downstage, with the attacker upstage, masking the shared knap.

The target is the abdominals: the victim tells the attacker exactly where.

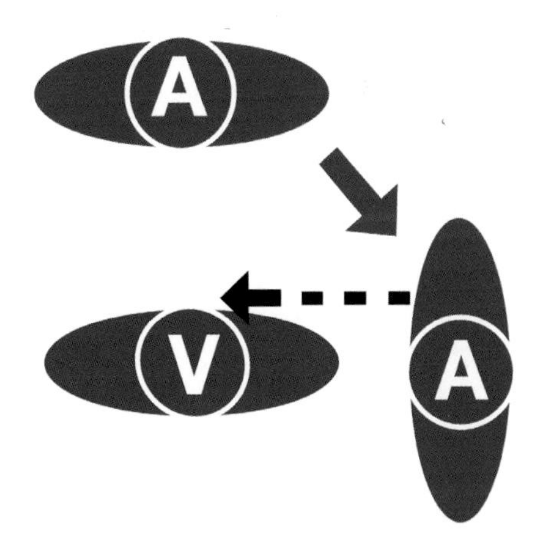

Figure 95: The staging of the open-palm strike to the stomach.

Eye Contact
They make eye contact, ensuring each partner is ready. If not, they attract their attention, before both shifting their focus to their target.

Preparation
The victim tightens their abdominals while making the preparation for a roundhouse punch, stepping forward on the opposite foot and lifting their fist (*see* Chapter 14). As soon as the attacker begins to avoid (green light), the victim releases the punch, stepping forward on the same side so that at the moment the attacker hits them their hips face forward, presenting a clear target.

The attacker prepares a hollow fist at target height.

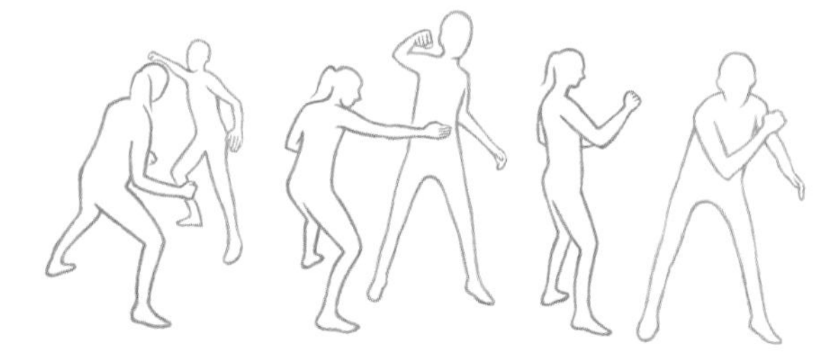

Figure 96: The open-palm strike to the stomach.

Action
Just before the victim finishes their roundhouse preparation, the attacker begins a bob and weave avoidance (*see* Chapter 14, for more detail). The avoidance moves on a forward diagonal so the attacker ends up beside the victim as they complete their step, at extended arm's length. As they avoid, their fist moves towards the victim's stomach. As soon as it is masked, it opens into a horizontal palm and claps it in a negotiated contact to the negotiated target, immediately withdrawing, closing the fist, pulling back into view. (Some practitioners prefer to strike with the palm side of a soft closed fist, finding it stings less. As with all techniques, personal preference plays a major role, as long as it does not compromise safety.)

On impact, the attacker's body needs to be beside and slightly facing the victim, to avoid

Common Errors

Attacker
Avoiding too close to the victim
Wrist bent as it claps the stomach
Misjudging the target and the contact
Misaligning the arm

Victim
Over-rotating the hips
Bending over in reaction
Vocal knap lacking clarity
Mistiming the reaction

stressing their shoulder joint. That shoulder must not be further downstage than the victim's stomach, as the potential for injury to the joint is high. The wrist, elbow and shoulder joints need to be aligned: if the hand is ahead, the wrist will bend back at the moment of impact, with a concomitant risk of injury. The hand must not 'claw' across the victim's abdominals, as this will risk leaving welts or detaching fingernails.

The palm claps, bounces back and closes, then retracts towards the attacker.

Reaction

The victim's fist finishes the path of their missed punch, and they keep their hips facing forward. If the hips rotate, there is a chance that the contact will happen on the wrong target, with an increased risk of injury. In their reaction to the contact their hips can add a little rotation to complete that visual story.

The stomach pulls back, the chest collapses slightly and the head stays up. The instinct is to fold over, head down, but dropping the face into the target zone increases the risk of contact.

The explosive vocal reaction is dictated by the reality of an abdominal strike, combined with specific pain, the emotional response to it and the technical needs of the auditorium.

OPPOSITE RIGHT: Four stages of the open-palm strike to the stomach.
TOM ZIEBELL

A flowing image of the open-palm strike to the stomach.
TOM ZIEBELL

BLOCKS

Work For

All staging.

Safety Principles

- Negotiation: the victim dictates where and how hard contact can be made.
- Soft on soft: presenting the softest parts of the arm or hand.

In reality, the impact from blocking a fast punch can be hard. Indeed, many blocks actively attack the punching arm, disrupting the punch and causing injury. The following theatrical blocks present the softest areas of the arms, in order to minimize that impact.

Position

The partners face each other in position to punch. Blocks are used with the various parrot punches, usually linked to an avoidance. The blocker's head should move away from the punch as they block, and usually the entire body shifts away, which will also reduce the potential impact.

The blocker knows the path of the punch and calculates where the block needs to be for the lightest of contacts, as their body steps off the line of the attack. The punching arm and block briefly co-exist in space beside each other. There

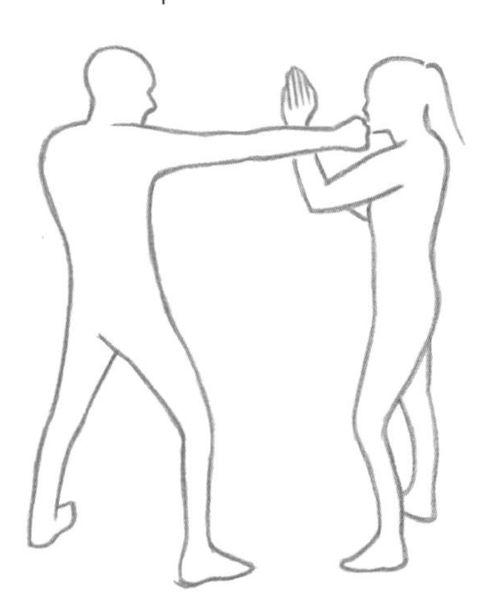

Figure 97: The same-side block.

is absolutely no need for heavy contacts; all these do is cause cumulative injury.

Blocks are made with relaxed arms, on either the outside or the inside of the attacker's forearm. Avoid the sides presenting the blade edges of the bones. The cupped palm is useful for blocks, but care must be taken to ensure that the thumb is always tucked to the side, to prevent a sprain or break.

These blocks do not beat through the attack. The same-side and the crash block meet the attack and stop. They are in opposition, and there is no attempt to deflect the attack. The across-the-body block can be in opposition, or can be an elliptical deflection, setting it up for the brush and replace.

All these blocks are described from a position inside the attack, so any contact is on the inside of the attacker's forearm. They can all be used on the outside of the attacker's forearm. In this case, care must be taken to avoid the joints of the arm, making contact instead on the muscled areas.

Eye Contact

The blocker makes eye contact, ensuring their partner is ready. If not, they attract their attention, before shifting their focus to the target zone.

Preparation

A block preparation is usually linked to the avoidance of an attack. This begins before the end of the attacker's preparation, so they do not have to wait at the red light before attacking. During the avoidance the block will begin to move, finishing just as the avoidance completes. Like a sword parry, the block usually crosses the blocker's centreline so that it's always deflecting out. This reduces the risk of jamming the fingers caused by lifting the block straight up.

The contact must be as light as possible. The area of contact is the muscle of the puncher's forearm, avoiding the wrist and elbow.

Action: Same-Side Block

The arm on the side of the attack lifts in a semicircular action, presenting the back of the forearm

A flowing image of the same-side block.
TOM ZIEBELL

OPPOSITE RIGHT: Four stages of the same-side block.
TOM ZIEBELL

or the cupped palm to the punching arm. If the palm is presented, the fingers and thumb must be tight together: a relaxed hand puts the individual fingers at risk. The move finishes beside the attacker's arm, placing the block just on the edge of the target zone.

Action: Across-the-Body Block

The arm on the opposite side of the incoming attack pushes across the blocker's centre, palm cupped, thumb tucked to the side. The block is placed on the edge of the target zone and light contact is made with the attacker's forearm. Do not fully extend the blocking arm, but aim for the

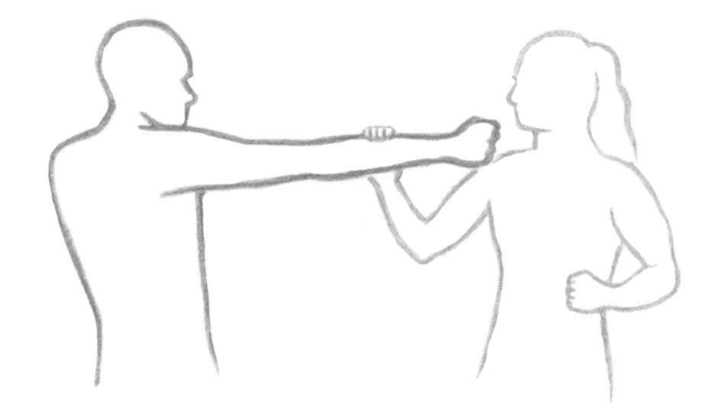

Figure 98: The across-the-body block.

A flowing image of the across-the-body block.
TOM ZIEBELL

RIGHT: Four stages of the across-the-body block.
TOM ZIEBELL

softest of contacts. Because of the cupped palm, it is possible there will be an audible knap: always check that the contact is not too hard. This block can be used as an opposition or as an elliptical deflection of the attack.

Action: Brush and Replace

This is a combination block, beginning with an across-the-body block followed by a same-side block. Unlike the single versions described above, in this version both hands brush along the punching arm rather than meeting it. The across-the-body block makes contact close to the elbow, brushing down the forearm in an elliptical deflection, before being replaced by the same-side block, repeating the same action and path. The

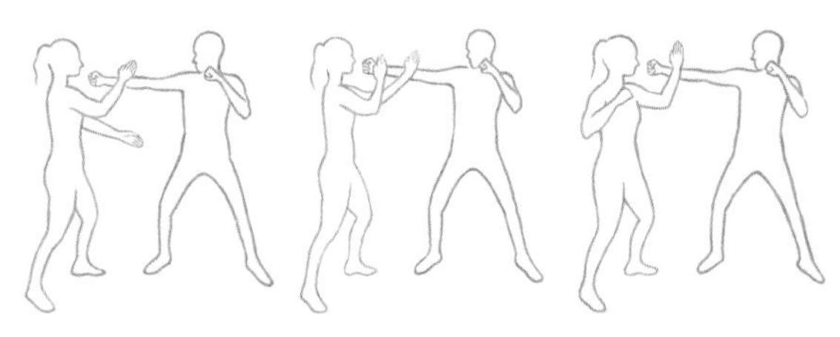

Figure 99: The brush and replace block.

A flowing image of the brush and replace block.
TOM ZIEBELL

RIGHT: Four stages of the brush and replace block.
TOM ZIEBELL

first block brushes the arm, releasing to become an attack preparation as it is replaced by the second block, which remains in contact.

Action: Crash Block

This block uses both hands or arms, together side by side. The back of the forearms or the cupped palms are placed between target and attack. The contact is always light and care is taken to keep fingers and thumbs together. As the block is made, the blocker steps in beside the attack before it gains power. It must be carefully choreographed

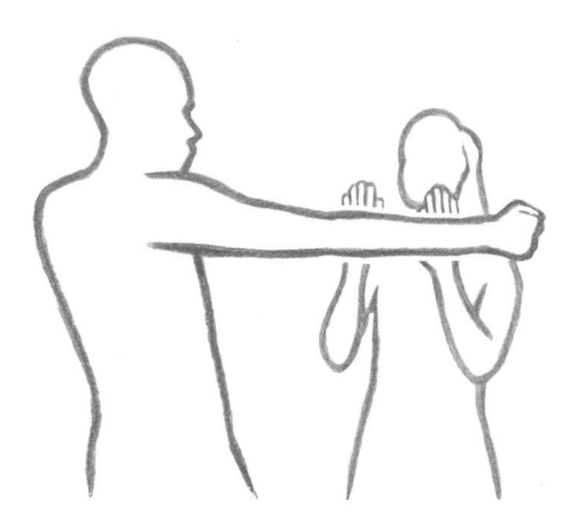

Figure 100: The crash block.

Common Errors

Blocker
Contact too hard
Pushing through the attack
Thumb sticking out
Brush and replace in the wrong order

A flowing image of the crash block.
TOM ZIEBELL

RIGHT: Four stages of the crash block.
TOM ZIEBELL

to avoid an accidental collision between the two performers. Contact is made with one hand on the upper arm, the other on the forearm, or with both hands on the forearm. The blocker avoids contact with the attacker's joints, reducing the risk of injury.

THE KICK TO THE GROIN

Works With

All staging.

Safety Principles

- Negotiation: the victim dictates where and how hard contact can be made.
- Soft on soft: shoelaces to gluteus.
- Withdraw the energy: as soon as contact is made it bounces back.
- Displace the target: the groin is replaced by the gluteus maximus.

In reality, the kick would drive at speed into the groin. For obvious reasons, this target is replaced by negotiated contact to the gluteus. Psychologically, this can be as difficult for the attacker as the victim, but starting slowly is the key to overcoming trepidation.

Position

The attacker stands before the victim, slightly offset, depending on the angle of the kick. The target is the gluteus (buttock): the victim tells the attacker exactly where to make contact. Kicking with the right foot, the target is the victim's right gluteus, and vice versa if using the left foot.

The target can be one gluteus or the other, depending on the physique of the victim and their

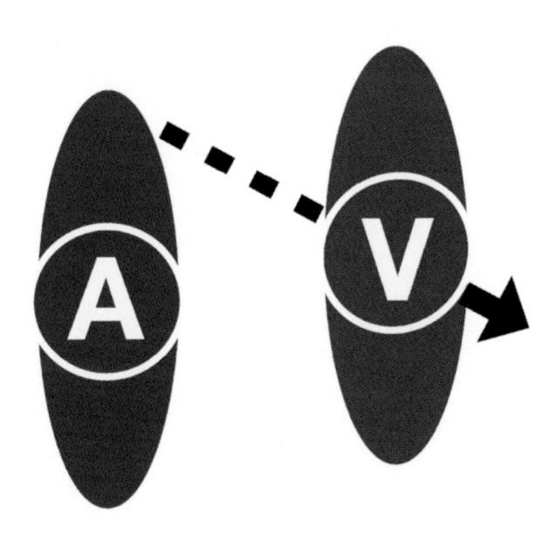

Figure 101: The staging of the kick to the groin.

RIGHT: Four stages of the kick to the groin.
TOM ZIEBELL

comfort. There is always the slight possibility of coccyx contact, but this depends on the individual's unique physicality. If there is any cause for concern, the kick is angled more to one side.

The obvious risk with this move is accidental contact with the groin, with the consequent pain. The pain is not gender-specific; the injury is equally uncomfortable for everyone. The adjustment of the pelvis (*see* below) greatly reduces that hazard. There is also much less chance of accidental contact if the attacker is shorter than the victim. If they are taller, the angle of the shin when extended increases the possibility of contact. The height difference can be mitigated by the attacker slightly bending the standing leg as they kick.

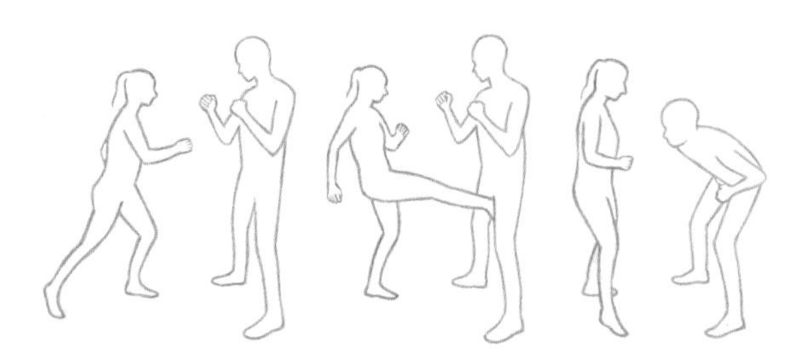

Figure 102: The kick to the groin.

Common Errors

Attacker
Misjudges the distance
Misjudges the target
Forgets to point the toes
Bends the leg as they kick

Victim
Does not step wide enough
Fails to tilt the pelvis up
Fails to tighten the glutes
Reacts too early

Eye Contact

The blocker makes eye contact, ensuring their partner is ready. If not, they attract their attention, before shifting their focus to the target zone.

Preparation

The victim takes a wide stance, giving clear access to the target. Tightening their glutes, actively tipping the bowl of the pelvis forward and up, they lift the most sensitive area clear of the attack.

The attacker steps their foot back, preparing for a swing kick. A snap kick creates a

A flowing image of the kick to the groin.
TOM ZIEBELL

heightened risk of groin contact; the lifting knee can angle the shin, rather than flattening it out. The flatter, extended leg of the swing kick reduces this hazard.

Action

The attacker swings their foot up between the victim's legs, foot flat, making negotiated contact with shoelaces to the negotiated target, the victim's gluteus. The foot immediately drops back to a balanced stance. The leg is straight when contact is made.

This contact negotiation always starts slow and light, gradually increasing until the victim confirms the level. Upon contact, the foot immediately withdraws, using only enough energy to create a clear knap. Because this target is close to easily damaged areas of the body, extreme care must be taken to target accurately. Partners must check in constantly for victim feedback on targeting and intensity.

The attacker must not bend the knee when they kick, because this will raise the angle of the shin, increasing the risk of painful contact.

Reaction

The victim's body lifts up slightly, hands dropping to their groin, legs clamping closed, as they collapse in a safe, choreographed descent. They must ensure that the attacker's foot has cleared before closing the legs.

It is not necessary to drop hard and fast. Often, pain is so overwhelming that it causes a slow, controlled subsidence.

The vocal response chosen reflects the intensity of the attack and the area attacked.

18
THE ILLUSION OF FALLING

WHY AND WHEN

The guidelines about how to use this book – as a reference during or after a stage combat course, and *not* as a substitute for having an instructor in the room – are particularly relevant when looking at techniques for falling. If they are explored outside of a supervised class environment, extreme care must be taken.

The reality is that, for the human animal, falling over is both frightening and dangerous. It is an unpredictable event in which they have lost control of their immediate future, and consequences can range from comic to tragic. Falling on stage can result in career-altering injury and must be approached with both technique and caution.

The fall is a moment when balance is lost and gravity takes control. Injury can occur because there is only a very brief moment when the body has time to prepare and redirect the energy of the fall before impact. Of the many positions the body can adopt, there are very few that actively protect against injury. Many performers are wary of falls due to previous experience or lack of experience. The following techniques were developed in response to the need to get performers safely to the ground repeatedly, without incurring injury.

These are not the same as the many extant martial arts techniques, which were developed to minimize the impact of real falls, or to redirect a fall into an opportunity in a fight situation. Neither is appropriate in a theatrical context. For the former, the performer wants to feel no impact at all. For the latter, a character usually has to look as if they have lost control and drop; it is less likely that they will need to appear to have ninja skills.

SAFETY

Falling on stage should always be a controlled descent, or the illusion of a fall. It is a structured technique that allows the performer to control every step of the journey from standing to lying prone. Momentary loss of control is a moment of increased risk.

The importance of safety is fundamental in stage combat, but the focus must be even sharper with controlled descents. There are a number of principles that are relevant in this context; these are discussed in detail below.

Body Close to the Ground

The body needs to be as close to the ground as possible before it is committed to the descent. The ground can seem a long way away when standing and this may be a psychological barrier for many performers. It will be less scary if they are closer to the ground. These techniques are designed to get the body lower in a controlled manner, before they have to get right down.

Taking the Energy Along the Ground

The energy must be taken along the ground, not into the ground. It may help to imagine a plane landing on a runway. It makes a gradual descent before making contact with the ground, then continuing to move along. It does not drop at a steep angle, hitting almost perpendicular to the ground, with all the energy crashing to an immediate stop. The shallower the performer's angle of descent, the less significant the impact will be and the easier it will be to control.

Soft on Soft

Contact with the ground is made with areas of muscle, or areas that can be structured to absorb impact safely. Areas of bone should be avoided. Large areas of muscle have a cushioning effect on the impact, reducing the chance of injury. With the front descent, the initial contact is with the hands, so these create a shape that acts in the same way as a crumple zone in a car. Bones are not designed to be load-bearing in all directions, and even a controlled descent can cause damage if energy enters the bone at an angle that it is not designed to withstand.

Protecting the Fragile Areas of the Body

Certain areas of the body are more prone to damage than others. Special attention must be paid to the face, the back of the head, the spine, the coccyx, the elbows, the wrists and the knees. These techniques are variously designed to specifically direct impact and energy away from these areas.

Fall to Safety

The performer takes responsibility for checking the area within which they are about to descend. This may mean creating moments when they can look back if it is a big step descent. If they assume it is safe to release the technique without checking, they greatly increase their risk of injury.

Exhale

When breath is held, the body tenses. When a tense body hits the ground, there is an increased risk of sprain, strain, fracture or dislocation. When breath is exhaled, the body relaxes; a relaxed body is less likely to be injured on impact with the ground. This may explain why the very drunk and the very young are so good at falling over without hurting themselves too badly.

WHAT WORKS?

These descents work in any orientation; the tricks that are hidden from the audience are internal to the technique and thus invisible. The following techniques are the basics, which are then customized to the individual. Each performer's physicality and flexibility are different, requiring adjustments to the line or angle of the techniques. Bones more or less protuberant in different areas, varying core mobility, and former or current injuries, all have an impact on the performer's application of soft on soft safety. Adjustments can only really be made with the help of a good teacher or fight director.

How to learn these techniques? The perennial question is, should the student start on mats and graduate to the floor, or learn directly on the floor? There are differing schools of thought, but these techniques are designed for contact with the ground and, as long as they are worked slowly and technically in the initial phase, there should be no real issues with impact. The complication with using mats is that it can introduce an intermediate step, whereby the student gains facility with the technique and speeds up, then still has to come to grips with the unpadded floor, but with a physical instrument that has just been tuned to a faster pace.

THE BIG STEP DESCENT (OR THE ILLUSION OF FALLING BACKWARDS)

Works With

All staging.

Safety Principles

- Get close to the ground.
- Energy along the ground.
- Soft on soft.
- Protect fragile areas of the body.
- Fall to safety.
- Exhale.

The learning process for this technique can be linear, as below, or can start in the middle then go back to the beginning. It depends on the preferences of the teacher or student. Some performers respond well to beginning flat, exploring contact with the floor and working out the soft on soft options, before concentrating on managing their flow of energy to the ground.

Position

Works in any orientation. It must be positioned so that the performer is descending into a safe zone, avoiding hazards. This means that it is always rehearsed slowly to begin with.

Figure 103: The big step descent.

RIGHT: Four stages of the big step descent.
TOM ZIEBELL

Common Errors

Victim
Not stepping back far enough
Not leaning forward enough to counter-balance
Putting the hands down
Sitting on the coccyx
Rolling back on the spine
Not tucking the chin down to protect the head
Holding the breath

The most common injury associated with falling over is a fractured wrist. Attempting to break a fall with the hands is an instinctive reaction. At the moment of impact, roughly 80 per cent of the body's weight is briefly concentrated through the wrists, which are not designed to be load-bearing. This technique keeps the hands forward, as if they are holding something in them, attempting to break the body's instinctive desire to put them down at the moment of contact.

Check the Space

The performers check the space they will descend into before proceeding. This is a predictive check, not only looking for fixed hazards, but also making sure that no one is about to move into the space. If there is any safety issue, the descent stops at this point.

BELOW: A flowing image of the big step descent.
TOM ZIEBELL

Technique Breakdown

- Take a step back: if this step is too small, the performer reaches a point where they lose their balance early and drop with a bump. If the step is too far back, they will not be able to shift their pelvis back behind their heel. It should be a comfortably large step that enables them to sit back behind their heel.
- Counter-balance forwards: the performer starts sitting back, imagining a stool behind their back heel. To avoid losing their balance early, and landing with a bump, they lean forwards at the waist, with the hands reaching forwards as if grasping for help. The more they lean as they sit, the closer they can get to the ground whilst remaining balanced. Counter-balancing allows the angle of descent to be as shallow as possible all the way down. Some performers find it useful to imagine trying to kiss their bent knee.
- Sit on the side of the straight leg: the majority of performers find it easiest sitting on the gluteus on the same side as the straight leg, as it is slightly closer to the ground. Whichever side they sit on, the contact should be as light as possible under the principle of taking energy along the ground. They should not sit directly on the base of the spine, as the coccyx is easily damaged. The action of sitting on one gluteus lifts the other side off the ground, ensuring it is possible to roll out avoiding the spine.
- Roll out: rolling from the gluteus up the back along the muscles that run alongside the spine creates a padded area to roll on, reducing the chance of damage to bone structures. Many performers find rolling on their spine uncomfortable. Accidentally hard impact with the ground can be very risky for the spine.
- Chin tucked, exhale: as they roll back, the performer tucks their chin towards their chest, minimizing the risk of slamming their head into the ground. The hands stay up and forwards, preventing the urge to put them down or hitting the elbows on the ground. The performer breathes out as they descend, ensuring the body is as relaxed as possible all the way to the stop point.

THE FRONT DESCENT (OR THE ILLUSION OF FALLING FORWARDS)

Works With

All staging.

Safety Principles

- Get close to the ground.
- Energy along the ground.
- Soft on soft.
- Protect fragile areas of the body.
- Fall to safety.
- Exhale.

This technique stands alone from the other controlled descents, having its own specific challenges, as the initial point of contact with the ground is with the hands, with all of the attendant issues. The technique is designed to do two things: getting the performer close to, and moving along, the ground at the point of impact; and, providing a graduated contact with the hand itself. This descent in particular is customizable, as many people find fast contact with their upper chest to the ground uncomfortable. An instructor will always provide the performer with a safe adjustment.

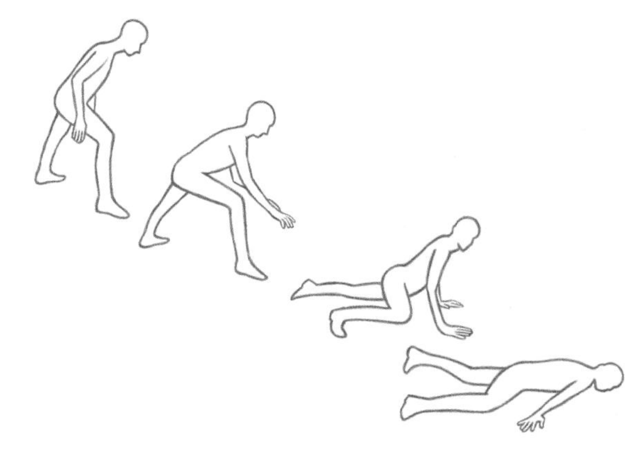

Figure 104: The front descent.

RIGHT: Four stages of the front descent.
TOM ZIEBELL

Position

Works in any orientation. It must be positioned so that the performer is descending into a safe zone, avoiding hazards. This means it is always rehearsed slowly to begin with.

Check the Space

The performers check the space they will descend into before proceeding. This is a predictive check, not only looking for fixed hazards, but also making sure that no one is about to move into the space. If there is any safety issue, the descent stops at this point.

Technique Breakdown

- Lunge forwards: the dominant leg lunges forwards just off the front line, on a slight diagonal – not too much, or it looks contrived. It should be just enough to the side to allow the chest to descend inside the line of the thigh.
- Bend forwards: continuing the illusion of forward energy, the performer hinges forwards at the waist, bringing the upper body much closer to the ground, helping to reduce the fear factor and any potential impact.
- Reach forwards with pyramid hands: both hands reach to the front as though the performer is throwing themselves into a press-up position. The hands must be splayed (fingers pointing forwards, not flat), so that the first ground contact is with the fingertips, then the hands collapse as they actively pull the body along the ground, with graduated contact running along the hand, through the palm to the

Common Errors

Victim

Lunging with the foot directly in front
Reaching with flat hands
Not turning the face to the side
Not bending at the waist and just falling forwards
Slamming straight down instead of reaching forwards
Landing on the knee
Holding the breath

A flowing image of the front descent.
TOM ZIEBELL

heel of the hand. The purpose is to avoid two outcomes: bending at the waist and dropping down hard on to open hands; and taking energy forwards along the ground, yet still slamming flat open hands straight down. The likely result of either move is to shock and potentially injure the wrists. Reaching forwards takes energy along the ground, while splaying the hands reduces the chance of shocking the wrists.

- Turn the face to the side: this will reduce the risk of hitting the chin on the ground at speed. It should be turned early enough so that it is side-on by the time the hands touch the ground, otherwise it will be too late. Ploughing the chin into the ground can lead to life-altering injuries.
- Pull the body along the ground: the hands make graduated contact with the ground, the body arching slightly. Contact is made with the front of the thigh, into the abdominals and the chest, as the hands slightly pull the body along the ground. If the body simply slams downwards, the impact shocks not only the wrists, but also the chest. Pulling along the ground minimizes impact. Sliding too far will make it unrealistic, and allowing the hands to slide forwards away from the body will mean that the chest slams down hard. The hands must reach, stick and pull.
- Slide the hands and foot clear: as the hands pull the body forwards, they slide away sideways when they pass the shoulders. If they stay braced beside the body, elbows up, the stress in the wrist and shoulder joints is painful. The lunging foot also slides out, releasing stress in the joints. Slide away on the inside edge of the toes, keeping the side of the knee from hitting the ground. The elevation of the knee an inch off the ground will not be obvious to the audience.
- Exhale: the performer should breathe out throughout the technique. Any tension in the body will make this move very difficult to execute well or safely.

THE SIDE DESCENT (CURTSY) (or the illusion of fainting)

Works With

All staging.

Safety Principles

- Get close to the ground.
- Energy along the ground.
- Soft on soft.
- Protect fragile areas of the body.
- Fall to safety.
- Exhale.

Position

Works in any orientation. It must be positioned so that the performer is descending into a safe zone, avoiding hazards, which means it is always rehearsed slowly to begin with.

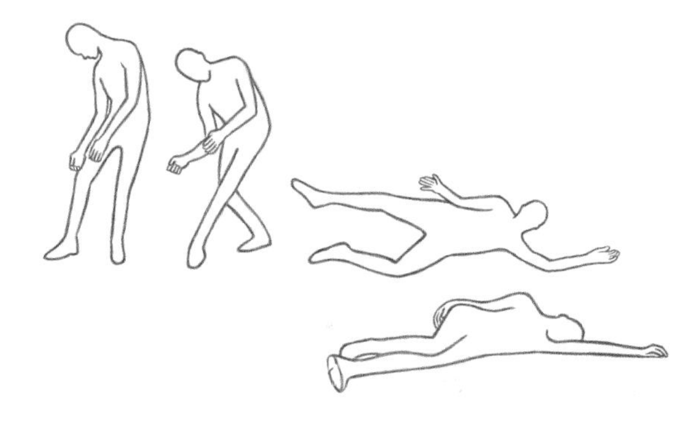

Figure 105: The side descent (curtsy).

Check the Space

The performers check the space they will descend into before proceeding. This is a predictive check, not only looking for fixed hazards, but also making sure that no one is about to move into the space. If there is any safety issue, the descent stops at this point.

Technique Breakdown

- Start to slump: imagine a puppet whose strings have been cut, causing its body to start to slump. As the knees begin to bend, the heels slightly point in the direction of the descent, the hip on that side starting to move in the same direction.

- Counter-balance: lean the head, upper body and hands in the opposite direction from the descent, as the body continues to sink lower.
- Curtsy: as the body gets lower it reaches a point of imbalance to one side, as the hip leans in that direction. At that moment the opposite foot slips behind the other foot in a curtsy. This shifts the body's balance point further along, getting further and closer to the ground in that direction.
- Roll out: make contact with the ground on the side of the thigh, rolling through the side of the gluteus and along the side of the back, and the latissimus dorsi. This is a graduated contact with the floor that minimizes the energy of the impact. Use the counter-balancing action to curl the side of the body: if the torso is straight, the flat impact will shock the ribs. It is possible to roll out on the side of the chest, but there is a slightly increased risk of impact. Each performers' unique physique requires them to customize the technique to avoid areas of their body such as prominent hipbones. Keep a dynamic energy in the knee closest to the ground so that it remains angled slightly upward during the roll-out, to avoid slamming it into the ground.
- Flop the arms over: the counter-balancing arms on the other side of the body now flop over in a semi-circle. The arm on the contact side rolls out, becoming a cushion for the performer's face, preventing accidental contact between floor and face. It is possible to slide the arm from finger, palm to arm, instead of flopping. Problematically, the start point places the hand in the position that it would naturally adopt if it was really trying to break the fall; the brain can give in to instinct and put the hand down, potentially leading to a broken wrist. Also, many floor surfaces leave the performer with friction burns along the arm.

Common Errors

Victim
Not counter-balancing enough
Not moving the hip in the direction of the descent
Upper body too upright
Curtsy step at the wrong moment
Rolling out on the back not the side
Sliding the edge of the hand
Dropping down hard instead of rolling along
Holding the breath

- Exhale: breathe out throughout the technique. Tension in the body will make this move very difficult to execute well or safely. It is also completely antithetical to what actually happens to a body when it faints.

A flowing image of the side descent (curtsy).
TOM ZIEBELL

OPPOSITE RIGHT: Four stages of the side descent (curtsy).
TOM ZIEBELL

THE SIDE DESCENT (PARACHUTE STYLE) (or the illusion of fainting)

Works With

All staging.

Safety Principles

- Get close to the ground.
- Energy along the ground.
- Soft on soft.
- Protect fragile areas of the body.
- Fall to safety.
- Exhale.

This version is similar to a parachute landing fall (PLF), with a graduated collapse to the ground along the body. However, the feet are slightly separated and there is no ending rollover as the performer is not trying to control an excess of speed.

It will feel to the performer as though there is a tiny moment of fall in the middle of this technique. As a result, it will be tempting to allow the side of the knee to crash into the ground, because it is at that moment that the brain thinks it is falling for real and tries to break the fall. To counteract this, the performer counterbalances strongly to the opposite side, keeping dynamic energy in the knee and consciously angling it slightly above the floor as contact is made.

As an exception to the rule, there is an argument for using mats to teach this version, whilst students work out how to manage the transition from downward motion to sideways motion.

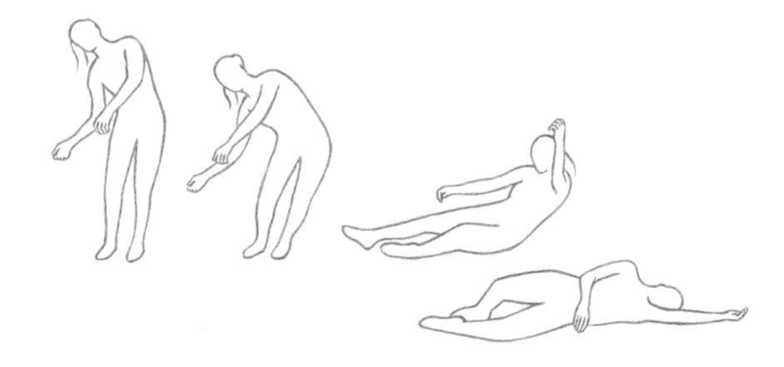

Figure 106: The side descent (parachute style).

Common Errors

Victim
Not counter-balancing enough
Not moving the hip in the direction of the descent
Upper body too upright
Collapsing the knee on to the ground
Rolling out on the back not the side
Sliding the edge of the hand
Dropping down hard instead of rolling along
Holding the breath

Position

Works in any orientation. It must be positioned so that the performer is descending into a safe zone, avoiding hazards, which means it is always rehearsed slowly to begin with.

Check the Space

The performers check the space they will descend into before proceeding. This is a predictive check, not only looking for fixed hazards, but also making sure that no one is about to move into the space. If there is any safety issue, the descent stops at this point.

Technique Breakdown

- Start to slump: imagine a puppet whose strings have been cut, causing its body to start to slump. As the knees begin to bend, the heels slightly point in the direction of the descent, the hip on that side starting to move in the same direction.
- Counter-balance: lean the head, upper body and hands in the opposite direction from the descent, as the body continues to sink lower. Counterbalance strongly.
- Roll out: make contact with the ground on the side of the calf, then the thigh, rolling through the side of the gluteus, along the side of the back and the latissimus dorsi. This is a graduated contact with the floor that minimizes the energy of the impact. Use the counter-balancing action to curl the side of the body: if the torso is

straight, the flat impact will shock the ribs. It is possible to roll out on the side of the chest, but there is a slightly increased risk of impact. Each performers' unique physique requires them to customize the technique to avoid areas of their body such as prominent hipbones. Keep a dynamic energy in the knee closest to the ground so that it remains angled slightly upward during the roll-out, to avoid slamming it into the ground.

- Flop the arms over: the counter-balancing arms on the other side of the body now flop over in a semi-circle. The arm on the contact side rolls out, becoming a cushion for the performer's face, preventing accidental contact between floor and face. It is possible to slide the arm from finger, palm to arm, instead of flopping. Problematically, the start point places the hand in the position that it would naturally adopt if it was really trying to break the fall; the brain can give in to instinct and put the hand down, potentially leading to a broken wrist. Also, many floor surfaces leave the performer with friction burns along the arm.
- Exhale: breathe out throughout the technique. Tension in the body will make this move very difficult to execute well or safely. It is also completely antithetical to what actually happens to a body when it faints.

OPPOSITE RIGHT Four stages of the side descent (parachute style).
TOM ZIEBELL

A flowing image of the side descent (parachute style).
TOM ZIEBELL

19
STAGE vs. CAMERA

Is performing unarmed combat essentially the same for the camera as it is for the stage? Well, in some ways it is, and is some ways it is not. The answer is as simple and as complex as that and, depending on which practitioner you speak to, you are as likely to get one answer as another. So where are the differences, large or small?

IS THERE THE SAME STRONG FOCUS ON SAFETY?

Yes there is. Nobody wants to see a performer get hurt, ever. However, some practitioners postulate that the performer has a stronger individual responsibility for their own safety while filming. They will argue for a paradigm shift: that in an accident on stage the responsibility more often lies with the attacker, while in an accident on screen it more often lies with the victim. The circumstances may be exactly the same, but there is a different view of who made the mistake. Filming is an astonishingly complex process, involving many individuals and departments, all under a great deal of financial pressure and time constraints. Within that pressured complexity, on some sets, it can be easy – not right, but easy – for the responsibility for their own safety to be left up to the performers. They must, for their own sake, clearly remember exactly which principle it is within each technique that keeps them and their partners safe. The fundamental principle underpinning the question, 'Can this be performed safely?' will also change. In the theatre, it may be 'Can this be performed safely eight times a week for the length of the run?'; on a film set, it might be 'Can this be performed once without hurting anyone?'

DO PERFORMERS USE THE SAME BODY OF TECHNIQUES?

Performers may use the same body of techniques, but these are often modified to work for the presence and position of the camera. The simplest example is that knaps are not used when fighting for the screen, as the sound effects are added in post-production; the performer no longer has to take responsibility for them, although they will of course still create a vocal score as they fight. This means that, beyond the need to create the illusion of contact by crossing the target line, they no longer need to worry about hiding technical elements within each moment of the fight. Instead, they can simply focus on telling the character's physical and emotional story.

IS INSTINCT MORE IMPORTANT THAN CRAFT IN FRONT OF THE CAMERA?

Not at all. A performance for camera is as much a crafted reality as a performance for a live audience. The main difference is that the technical constraints within which the performance is created are different. Instead of thinking how to ensure that all members of the audience hear the text, the focus is on working with the microphone. Rather than worrying about finding their light and not falling off the stage, the fighters are concerned with hitting their marks and not hitting the camera. Strong fight performers develop an instinctive sense of where the camera is, and will use that awareness to incorporate subtle adjustments into the fight, on the fly, to make it work specifically for the position of the camera on that take. If anything, it could be argued that technical accuracy is more important for the camera. Where aggression and speed may sustain the illusion on stage, loose technique while filming can make the shot unusable.

WHEN HITTING MARKS, ARE SIGHTLINES STILL A MAJOR CONSIDERATION?

Yes, but it is not the same as in a live performance. In place of selling the violence effectively for many sets of eyes in different locations, the screen fighter is usually working for the one point of view (POV) of a single camera. Sometimes they have to consider multiple cameras, ensuring each move works for as many of them as possible, but it is far more common to have to convince one camera. Occasionally, there may be a series of cameras, placed in a sequence to record each moment as the fight hits different sets of marks. In many ways, this is easier than working with an audience and physically more akin to a real fight. The focus is on making each moment look extremely realistic – there is no more need to stretch techniques out to work for a wide audience, to telegraph moves or to work at a speed that audience members can read. However, it is no less technical in its demands, as each move must be made to work for that exact camera position and that lens size.

ARE THE ENERGY LEVELS THE SAME?

Given appropriate rehearsal time, strong performers can fight extremely fast. On stage this can become something of a blur for the audience, and fights often have to be slowed down slightly to allow the story-telling to 'breathe'. However, a high level of energy is absolutely what is required when fighting on screen. There is something about the experience of viewing a fight through the medium of a camera that can make it seem under-energized. It is an oft-heard maxim in stage combat circles that the camera slows action down, and it is therefore necessary to fight as fast as possible when filming. However, it is more the case that the camera sees the truth. This means that any attack that is not absolutely, fully physically committed to by the performer will inevitably seem slow, because it is not true to the character's desperate desire to survive the fight. Each physical choice must not only be played with the speed that the character would need in order to succeed, but must also be fully energized in all parts of the body, not simply in the attacking limb or by moving a single body part in the avoidance of an attack. This is the same principle discussed in Chapter 9, but it is exponentially true when fighting for camera; the character's entire body must be fully involved in every moment of the fight.

IS IT NECESSARY TO GET THE ENTIRE FIGHT RIGHT EVERY TIME?

No, it is not. In fact, this question highlights a number of differences in practice between the two media. It is unusual for a performer to have to perform the whole fight for the camera. This is primarily because, wherever the camera is set, it is unlikely that every moment of the choreography can be made to work for that position. It may be run fully once or twice to allow the director and DOP to see it and begin to make their shooting choices, but once filming begins it will probably be broken down into shorter sections of a few moves at a time. The advantage of this is that the performer has to remember only a small element of the fight and give it everything they have got, then they can dump that information completely to focus on the next component. The process also allows for retakes until every moment has been successfully captured to the satisfaction of the various departments.

IS THERE AS MUCH REHEARSAL TIME FOR CAMERA AS THE THEATRE?

There is of course no defined allocation of time established for rehearsing a fight. In both contexts, the single most important element is money. The level of funding will define how much time can be made available for preparing and shooting the fights. Only then will other considerations, such as the availability of performers or the director's interest in the action, have an impact on the choices made. Some productions provide a great deal of prep time for the stunt team and fight arrangers, investing resources in the hope of capturing great action sequences. However, it seems to be a more common experience for filming to involve short but intense rehearsal periods. Indeed, it is not unusual for the action to be created and worked in a brief period of less than an hour, and then immediately shot. This latter process places a great strain on all involved, and is one compelling reason why performers should absolutely keep their fight training current, to enable them to be adaptable and rise to the challenge if called upon.

HOW SHOULD A PERFORMER TRAIN TO BRING 'TRUTH' TO THEIR CAMERA FIGHT PERFORMANCE?

So what is 'truth' in performance? This one question alone has led to many volumes of discourse and debate, and created and destroyed reputations. Untangling the complexities of the many schools of thought would be a huge task, but perhaps there is one simple answer to clarify the issue: it is truth if the viewer believes it. In that case, what is required to engender that belief, beyond the performer's ability to create a character and bring them to responsive life, or indeed their ability to act, but act specifically for the technical demands of the screen? It goes without saying that fight training will imbue an invaluable level of confidence in a performer entering the pressured environment of a film set, particularly if they have prior experience of adjusting a fight to a moving camera. They will also need physical stamina to survive the rigours of a fight, combined with a robust mental response to the situation of shooting, which always demands a certain flexibility and a focused discipline. The likelihood is that the filming situation will change very quickly, often more than once. The performer will be required to absorb rapid shifts both physically and mentally, while maintaining the ability to produce the material needed. That particular aspect of fight work is far less demanding in the theatre, where, once the choreography and the performance parameters have been set, they are much less likely to change.

WILL THE PERFORMER MAKE THE SAME ACTING CHOICES IN THE FIGHT WHETHER IT IS LIVE OR RECORDED?

Everything described in Chapter 3 applies equally to fighting for the camera. However, because the camera can watch the character fighting in close-up, all of the acting choices need to be as precise and detailed as possible. For example, the character's inner monologue needs to be a fully realized and connected sequence of thoughts, each responding to a moment, analysing it and making a decision that leads to an action, then linking to the next moment and then the next. The performer must create and experience those thoughts, because the camera will see very clearly if they fail to do so. Unless every element is fully focused and embodied, the performance will feel fake. A fight is an argument, not a debate. In live performance, the brain of the audience member will often forgive a slight element of apparent choreographic structure, as long as it is masked with aggressive intent, but that will not work for camera. Each character must continue with the intent to attack, until they are forced to defend, and usually do that with the intent to try and attack again as soon as possible.

WHAT HAPPENS IF THE PERFORMER MAKES A MISTAKE?

On stage, if an audience member happens to be looking at that part of the fight, they will almost certainly see the error – although full physical and emotional commitment to the moment can often fool them into believing they have seen something they have not, and vice versa. In filming, the performer simply continues until they hear the director say 'Cut', secure in the knowledge that there will almost certainly be other coverage of the moment from different takes or set-ups, and that any mistake will end up on the cutting-room floor.

WHAT IS THE MOST IMPORTANT DIFFERENCE BETWEEN SCREEN AND STAGE?

Arguably, the most important difference is framing; put another way, it is what the observer can see. On stage, almost everything is seen by someone, even if the company are very skilled at throwing focus and directing the audience's attention. With the camera, if it is not in frame, it does not exist. This means that an understanding of lens lengths and their impact on depth of field and frame size is important – or, at least, knowing who to ask and at what stage in the filming process it is appropriate to do so. As the jigsaw of the fight is created, ready for the editor to eventually put together, there must be a clear understanding of what information is required for each piece of the puzzle to fit cleanly with the next piece. The focus on detail can be paramount, particularly as the frame gets tighter. The fight still requires the character's aggressive energy, but it must be technically precise when utilized.

Although the two different media use essentially the same corpus of techniques, there are a number of important differences. Whilst the basic process of creating the illusion of contact by crossing or covering the target line is the same, on screen those techniques are supported and boosted by a variety of post-production technologies that can enhance their effectiveness. Performers in recorded media need to aggressively energize their actions and reactions, and yet perform with extreme technical precision, all the while remaining adaptable to the moment-by-moment adjustments required to remain oriented to a moving camera. They rarely have to perform more than a few beats of the fight at one time and, if they make a mistake, the editor can usually cut around it. However, the pressure on a film set is generally far greater than that in a theatre.

There is a fundamental difference between a film viewer's experience of a fight compared with that of a theatre audience. Unlike the theatre audience member, the viewer of a film is given no choice where to look, as their eyes are guided through the action by the director and editor. In addition, they will see moments in much closer detail than can be achieved in a live performance. Although it is possible to craft a fight with great specificity, because the camera, by its very nature, demands complete emotional and physical commitment to every beat of the story, the performers really have to inhabit every moment. If there is any slight sense of choreography, of them knowing the dance, it will be magnified by the filming process and be immediately apparent to the viewer. The performer cannot afford to be in their comfort zone in any sense; they must push themselves to be the best they can in all aspects of the role, because, once it has been recorded, their performance will likely outlive them.

CONCLUSION

The wise performer continues to train long after their initial period of intensive learning has been completed. All aspects of their craft deserve ongoing attention, to ensure that they are up to any work-related challenges that may, of a sudden, come their way. As is often the case in the performance industries, work can arrive at short notice, with little opportunity to prepare, so it is very important to keep specific skillsets sharp.

All stage combat training organizations suggest that performers renew their stage combat qualifications every three years. This is not an arduous process and it will pay dividends in the level of confidence the performer takes into a professional fight audition or rehearsal. The BASSC renewal process involves a day retraining for each weapon certificate held, culminating in a simple, external adjudication.

This is of course the minimum suggested. There are many workshops and courses held each year and it is worth considering adding new weapons skills on a regular basis, or deepening knowledge already held. Most countries have at least one, and often more than one, training organization available, and it may also be of benefit to sample different teachers and organizations as you search for an approach that works for you individually.

It is unfortunate that, amongst all of the performer's tools, stage combat is often seen as peripheral and considered least when it comes to time for further training. All elements of a performer's training are important, but of them all, stage combat is the only one which is likely to lead to potentially career-changing injury if used incorrectly. For that reason alone, serious consideration should be given to keeping the skillset up to date.

GLOSSARY

Action Term used by the director to begin recording on a film set.

Archer's preparation Preparation for the cross punch, which looks very similar to an archer drawing a bow.

Artistic team An alternative term for the creative team, used by those who feel that that term implies that other teams in the production process are considered less creative. *See* also Creative team.

Auditorium The space where the members of the audience sit to watch a performance.

Autonomic reflex Any of a number of different, automatic reflexes that keep the body functioning, and which operate outside of a person's conscious control.

Avulsion fracture A fracture where the bone is damaged by the strong pull of a tendon or ligament detaching a section of it.

Balcony *See* Gallery or Gods.

Beat The minimum sub-division of action possible within a unit of action, within a scene.

Chambering energy Making a preparation for an attack by placing the body into such a position that energy is stored in the muscles ready to be released into an explosive action.

Character An individual role within a performance.

Characterization The act of creating a fully formed depiction of a person for dramatic performance.

Cheating Adjusting the position of the performers to make a moment work better in a technical sense, without the audience realizing, even though it may not be an entirely natural choice.

Choreography The formal sequence of moves comprising the finished fight. Once set and signed off by the director and production manager it can only be safely altered by the fight director.

Comminuted fracture A fracture that leaves the bone broken into a number of pieces.

Concept team An alternative term for the creative team, used by those who feel that that term implies that other teams in the production process are considered less creative. *See also* Creative team.

Consent A fundamental aspect of all stage combat work. Nothing should be done to any performer without their explicit consent. If at any point they withdraw their consent for any aspect of the work in progress, that withdrawal must be acknowledged and acted upon immediately.

Contact A family of techniques that make physical contact with the victim. All of the fundamental safeties are developed in rehearsal, and are internal to the technique. Consequently, there is nothing to hide from the audience, making these moves ideal for in-the-round or thrust staging.

Core General term to describe the muscles of the abdomen and the mid and lower back. Both the surface and the deeper muscle groups act to initiate and to stabilize movement through the body. Not only does a strong and stable core support a performer's movement choices, it also provides support for breath and vocal work, enabling that performer to be responsive both technically and in their character work.

Cover Alternative term for an understudy, a performer who is prepared to step into a role at the last minute in case of emergency.

Coverage All the material recorded for a screen production. Having sufficient coverage means that enough takes have been made for all of the requisite shots and angles, including close-ups and pick-up shots.

Covering the line Alternative term for spiking the line.

Creative team The collective term for the director, and all of the designers and choreographers involved in the production. *See* also Artistic team and Concept team.

Cross the line A fighting-for-camera term which specifically describes the process of a weapon or body part crossing the line between the target and the camera, creating the illusion of contact. It should not be confused with the film-maker's term 'crossing the line', which refers to shooting from the wrong side of the performer, creating difficulties in editing specific shots together.

Cueing system The sequence that determines which element of a technique happens in which order, thus maximizing the safety of the performers. *See* Chapters 5 and 10.

Cut The term used by the director to stop recording on a film set.

Cutting room floor A colloquial term used to describe any unused elements of a recorded performance.

Depth of field The distance between the foreground and the background of a shot, within which the performer is in focus.

Displaced fracture A fracture that breaks the bone into two or more pieces, leaving them unaligned.

Displacement of target *See* Glossary of Safety Principles, Chapter 5.

Distance The performer is either close enough to hit their partner, or they are not – in other words, they are in or out of distance. Being in or out of distance will affect the techniques and safety principles they use for that moment. *See* Glossary of Safety Principles, Chapter 5.

Distance check An element of many upstage/downstage techniques, where the arm not being used to launch an attack – usually the non-dominant arm – is extended to confirm that the victim is not close enough to actually hit.

DOP Director of photography, or cinematographer, who controls the camera and lighting crews on a film set. They collaborate with the director to create the visual look and style of the shots.

Dove of peace *See* Glossary of Safety Principles, Chapter 5.

Downstage The section of the stage closest to the audience for proscenium arch, end-on and thrust staging configurations.

Dress circle *See* Royal Circle.

Dress rehearsal A rehearsal session during which the performance is run in the venue exactly as it will later be run for the audience.

End-on staging *See* Proscenium (arch) staging. *See* also Chapter 6.

Eye contact The safety principle that encourages performers to check in with each other by making eye contact at appropriate and agreed moments in the choreography. It creates the opportunity for them to stay in synch with each other, and to assess whether their partner is ready for the next beat of the fight. *See* Chapters 5 and 10.

Fight arranger Commonly used term for the fight choreographer on a film set. This role is both different from, and subordinate to, that of the stunt coordinator.

Fight call A pre-show rehearsal allocated specifically for those performers who are fighting within a performance. During the fight call, all of the fights are rehearsed, giving the performers time to refresh their recall of the choreography and any other relevant elements. Enough time will be given for each fight to be run at least twice, once slowly and once at speed.

Fight director The term used by Equity to denote the fight choreographer for a live performance. Note that not all fight directors have sufficient qualifications to join Equity's register of fight directors.

Fight/flight The body's short-term chemical response to acute stress, an over-arousal of the nervous system caused by the perception of danger. *See* also Freeze/fold.

Film set The venue, either interior or exterior, for shooting a section of a film. This is usually built specifically for the purpose, or adapted.

Footlights Theatre lights set into or along the front of the stage, originally used to reduce shadows on the faces of performers, created by overhead lighting. Rarely used in modern theatres, except for specific effects.

Fracture Damage to a bone caused by excessive physical stress, resulting in anything from a hairline crack to a complete disintegration of the material. *See* also Avulsion fracture, Comminuted fracture, Displaced fracture and Non-displaced fracture.

Frame Exactly what the camera sees from side to side and top to bottom, without moving. If the performer is in the frame, they are seen; if they are outside the frame, they are not seen.

Freeze/fold The body's alternative short-term response to acute stress. The body either becomes immobile and tense, or collapses completely. *See* also Fight/flight.

Gallery Also known as the Balcony, the highest level of raised audience seating in the auditorium. *See* also Gods.

Gate control theory A theory that posits that the central nervous system gives priority to non-pain-related sensory stimuli over pain-related stimuli, thus allowing a perceived reduction in pain by stimulating the touch sensation at the originating site of pain.

Given circumstances The sum total of all the factors heating the crucible of the character's story. The information is mined from the text, often using the questions 'Who, What, Where, Why, When?'

Gods An idiomatic term used to describe the highest audience seating level in the auditorium. *See* also Gallery or Balcony.

Golgi tendon reflex *See* Inverse myotatic reflex.

Grand circle *See* Upper Circle.

High arousal *See* Fight/flight.

High house An auditorium with multiple levels of audience.

Hitting marks The act of a performer walking into frame and stopping exactly where they are supposed to for the shot. *See* Mark.

House An alternative term for the auditorium.

Illusion of contact Creating the right circumstances to help the audience believe that a character was hit by a fist/foot/weapon, without the performers actually making physical contact. *See* Chapter 10.

Immersive theatre A theatrical format designed to include the audience in the development and playing out of the characters' stories, in a non-traditional performance space.

In-the-round staging A stage area completely surrounded by audience seating. This is usually circular or square, or some variation thereof. The performers' entrances on to stage usually run through the audience. *See* Chapter 6.

Inverse myotatic reflex A protective mechanism that causes a muscle to relax before the tendons can tear due to unexpected tension.

Kiai A martial arts term describing the vocalized release of the attacker's energy at the point of an attack.

Kitchen sink drama A form of mid-twentieth-century theatrical realism, specifically focused on the working class, reflective of a broader movement in all forms of British cultural media.

Knap The simulated sound of a violent contact, created by striking one body part against another. *See* Chapter 11.

Laban A short-hand term for Laban Movement Analysis (LMA), a methodology for describing and analysing physical movement, originally developed by Rudolf Laban.

Lighting A generic term to describe the designed lighting states for a performance. These have an impact on fight work only when they restrict the performer's ability to see clearly during a fight, either by being too bright or too dim.

Low arousal *See* Freeze/fold.

Magic thread *See* Target line.

Mark A filming term for a mark created with tape, chalk, or anything appropriate, which tells the performer where to stand to be in focus and frame, for the shot. *See* also Hitting marks.

Marking a fight Running a fight slowly; although this is not done at full speed, it should always be done with full intentions.

Music of the fight *See* Vocal score.

Myotatic reflex Also known as the stretch reflex, a protective mechanism that causes a muscle to contract to prevent damage caused by over-extension.

Negotiation *See* Glossary of Safety Principles, Chapter 5.

Nociceptive A medical term used to describe pain arising from actual or potential harm to the physical body. It is the most common type of pain, attributable to a specific incident, with a defined period of healing.

Non-contact The term used to define a family of techniques that have the illusion of contact, but do not actually touch the victim.

Non-displaced fracture A fracture that cracks the bone part-way or entirely through, but leaves it in alignment.

Objective The character's aim, scene by scene, determined by asking, 'What does this character want right now?'

Pain perception threshold The point at which an increasing physical stimulus begins to be perceived as pain, rather than simply sensation.

Pain tolerance threshold The point at which an increasing level of pain can no longer be borne.

Parachute hand A hand placed behind a victim's elbow to help them slow down and stay upright.

Paradigm An analytical framework designed to encompass a discipline's methodologies and world view.

Parrot space Refers to the spaces above the victim's shoulders, beside their face, in humorous reference to the piratical habit of carrying a parrot perched on one shoulder. The parrot spaces are used as displaced targets for profile attacks to the head.

Phrase The separate sections of choreography, defined by a pause between each section, long enough that the impulse to fight has to be renewed by the characters, rather than simply run on from the previous physical impulse. The separations between the phrases often provide an opportunity for text to interleave with the action.

Point of view (POV) Point of view: usually used to describe the physical location of the camera or audience member.

Post (production) A catch-all phrase used to describe the period in the film-making process when the film is edited, and music, sound and digital special effects are added.

Prize fights A public performance by fighters seeking to attain a higher ranking within 'The Company of Maisters of Defence', primarily in sixteenth-century England. A profitable and popular form of entertainment, which shared many of the same performance spaces as the acting companies of the time.

Proprioception A performer's internal awareness of their body's position, balance and movement, moment by moment.

Proscenium (arch) staging A traditional seating format placing all of the audience in the same physical relationship to the stage, exactly as in a cinema. *See* Chapter 6.

RADA The Royal Academy of Dramatic Art, founded in 1904, one of the world's most prestigious drama schools.

Red light/green light *See* Glossary of Safety Principles, Chapter 5.

Rehearsal A set period of time during which the performers work on preparing the performance. Fight rehearsals are time slots specifically allocated to fight work alone.

Restoration comedy A style of comedy associated with the restoration in England of the Stuart monarchy in 1660, in vogue for roughly fifty years. The style, loosely known as 'Comedy of Manners', has been alternately praised and damned for its focus on impropriety, licentiousness and wit. It is notable for the appearance of the first professional female performers.

Reversal of energy *See* Glossary of Safety Principles, Chapter 5.

Risk assessment A written appraisal of the potential risks attendant on a proposed activity, containing an assessment of who is at risk, the level of that risk, and any actions taken to mitigate both their exposure and the danger itself.

Royal circle Also known as the Dress Circle, the first level of raised audience seating above the Stalls.

Safe gesture A gesture that is mutually agreed between the performers prior to any activity taking place, to be used by the victim to indicate that they want their partner to immediately stop what they are doing and back away. It must be something that their character would not normally do, so that it may not be mistaken for a gesture that might arise from improvised struggle. A safe gesture is chosen for any situation that could lead to the performer being unable to speak.

Safe word A previously, mutually agreed upon word, to be used by the victim to indicate that they want their partner to immediately stop what they are doing and back away. It must be a word that their character would not say, to prevent it being mistaken for paraphrased text.

Safeguarding A measure designed to prevent someone from being placed in harm's way.

Set (film) *See* Film set.

Set (theatre) The physical environment on stage within which the performance takes place. Usually used to describe both constructed elements such as rostra, and also furniture.

Set-up The position of the camera and lighting for a particular shot.

Shot What the camera can see for the span of the recording. There will usually be multiple takes of each shot. There are many different types of shot used according to the storytelling needs of the moment.

Side-coaching Directing a performer while they are actually acting in a rehearsal, without interrupting the work, allowing them to make adjustments and continue to remain immersed in the character's experience.

Sightline The line of sight from a seat in the auditorium to the performance area. The important sightlines are those from the extreme sides and height of the auditorium, as they will define which techniques are playable in that space.

Site-specific staging A performance created for a particular non-theatrical venue.

Soft on soft *See* Glossary of Safety Principles, Chapter 5.

Spiking the line The process of a weapon or body part stopping momentarily on the line between the target and the camera, creating the illusion of contact. Also known as covering the line.

Stakes What a character stands to gain or lose as a consequence of their actions and the actions of others.

Stalls Ground-level audience seating in the auditorium.

Standard combats A series of pre-choreographed sword-fighting phrases, individually named and learned, and used by most working performers in the nineteenth and early twentieth centuries. They could be strung together in any order to create a fight of the necessary length with minimal rehearsal. It was not unknown, if the fight was well received, for the star to add phrases mid-performance.

Stertorous breathing Loud and laboured breathing. In vocal terms known as 'audible intake'.

Superman punch A colloquial term for the cross punch, in reference to the final image of the punch, which resembles the classic Superman flying pose.

Super-objective The over-arching aim of the character, which links together all of their different objectives during the play. Sometimes used interchangeably with the term through-line.

Take A film recording from the moment the director calls 'Action' to the moment they call 'Cut'. There will often be multiple takes of the same shot until the director is happy with the result.

Target line The imaginary line drawn from the camera lens, or from the centre of the audience, to the target. This line is perceived as continuing upstage through the target. The illusion of contact is achieved by the attack either stopping on the line to obscure the target, or crossing the line either horizontally or vertically, upstage or downstage of the target. Sometimes referred to as the magic thread.

Target zone The actual space into which the attacker is aiming, as opposed to where the audience believes they are aiming.

Technical rehearsals The sessions during which all of the technical components (lighting, sound, costume, set, props) are brought together for the first time, and rehearsed until all elements mesh smoothly.

Through-line A central theme that links everything together. Sometimes referred to as the spine.

Throwing focus An idiomatic expression describing a performer's ability to direct the audience's attention elsewhere on stage.

Thrust staging Staging that extends out into the auditorium, creating a seating format where the audience are placed on three sides of the playing area. *See* Chapter 6.

To action To apply an active or transitive verb to each specific beat within the text. A performer's tool to clarify exactly how each moment affects a character and how they attempt to affect other characters or events.

Traverse staging Staging in which the audience are seated on opposite sides of the playing area, facing each other. *See* Chapter 6.

Understudy A performer prepared to step into a role at the last minute in case of emergency, alternatively known as cover.

Unit A distinct block of action within a scene. The idea of breaking scenes down into connected units of action originated in the work of Russian theatre director Konstantin Stanislavski, whose approach to performance was later interpreted by American practitioners. Each unit can be further broken down into beats.

Upper circle Sometimes referred to as the Grand Circle, the second level of raised audience seating in the auditorium.

Upstage The section of the stage furthest away from the audience for proscenium arch, end-on and thrust staging configurations.

Victim control *See* Glossary of Safety Principles, Chapter 5.

Vocal instrument A term used in the industry to describe the performer's voice, both the actual physical structure and the sound of the voice itself.

Vocal score A commonly used term for the vocal choreography of the fight, encompassing pain, effort and the character's emotional responses to the violence. *See* Music of the fight.

Voms A shortening of the term vomitorium, which is a path by which the audience or performers enter and leave a performance space. This colloquial term is usually applied to entrances for in-the-round venues.

BIBLIOGRAPHY

Alonso, J. (2011), 'The Brain as a Pattern Recognition Machine', *Seeing Complexity*, 2 September. Available at: seeingcomplexity.wordpress.com/2011/02/09/the-brain-as-a-pattern-recognition-machine/

Aylward, J. D. (1953), *The House of Angelo,* London: The Batchworth Press, pp. 19, 26–27, 31, 35, 65, 159–161

Banozic, A., Miljkovic, A., Bras, M., Puljak, L., Kolcic, I., Hayward, C. & Polasek, O. (2018), 'Neuroticism And Pain Catastrophizing Aggravate Response To Pain In Healthy Adults: An Experimental Study', *The Korean Journal Of Pain*, Vol. 31 (1), January, pp. 16–26. Available at: www.ncbi.nlm.nih.gov/pmc/articles/PMC5780211/

Bellinger, M. (1927), 'What The Roman Play Was Like'. In: *A Short History of the Drama*, New York: Henry Holt & Co. pp. 92–96

Berry, H. (1991), '*The Noble Science. A Study and Transcription of Sloane Ms. 2530*', *Papers of the Masters of Defence of London, Temp. Henry VIII to 1590*, London: Associated University Presses, pp. 1, 12–13, 33

BJJEE (2018), 'How Dangerous Is Being Choked Out? Plus The Difference Between Strangle And Chokehold', *Brazilian Jiu-Jitsu Eastern Europe*, 28 May. Available at: www.bjjee.com/articles/how-dangerous-is-being-choked-out/

Bradford, W. (2019), 'The Shocking Aspects Of Theater In Ancient Rome', *ThoughtCo*, 15 June. Available at: www.thoughtco.com/theater-in-ancient-rome-2713183

Brereton, J. (2014), 'Singing In Space(s): Singing Performance In Real And Virtual Acoustic Environments – Singers' Evaluation, Performance Analysis And Listeners' Perception', August, pp. 138–139. Available at: pdfs.semanticscholar.org/4a60/7191860a82161eaca928963bb67d8dc73caa.pdf

Brouhard, R. (2019), 'Is Choking The Same As Strangulation?' *VeryWell Health*, 15 August. Available at: www.verywellhealth.com/is-choking-the-same-as-strangulation-1298889

Chicago Theatre, 'Standards', 2017. Available at: www.notinourhouse.org/#

Coetzee, M-H. (2001), 'Voicing The Visceral: An Interview With Erik Fredericksen and K. Jenny Jones'. In: Dal Vera, R. ed., *The Voice in Violence: And Other Contemporary Issues in Professional Voice and Speech Training*, Cincinnati: Voice and Speech Trainers Association, Inc, pp. 97, 102

Cohen, R. (2002) *By The Sword*, London: Macmillan, p. 224

Collins (2019), 'Strangle', In: Cobuild Advanced English Dictionary, HarperCollins Publishers. Available at: www.collinsdictionary.com/dictionary/english/strangle

Cooney, M. J. (2017), 'How To Explain Your Pain To A Doctor', *Spine Universe*, 20 September. Available at: www.spineuniverse.com/blogs/cooney/how-explain-your-pain-doctor

Cordain, L., Gotshall, R. W., Eaton, S. B. & Eaton 3rd, S. B. (1998), 'Physical Activity, Energy Expenditure And Fitness: An Evolutionary Perspective', *International Journal of Sports Medicine*, July, Vol. 19 (5), pp. 328–335. Available at: thepaleodiet.com/wp-content/uploads/2015/08/Physical-Activity-Energy-Expenditure-and-Fitness-An-Evolutionary-Perspective-The-Paleo-Diet.pdf

Dafny, N. (1997), 'Pain Principles'. In: *Neuroscience Online*, UTHealth, Section 2, Chapter 6. Available at: https://nba.uth.tmc.edu/neuroscience/m/s2/chapter06.html

Dunn, R. & Lopez, R. (2019), 'Strangulation Injuries'. In: *StatPearls* [Internet], 3 July. Available at: www.ncbi.nlm.nih.gov/books/NBK459192/

Ferrara, N. (2019), 'Is Dynamic Stretching Better Than Static Stretching?', *Healthy But Smart*, 5 June. Available at: healthybutsmart.com/dynamic-vs-static-stretching

Fisher, E. (2018), 'The Benefits Of Warming Up Before Exercise', *BRN Fitness*, 2 March. Available at: brnfitness.com/blog/benefits-warming-exercise/

FJCA, (n.d.), 'Facts Victims Of Choking (Strangulation) Need To Know!', Family Justice Centre Alliance. Available at: dhss.alaska.gov/ocs/Documents/childrensjustice/strangulation/20.Strangulation%20Brochure.pdf

Groves, B. (2007), '"Now Wole I A Newe Game Begynne": Staging Suffering In King Lear, The Mystery Plays and Grotius' Christus Patiens'. In: Cerasano, S. P. ed., *Medieval and Renaissance Drama in England*, Vol. 20, Cranbury: Associated University Presses, pp. 136–138

Hansen, G. R. & Streltzer, J. (2005), 'The Psychology Of Pain', *Emergency Medicine Clinics Of North America*, 23, pp. 339–348. Available at: williams.medicine.wisc.edu/painpsychology.pdf

Henschke, N. & Lin, C. (2011), 'Stretching Before Or After Exercise Does Not Reduce Delayed-Onset Muscle Soreness', *British Journal of Sports Medicine*, Vol. 45 (15), December, pp. 1249–50. Available at: www.researchgate.net/

publication/51721354_Stretching_before_or_after_does_not_reduce_delayed-onset_muscle_soreness

Hough, P. A., Ross, E. Z. & Howatson, G. (2009), 'Effects Of Dynamic And Static Stretching On Vertical Jump Performance And Electromyographic Activity', *Journal of Strength and Conditioning Research*, Vol. 23 (2), March, pp. 507–512. Available at: https://journals.lww.com/nsca-jscr/fulltext/2009/03000/Effects_of_Dynamic_and_Static_Stretching_on.21.aspx

Johnson, E., George, C. B., Konstantinos, C. S. & Panayotis, S. (2008), Functional Neuroanatomy Of Proprioception, *Journal of Surgical Orthopaedic Advances*, 17 March, pp 159–64. Available at: www.semanticscholar.org/paper/Functional-neuroanatomy-of-proprioception-Johnson-Babis/b578f1892c9e6ca8078f9c9bf4e3a1468c865da0

Johnstone, A. (2017), 'The Amazing Phenomenon Of Muscle Memory', Oxford University, 14 December. Available at: medium.com/oxford-university/the-amazing-phenomenon-of-muscle-memory-fb1cc4c4726

Kanner, R. (2009), 'Definitions' (Chapter 1). In: Argoff, C. E. & McCleane, G. eds., *Pain Management Secrets,* 3rd Ed. Mosby, pp. 9–14

Knight, J. (2019), 'What Are The Different Types Of Stretching?', NielAsher Continuing Professional Education, 29 May. Available at: www.nielasher.com/blogs/video-blog/what-are-the-different-types-of-stretching

Lipscomb, S. (2019), 'Sound And Vision: Using Music In Film To Manipulate Emotions', World Science Festival 2019. Available at: www.worldsciencefestival.com/2013/09/art_of_the_score_the_mind_music_and_moving_images-2/

Lorenzi, R. (2003), 'Ancient Egyptian Priest Settlement Uncovered', *ABC Science*, 15 July. Available at: www.abc.net.au/science/articles/2003/07/15/901864.htm

Lothian, J. (2011), 'Lamaze Breathing – What Every Pregnant Woman Needs To Know', *The Journal Of Perinatal Education*, Vol. 20 (2) Spring, pp. 118–120. Available at: www.ncbi.nlm.gov/pmc/articles/PMC3209750/

Lowry, M. & Walsh, R. (2001), 'Voice/Combat Conversation'. In: Dal Vera, R. ed., *The Voice in Violence: And Other Contemporary Issues in Professional Voice and Speech Training*, Cincinnati: Voice and Speech Trainers Association, Inc, pp. 107–108

Mahon, C. (2018), 'New Illusion Experiment Claims Brain Can Retroactively Change Perceptions Of Reality', *Outer Places*, 10 October. Available at: www.outerplaces.com/science/item/18937-calltech-illusory-rabbit-experiment

Markowsky, G. (2017), 'Information Theory', *Encyclopaedia Britannica*, 16 June. Available at: www.britannica.com/science/information-theory

Martinez, J. D. (1996), *The Swords of Shakespeare*, North Carolina: McFarland & Company, Inc. p. 21

Merriam-Webster (2019), 'Strangle'. In: Merriam-Webster. Available at: www.merriam-webster.com/dictionary/strangle

Munro, M. (2001), 'Introduction To The Papers On Voice In Violence'. In: Dal Vera, R. ed., *The Voice in Violence: And Other Contemporary Issues in Professional Voice and Speech Training*, Cincinnati: Voice and Speech Trainers Association, Inc, p. 14

MyDr.com.au (2012), *Pain And How You Sense It*. Available at: www.mydr.com.au/pain/pain-and-how-you-sense-it

Newcomb, J. & Meyer, U. (2001), '"I'm A Singer, Not A Fighter!" A Few Brief Thoughts On Voice, Violence And The Opera'. In: Dal Vera, R. ed., *The Voice in Violence: And Other Contemporary Issues in Professional Voice and Speech Training*, Cincinnati: Voice and Speech Trainers Association, Inc, pp.111–112

Nordqvist, C. (2017), 'What Is A Fracture?', *Medical News Today*, 14 December. Available at: www.medicalnewstoday.com/articles/173312.php

Olsen, C. (2013), 'Danger Cues You Can See To Prepare You For Self-Defense', *Pacific Wave Jiu-Jitsu*, 11 March. Available at: pacificwavejiujitsu.com/blog/danger-cues-you-can-see/

Olson, L. (2001), 'Some Personal Discoveries Regarding Vocal Use In Stage Combat'. In: Dal Vera, R. ed., *The Voice in Violence: And Other Contemporary Issues in Professional Voice and Speech Training*, Cincinnati: Voice and Speech Trainers Association, Inc, pp. 31–32

Oman, C. (1958), *David Garrick*, Bungay: Hodder & Stoughton, pp. 208, 375

Page, P. (2012), 'Current Concepts In Muscle Stretching For Exercise And Rehabilitation', *International Journal of Sports Physical Therapy*, February, Vol. 7 (1), pp. 109–119. Available at: www.ncbi.nlm.nih.gov/pmc/articles/PMC3273886/

Popkin, B. M., D'Anci, K. E. & Rosenberg, I. H. (2010), 'Water, Hydration And Health', *Nutrition Reviews*, Vol. (8), 1 August, pp. 439–458. Available at: www.ncbi.nlm.nih.gov/pmc/articles/PMC2908954/

Puce, A. (2013), 'Perception Of Nonverbal Cues'. In: Ochsner, K. & Kosslyn, S. eds, *The Oxford Handbook of Cognitive Neuroscience*, Vol. 2: The Cutting Edges. Oxford Handbooks Online, 1 December. Available at: www.oxfordhandbooks.com/view/10.1093/oxfordhb/9780199988709.001.0001/oxfordhb-9780199988709-e-017

Raphael, B. (2001), 'Staged Violence: Greater Than The Sum Of Its Parts'. In: Dal Vera, R. ed., *The Voice in Violence: And Other Contemporary Issues in Professional Voice and Speech Training*, Cincinnati: Voice and Speech Trainers Association, Inc, pp. 22, 26, 28

Ricard, P. (2014), 'Pulmonary System' (Chapter 4). In: Paz, J. & West, M. eds, *Acute Care Handbook for Physical Therapists*, 4th Edition. Available at: www.sciencedirect.

com/book/9781455728961/acute-care-handbook-for-physical-therapists

Richards, J. (1977), *Swordsmen of the Screen: From Douglas Fairbanks to Michael York*, London: Routledge & Kegan Paul Ltd., pp. 42, 44–45

Riecken, K. (2016), 'The Benefits Of Static Stretching Before And After Exercise', *Training Peaks*, 1 July. Available at: www.trainingpeaks.com/blog/the-benefits-of-static-stretching-before-and-after-exercise/

Roberto, M. (2013), *How Business Leaders Avoid Conflict (Collection)*, FT Press, p. 381

Ryker, K. (2001), 'To Train And Test The Voice In Violence'. In: Dal Vera, R. ed., *The Voice in Violence: And Other Contemporary Issues in Professional Voice and Speech Training*, Cincinnati: Voice and Speech Trainers Association, Inc, p. 67

Sein, M. T. (2018), 'Acute vs. Chronic Pain', *Pain-health*, Veritas. Available at: www.pain-health.com/conditions/chronic-pain/acute-vs-chronic-pain

Semino, E. (2010), 'Descriptions Of Pain, Metaphor, And Embodied Simulation', *Metaphor And Symbol*, Vol. 25 (4) September, pp. 205–226. Available at: www.researchgate.net/publication/254306724_Descriptions_of_Pain_Metaphor_and_Embodied_Simulation

Shimojo, S. (2014), 'Postdiction: Its Implications On Visual Awareness, Hindsight, And Sense Of Agency', *Frontiers In Psychology*, 31 March, Vol. 5 (196). Available at: www.ncbi.nlm.nih.gov/pmc/articles/PMC3978293/

Shoukat, H., Arshad, H. S., Sharif, F., Fatima, A. & Shoukat, F. (2017), 'Effects Of Different Stretching Times On Range Of Motion In Patients With Hamstring Tightness: A Randomized Control Trial', *Annals of King Edward Medical University*, Vol. 23 (4), 24 December, pp. 554–559. Available at: researcherslinks.com/current-issues/Effects-of-Different-Stretching-Times-on-Range-of-Motion-in-Patients-with-Hamstring-Tightness-A-Randomised-Control-Trial/25/1/1130/html

Simon, A. (2019), 'Why Do We Need To Warm Up Before Exercise?', *Push Doctor*, 19 June. Available at: www.pushdoctor.co.uk/blog/why-do-we-need-to-warm-up-before-exercise

Small, I. (2019), 'What I Learnt About Deliberate Practice From The Comedian Jerry Seinfeld', *Iesha Small: Use Your Uniqueness To Add Value*, 20 March. Available at: ieshasmall.com/seinfeld/

Sommerstein, A. (2010), 'The Tangled Ways Of Zeus: And Other Studies In And Around Greek Tragedy', Oxford Scholarship Online. Available at: www.oxfordscholarship.com/view/10.1093/acprof:oso/9780199568314.001.0001/acprof-9780199568314-chapter-3

Stephens, R. & Umland, C. (2011), 'Swearing As A Response To Pain – Effect Of Daily Swearing Frequency', *The Journal of Pain*, Vol. 12 (12) December, pp. 1274–1281. Available at: www.bioestadistica.uma.es/baron/bioestadistica/articulos/swearingPain.pdf

Stretchify, (2013), 'Ballistic Stretching', *Stretchify*, 26 June. Available at: www.stretchify.com/ballistic-stretching/

Thomas, T. (1973), *Cads and Cavaliers: The Film Adventurers*, New Jersey: A. S. Barnes & Co, pp. 122–123

Topham, I. (2018), 'Oldham Coliseum', *Mysterious Britain & Ireland*, 2 December. Available at: www.mysteriousbritain.co.uk/hauntings/oldham-coliseum/

Turner, B. (2019), 'The Building Blocks Of Consent – Create A Framework For Change', *UK Theatre*, December 2019. Available at: uktheatre.org/who-we-are-what-we-do/uk-theatre-blog/the-building-blocks-of-consent-creating-a-framework-for-change/

Utley, K. (2014), 'Health Issues Result From Strangulation', Training Institute On Strangulation Prevention, 30 April. Available at: www.strangulationtraininginstitute.com/health-issues-result-from-strangulation/

Vasiliades, T. (2004), 'The Alexander Technique: An Acting Approach', *Soul of the American Actor*, Vol. 7 (3), Fall. Available at: www.alexandertechnique.com/articles/acting3/

Villines, Z. (2016), 'What Happens After A Lack Of Oxygen To The Brain', *SpinalCord.com*, 13 June. Available at: www.spinalcord.com/blog/what-happens-after-a-lack-of-oxygen-to-the-brain

Voice Foundation (2006), 'Understanding Vocal Fold Scarring'. Available at: voicefoundation.org/health-science/voice-disorders/voice-disorders/vocal-fold-scarring/1428-2/

Walker, O. (2016), 'Warm Ups', *Science For Sport*, 14 May. Available at: scienceforsport.com/warm-ups

Wiley, E., Munro, M. & Munro, A. (2001), 'Orchestrating The Music Of A Fight'. In: Dal Vera, R. ed., *The Voice in Violence: And Other Contemporary Issues in Professional Voice and Speech Training*, Cincinnati: Voice and Speech Trainers Association, Inc, pp. 34–35

Williams, A. C. de C. & Craig, K. D. (2016), 'Pain: Updating The Definition Of Pain', *Pain Journal Online*, November 2016. Available at: www.aaalac.org/BOD/AdhocNewsletter/Updating_the_definition_of_pain_Pain2016.pdf

Wlassoff, V. (2014), 'Gate Control Theory And Pain Management', *Brain Blogger*, 23 June. Available at: www.brainblogger.com/2014/06/23/gate-control-theory-and-pain-management/

Wolf, T. (2009) *A Terrific Combat!!!* Lulu Press, pp. xiii–xiv, 235

Worthington, V. (n.d.), 'The Physiology Of A Rear Naked Choke, Or: What Happens When You Get Choked Out', *Breaking Muscle*. Available at: breakingmuscle.com/fitness/the-physiology-of-a-rear-naked-choke-or-what-happens-when-you-get-choked-out

Yu, L. & Yu, Y. (2017), 'Energy-Efficient Neural Processing In Individual Neurons And Neuronal Networks', *Journal Of Neuroscience Research*, Vol. 95 (11) November, pp. 2253–2266. Available at: onlinelibrary.wiley.com/doi/full/10.1002/jnr.241318

Yusuf, S. (2019), 'Evolution Of Pain: When Did Living Things Start Feeling Pain?', *Science ABC*. Available at: www.scienceabc.com/humans/evolution-pain-living-things-start-feeling-pain.html

Zarrelli, N. (2016), 'How The Hidden Sounds Of Horror Movie Soundtracks Freak You Out', *Atlas Obscura*, 31 October. Available at: www.atlasobscura.com/articles/how-the-hidden-sounds-of-horror-movie-soundtracks-freak-you-out

Zasler, N., Horn, L. & Martelli, M. (2007), 'Medical Assessment & Management', *Brain Injury Medicine: Principles & Practice*, New York: Demos Medical Publishing LLC, p. 712

Zehr, E. P. (2015), 'Miyamoto Musashi And Vision In Martial Arts', *Psychology Today*, 17 June. Available at: www.psychologytoday.com/gb/blog/black-belt-brain/201506/miyamoto-musashi-and-vision-in-martial-arts

INDEX

abdominals 194, 210–1, 213–4, 216–9
accident theory 44
acoustics 72, 102
across the body block **221–2**
acting 35
acting beat 96
action 29–30, 85, **98**, 100, 249
active stretching **114**
A-delta fibres 78
airway 177
Ancient Egypt 13
Ancient Greece 13
Angelo, Domenico 15
Angelo, Henry 17
archer's preparation 246
articulators 180, 185, 189
artistic team 25, 45, 73, 246
attack 95
audience 23, 33, 65, 69–70, 72, 89, 97–8, 144, 147, 159, 161–2, 165, 167, 170, 172, 189, 193, 242, 244
auditorium 58, 61, 100, 102, 137, 187, 246
autonomic reflex 246
avoidance 41, 54, 142, 144, 221
avulsion fracture 115, 246

backhand profile slap 63–6, **130–1**
backhand profile sweep slap 63–6, **134–5**
backhand upstage/downstage slap 63, **124–5**
backstory 100
ballistic stretching **115–6**
beat 29, 246
belt and braces 44
Bertrand, Baptiste 17
Bertrand, Felix 17
big step descent 63–6, **231–2**
blade of foot 163
blocks 54, 63–6, 149, **220–4**
bob and weave 144, **218**
body language 96
boxing 137
brain 47, 60, 62, 69, 91, 110, 137, 177, 211, 214, 217, 236, 239, 243
breath 72, 78, 80, 99, **101–3**, 177
breath support 72
British Academy of Stage and Screen Combat (BASSC) 45, 245
brush and replace block **221–3**

C clamp grip 200–2, 205
C pain fibres 78
camera 38, 50, 123, 137, 159, **241–4**
carotid arteries 177
cascade 44
character 18, 27–8, 37–8, 49, 70, 77, 79–81, 85, 87–8, 90–2, 96, 99, 180, 242, 246
character impulse 100, 103
character logic 31
chest knap **105**
choke from behind 52–4, 63–6, **183–5**
chokes 63–6, **177–91**
choreographic analysis 29
choreography 18, 28, 38–39, 49, 73, 91, 100, 103, 116–7, 243–4, 246
circle of life 183–5, 187–8
circles of attention 34
clap knap **105**
classroom 46
close to ground **51**, 229, 231, 233, 235, 237
coccyx 53, 194, 206, 209, 226, 232
COLDER 83
comminuted fracture 79, 246
communication 194
concept team 45, 246
consent 45, 52, 177, 193, 203, 206, 246
contact 63–6, 191, **193–227**, 246
contact elbow strike 53–5
contact kick 53–5, **206–10**
contact punch 54–5, 137, **213–7**
contact slap 121
controlled descents 51–4, 63–6, **229–39**
core muscles **89–90**, 93, 246
costume pull 53, 55, 63–6, **199–201**
counter-balance 232, 235, 237–8
craft 38, 41, 61, 101–102, 123, 241
crash block 221, **223–4**
creative team 246
crescent kick 53, 63, **165–7**
cross parrot 148
cross punch 53, 60, 63, 65, 127, **149–1**
cueing system 48, **95–9**, 246
cursing 79
curtsy descent **235–7**
customize 106

deltoids 194
depth of field 244, 246
director 21–2, 24, 39, 49, 65, 74, 242
director of photography (DOP) 242, 246
displace target 44, **51**, 121, 128, 130, 132, 134, 137, 142, 147, 149, 152, 156, 159, 167, 170, 172, 185, 190, 225
displaced fracture 79, 246
distance check 122, 124, 126, 140, 247
dominance 103
double tap 178
dove of peace **51**, 178–9
drama school 18
dynamic stretching **114**–7

ear pull 53, 55, 63–6, **204–6**
eardrum 201, 205
editor 244
Edwardian era 24
elbow strike
latissimus dorsi 51, 63–6, **190–1**
stomach 51, 63–6, **185–7**
Elizabethan theatre 15
elliptical deflection 221–2
emotional logic 31
emotional response 101
end-on staging 58–60, **63**, 247

energy along the ground **52**, 229, 231–3, 235, 237
energy logic 31
Equity register of fight directors 17,43
exhale **52**, 230–1, 233, 235, 237, 239
eye contact 46, 48, 52, **96**, 100, 247

fainting **235–9**
fall to safety **51**, 230–1, 233, 235, 237
falling **229–39**
falling backwards **231–2**
falling forwards **233–5**
falling sideways **235–9**
fencing masters 17
fight arranger 243, 247
fight call 21, 44, 178, 194, 247
fight director 10, 17–8, 21–2, 28, 39, 43, 46, 50, 57, 61, 63, 64–5, 74, 88, 93, 193
fight masters 15
fight performance test 18, 38
fight/flight 81–2, 247
film industry 24
filming 50, **241–4**
first party knap **107**
flick-hand stomach punch 63, **215–7**
fracture 79, 247
framing 244, 247
freeze/fold 81, 247
front descent 63–6, **233–5**

Garrick, David 15, 17
gate control theory 79, 247
given circumstances 33, 81, 85, 247
gluteus maximus 194, 206, 208, 211, 225–6, 232, 236, 238
Go Rin No Sho 96
golgi tendon reflex 115, 247
groin kick 63–6, **225–7**
grunts-per-minute (GPM) 71

hair pull 53, 55, 63–6, **201–3**
hamstrings 194, 206
health and safety 39
high arousal 81, 247
high house 22, 58, 64, 149, 247
hitting marks 241–2, 247
hollow fist 137, 194, 213, 215, 218
hollow fist stomach punch 63–6, **213–4**
hook hands 184, 188–9, 200
hook punch 53, 63, **138–9**, 149
hydrated 49
hyper-extension 143

illusion 22, 25, 100
illusion of contact 40–1, 57, 100, 128, 130, 132, 134, 144, 149, 161–2, 165, 167, 170, 172, 244, 247
immersive theatre 25, 247
improvise 49
inner monologue 243
inside crescent kick 166, **165–7**
instinct 38, 41, 61, 69, 101–2, 241
interrupted action 217
in-the-round 25, 58, 60, **66**, 110, 144, 193, 247
intimacy coordinator 46
intimacy director 46
inverse myotatic reflex 115, 247
isolation 49, **89**
isometric stretching **115**

jab punch 22, 53, 63, **144–6**, 155, 159
Jacobean theatre 15

kick to thigh
lying down 63–6, **208–10**
standing 63–6, **206–8**
kicks 63–6, **159–74**
kitchen-sink drama 35, 247
knap 100, **105–11**, 248
knee 210–2, 235, 237–9
knee to stomach 53–5, 63–6, **210–2**

Laban 40, 248
Lamaze 80
lapel grab 199
latissimus dorsi 194, 236, 238
limp 79
LOCATES 83
London Masters of Defence 15
look at the target **96–7**, 100
low arousal 81, 248

Macready, William 17
marking the fight 93
marks 241–2, 247
Marshall, Henry 24
matinee 44
mats 230, 237
McGill Pain Questionnaire 83
mental health 45
mental health first aid 45
misdirection 64, 110
motor learning 28, 47
muscle memory 47
music of the fight **69–75**, 248
myotatic reflex 115, 248

mystery play 14

negotiation **52**, 178, 180–1, 183, 187, 193–5, 197, 199, 201, 204, 206, 208, 210, 213, 220, 225, 227
nociceptive pain 78, 248
non-displaced fracture 79, 248

objectives 28–30, 248
obstacles 32
open-palm stomach strike 63, **217–9**
opera 73
opposition 221–2
out of distance **53**, 121, 122, 124, 126, 137,138, 140, 142, 144, 149, 154, 159, 160, 162, 165
outside crescent kick 166, **165–7**

padding 193–4
pain 69–72, **77–85**, 87, 100, 102, 177
pain threshold **78**, 248
pain train 85
parachute descent **237–9**
parachute hand 200–3, 205–6, 248
parachute landing fall (PLF) 237
parrot punch 44, 51, 54, 63–6, **147–9**, 220
parrot space 128, 130, 147, 152, 248
passion play 14
passive stretching **114**
permission 193
physical logic 31
picturization **87–93**
PNF stretching **115**
point of view (POV) 22, 123, 137, 159, 242, 248
post-production 244, 248
predictive check 195, 197, 200–1, 203, 205–6, 232, 234–5, 238
preparation **97–8**, 100
prizes (playing) 15, 248
producer 39, 44
profile kick
head 51, 63, 65, **167–9**
head (kneeling) 63, 65, **170–2**
stomach 51, 63, **172–4**
profile slap 51, 58–59, 63–6, **128–9**
profile sweep slap 51, 58–9, 63–6, **132–3**
proprioception 40, 248
proprioceptive neuromuscular facilitation 115
proscenium arch 25, 58–9, **63**, 248

protect fragile areas **53**, 230–1, 233, 235, 237
psychology 79, 81–2
pull to safety **53**, 199, 201, 204
pulling the blow 55
punches 63–4, 87–8, 90, **137–57**
push kick 160, 163
push to safety **53**, 195, 197
pyramid hands 234

reaction 95, **98–100**
realism 24
reality 40
red light fever 38, 49
red light/green light 44, **54**, 96, 142–3, 147, 149, 218, 221, 248
rehearsal 18, 93, 149, 178, 183, 193–4, 243, 248
relationship 32, 81
relaxed grip 201
releases **177–91**
restoration comedy 35, 248
reversal of energy **54**, 178, 180, 183, 187–8
risk assessment 44–5, 50, 248
Roman theatre 14
roundhouse kick 63–6, **172–4**
roundhouse punch 40, 51, 53–4, 63–6, **142–4**, 218
Royal Academy of Dramatic Art (RADA) 24, 248

safe gesture 178, 183, 187, 248
safe word 178, 248
safety 27, **43–55**, 87, 92, 96, 98, 121, 144, 159, 177–8, 193–4, 229–30, 241
same side block **221–2**
second party knap **107**
secondary symptoms **82**
Shakespeare 14
shared energy 180
shared energy push 53–4, 63–6, **197–8**
shared knap **108**, 154, 159, 217
shoulder 211, 219
side-coach 38, 249
side descent
  curtsy 63–6, **235–7**
  parachute 63–6, 172, **237–9**
sightlines 21–2, **57–63**, 65, 131, 137, 149–50, 153, 159, 171, 178, 242, 249
site specific 25, 249
six elements **99–101**
slaps 63–4, **121–35**
sleeper hold 54, 63–6, **187–9**, 190
slow-motion 93
snap kick 160, 226
Society of American Fight Directors (SAFD) 17
Society of British Fight Directors (SBFD) 17, 43
soft on soft **54**–5, 149, 194, 206, 208, 210, 213, 220, 225, 230–1, 233, 235, 237
soft striking implement **55**, 194
soundtrack 69
spike 144, 249
spine 232
stage management 39, 44–5, 49, 194
stakes 29, 32–3, 249
standard combats 24, 249
stand-up comedian 70
Stanislavski 34
static stretching **114**, 116–7
stomach punch (non-contact) 51, 63–5, **156–7**
stomp kick 51
straight punch in profile 51, 63, 65, **152–3**
strangle 52–5, 63–6, 87, 177, **178–80**
stretch **113–8**
stretch reflex 115
studio theatre 22
suffering 81
superman punch 249
super-objective 29–30, 249
sweep break 63–6, **181–2**
swing kick 160, 226

tactics 32
tap out 178
target line **61**, 137, 144, 159, 161–2, 165, 167, 169, 170, 172, 174, 241, 244, 249
target zone 100, 249
Tarlton, Richard 15
teacher 46, 50
technical head 37
technical skillset 28, 35
television 24
theatre museum 24
thigh knap **107**
third party knap **108**
threat 99
through-line 31, 249
thrust 25, 58, 60, **64**, 110, 144, 193, 249
timing 99–100
traverse 25, 58–60, **65**, 110, 193, 249
trigger 45
Tudor 14
two hand push 198

understudy 44, 249
unit 29, 249
uppercut punch 53, 63, **154–5**
upstage/downstage backfist punch 53, 63, **140–1**
upstage/downstage crescent kick 53, 63, **165–7**
upstage/downstage kick
  head 53, 63, **160–2**
  stomach 53, 63, **162–4**
upstage/downstage slap 53, 57–8, 63, **122–3**

V slap **129**
victim control **55**, 178, 180, 187, 199, 201, 204
Victoria and Albert museum 24
Victorian era 24
vocal choreography 72, 75
vocal delivery 177
vocal instrument 27, 52, 72–5, 80, 178–80, 184–5, 188–9, 249
vocal knap 212, 216
vocal reaction 100, 157, 214, 217, 227
vocal safety **72–3**
vocal scoring 49, 69, 249
vocal violence 73
vocal warm-up 75
vocal work 39, 71, 78, 80, 99
voice coach 74
vom 60, 249

warm up 46, **113–8**
West End 22
whiplash 145, 155, 162, 169
wide-angle upstage/downstage slap 53, 58, 63, **126–7**
withdraw the energy **55**, 194, 206, 208, 210, 213, 225
Woffington, Peg 15
wrist 214, 216, 219, 232, 234–5

zero energy push 53–4, 63–6, **195–6**